SECRET
SOCIETIES

SECRET SOCIETIES

THEIR INFLUENCE AND POWER
FROM ANTIQUITY TO THE PRESENT DAY

MICHAEL HOWARD

Destiny Books
Rochester, Vermont

Destiny Books
One Park Street
Rochester, Vermont 05767
www.DestinyBooks.com

Destiny Books is a division of Inner Traditions International

Originally published in the United Kingdom in 1989 by Random House under the title *The Occult Conspiracy*
First U.S. paperback edition published in 1989 by Destiny Books under the title *The Occult Conspiracy: Secret Socieites—Their Influence and Power in World History*
Second U.S. edition published in 2008 by Destiny Books under the title *Secret Societies: Their Influence and Power from Antiquity to the Present Day*

LIBRARY OF CONGRESS CATALOGING-IN-PUBLICATION DATA

Howard, Michael, 1948–
  Secret societies : their influence and power from antiquity to the present day / Michael Howard. — 2d ed.
    p. cm.
  Originally published: The Occult Conspiracy. Rochester, Vt. : Destiny Books, 1989.
  Includes bibliographical references and index.
  ISBN-13: 978-1-59477-203-0 (pbk.)
  ISBN-10: 1-59477-203-7 (pbk.)
  1. Occultism. I. Title.
  BF1042.H64 2008
  366.09—dc22
                                                                  2007036376

Printed and bound in the United States by Lake Book Manufacturing

10 9 8 7 6 5 4 3 2 1

Text design by Jon Desautels and text layout by Virginia Scott Bowman
This book was typeset in Garamond Premier Pro with Copperplate as the display typeface

To send correspondence to the author of this book, mail a first-class letter to the author c/o Inner Traditions • Bear & Company, One Park Street, Rochester, VT 05767, and we will forward the communication.

CONTENTS

PREFACE   vii

1. THE ANCIENT MYSTERIES   1

2. THE CURSE OF THE TEMPLARS   24

3. THE ROSICRUCIAN CONNECTION   48

4. THE AMERICAN DREAM   84

5. GERMAN NATIONALISM AND THE
    BOLSHEVIK REVOLUTION   112

6. NAZISM AND THE OCCULT TRADITION   151

7. SECRETS IN THE VATICAN   172

8. THE OCCULT AND MODERN POLITICS   196

9. THE NEW WORLD ORDER   217

CHRONOLOGY   237

BIBLIOGRAPHY   245

INDEX   253

Dedicated to the memory of Archduke Franz Ferdinand
and Archduchess Sophia von Habsburg

Lancti coniugo fatis iungunter eisdem

———◆———

Rumor is not always wrong.

TACITUS

*The world is governed by very different personages from what is
imagined by those who are not behind the scenes.*

BENJAMIN DISRAELI

*It is a strange desire to seek power and to lose liberty or to seek
power over others and to lose power over a man's self.*

FRANCIS BACON

———◆———

PREFACE

It is the generally accepted view among those who have very little knowledge of the matters discussed in this book that occultism is the province of a minority of deluded individuals. Those who study or practice the occult are generally dismissed by the public, usually on the basis of sensational media stories, as cranks, charlatans, sexual deviants, or lunatics. Anyone involved in the twilight world of the occult must, so the argument goes, be weird or unusual because the practice of occultism conjures up in the popular imagination visions of incense-filled temples, naked virgins on altars, bizarre rituals, secret initiations, and, if Christian propaganda can be believed, the worship of Satan and the powers of darkness.

Those rational intellectuals who are the leading critics of occultism will therefore be surprised to learn that the word *occult* can be defined simply as "hidden." It is used in that sense in astronomy to describe a planet that is "occulted" or hidden from view by another planet. Occultism is therefore the study of the hidden, and this makes it sound far less sensational and mysterious. In practice, those who follow the esoteric path are heirs to an ancient tradition of forbidden knowledge that is thousands of years old. Experienced occultists who have probed the inner mysteries of this arcane tradition are the guardians of an Ancient Wisdom that is the secret teaching behind all established religions. While occultism, like all religious systems, has its fair share of eccentrics, it also boasts members who are respectable people of high social standing.

A dyed-in-the-wool materialist who dismisses the occult as pure fantasy will be even more shocked by the central thesis of this book. Offering evidence gathered from both orthodox and unorthodox sources, it will prove that many of the famous historical personalities of the last two thousand years, including statesmen, politicians, religious leaders, and royalty, were actively involved in mysticism and magical practices. In addition, it will show that many of the major historical events of the period have a hidden significance that can be explained only in terms of an occult conspiracy. Because of its wide-ranging and far-reaching influence, this conspiracy and its revelation are integral to any true understanding of world history and the development of Western civilization.

To the average citizen, the political system of the country he lives in involves only the mundane. Politics is generally concerned with economics, education, social welfare, the defense of the nation, the legal system, and the daily governance of the country. International politics, on the other hand, touches upon larger issues, including treaties between nations, global economic structures, and the awesome responsibility of preserving world peace in the face of an escalating arms race. When we see the smiling faces of international statesmen and religious leaders on the television or in the newspapers it is difficult to imagine that behind the diplomatic facade exists a very different world—one of secret societies and occult fraternities peopled by shadowy figures who have often been obsessed with the pursuit of power. Since the days of the pharaohs in ancient Egypt, the occult has entangled in its web the black arts of espionage, subversion, and revolution. Today, it still affects politics, although there are few who are aware of its influence or that those who control it are often well-known faces and household names.

The purpose of this book is not sensationalism for its own sake, although many who are not conversant with the hidden world of secret societies and parapolitics may criticize it on those grounds. In presenting the facts about the influence of occultism on politics, I have tried to avoid falling into the trap of overdramatizing certain historical events. Once, however, we step from the well-worn path that the conventional historian treads and examine the real motives that engineered key situations in Europe during the last two thousand years, we enter the realm of a "secret" history—an alternative history that has seldom been chronicled and remains the study of a few dedicated researchers of the arcane and the esoteric. It is this secret history—melodramatic as it may appear to the outside world, which is only dimly aware of its existence—that is the subject matter of this book. It is the background upon which the participants in the occult conspiracy play their sometimes sinister games with the lives of millions of ordinary men and women.

In many cases, the influence of the puppet masters can be recognized as benevolent and the pattern that emerges is one that, overall, has been instrumental in the progress of human civilization. As the historical story unfolds, however, it will become clear that the pursuit and exercise of power, especially absolute power, can become a corrupting force that leads astray those who have high ideals and the purest of aspirations. History is littered with the remnants of grand plans that crumbled to dust because of human frailty. The road to Utopia is too often paved with the bones of the common man martyred in the cause of freedom.

Occult knowledge is a double-edged sword, and those who seek to unravel its secrets and discover its mysteries should be aware of the grave responsibility that comes with that task. Unfortunately, in these pages you will meet those who have not been worthy of the quest and the task they were given by higher spiritual authority. Yet you will also discover that through the acquisition of the Ancient Wisdom it is possible the aspirations of humanity can be fulfilled, provided those who guide the destiny of our nations are not diverted from the narrow path they tread by the lure of temporal power at the expense of spiritual integrity.

I thank the following for their help during the writing of this book:

the staff of the British Library reading room at the British Museum, the Westminster Public Reference Library, the Folklore Society Library, the librarians of the British Federation of International Co-Freemasonry, the Theosophical Society (United Kingdom), and Robin Ramsey of *Lobster* magazine.

THE ANCIENT MYSTERIES

To understand the origins of the occult conspiracy as it first openly manifested in medieval Europe through the secret societies of the period, it is advisable to examine their ancient roots, which can be traced back to ancient Egypt and the classical civilizations of Rome and Greece. During the Middle Ages, several secret societies based on occult doctrines emerged and claimed antecedents dating back almost to the beginning of human history. The mystical ideas they espoused had their origins in the earliest religious beliefs known to humankind. These pagan beliefs survived the formation of the major world faiths of Judaism, Christianity, and Islam by adopting the outward forms of these religions and operating within them as a heretical, secret, and esoteric tradition.

With the persecution of alternative spiritual beliefs such as witchcraft and Christian heresies in medieval Europe, the guardians of this Ancient Wisdom went underground and formed secret societies to preserve their pagan ideals. The two major secret societies formed in this period, although they revealed themselves in a public form only in the sixteenth and seventeenth centuries, were Freemasonry and the Order of the Rosy Cross. The beliefs and practices of these two clandestine fraternities provide an insight into the workings of the occult conspiracy and the sociopolitical vision that exists at its heart.

While the Order of the Rosy Cross, or the Rosicrucian Order, is still a secret society and has received very little publicity in modern times, considerable public attention has recently been drawn to Freemasonry, which has been singled out as a potentially corrupting influence in modern society because its membership includes businessmen, judges, and police officers whose Masonic oaths and activities are regarded as the ideal cover for nepotism. To the outside world, Freemasonry is depicted as a superior working men's club for the professional person who wants to progress in his career through membership in an elite social group. Masons allegedly show favors to each other in business deals and job applications, while the prominence of lawyers and police officers in Masonic lodges indicates to the suspicious that the course of justice could be perverted by rich men gathering in darkened lodge rooms.

The Freemasons have responded to these allegations by denying that membership in their lodges offers any special rewards in the business or professional world. They have attempted to present a respectable image to the outside world using the argument that their Craft is not a secret society but a society with secrets. Yet despite this public relations exercise, the popular image of Freemasonry is still a group of middle-aged businessmen meeting once a month, wearing fancy dress, and performing mumbo-jumbo schoolboy rituals. In many cases, the activities of the modern Masonic lodge may be just an eccentric pantomime. If Freemasonry is so laughable, however, why, over the centuries, has it attracted some of the most brilliant minds, including leading scientists, prominent politicians, writers, intellectuals, artists, financiers, and even royalty? The answer must lie in its inner teachings that are seldom discussed in public.

At a recent Church of England synod, a report on Freemasonry was presented to the assembled clerics and lay people for debate. Several speakers denounced Masonry as contrary to the teachings of Christianity and condemned Christians, especially clerics, who might be members. One speaker even went so far as to attack Masonry as "blasphemous" because he claimed its central initiation ritual, which involves a symbolic death and rebirth enactment, was a travesty of the Christian belief in the crucifixion and resurrection of Jesus of Nazareth. Since its inception, Freemasonry has been the target of Christian wrath, although later in this book it will be revealed that the Roman Catholic Church itself has been infiltrated by agents of the secret societies.

Why should Christians be so critical of Freemasonry, apart from the obvious reason that the Church is opposed to any alternative belief system that might threaten its spiritual monopoly? Again, the answer to this question lies in the "secrets" of Freemasonry. If these were readily available to the general public, it is doubtful that their meaning would be understood by those who were not versed in the doctrines of occultism and ancient religion. In fact, it is doubtful that many of the ordinary lodge members understand what Freemasonry's secrets represent. In the inner circle of Masonry, among those who have obtained higher degrees of initiation, there are initiates who understand that they are the inheritors of an ancient and pre-Christian tradition handed down from pagan times. The medieval Masons inherited this secret tradition in the form of symbolic teachings expressing spiritual truths. These teachings originated in the pagan mysteries that were followed in the ancient world.

To understand these secret teachings—which also places into a spiritual context the involvement of the medieval secret societies in international politics—it is necessary to examine the alleged origins of Freemasonry in the pre-Christian period. The information about these origins is preserved in the writings of Masonic historians, in the theories put forward by occultists who have investigated the symbolism of Freemasonry, and in the academic accounts of the pagan religions that influenced the medieval esoteric tradition.

Historically, it is known that speculative (versus operative) Freemasonry developed from the early medieval guilds of masons who built the Gothic cathedrals of Europe. The guilds these craftsmen formed operated as mutual self-help groups similar to modern trade unions. Members used secret symbols—the so-called masons' marks found in old churches, passwords, and a special handshake—so they could recognize each other. It is generally believed in occult circles that these medieval stonemasons had inherited esoteric knowledge from their pagan antecedents and incorporated this knowledge into the sacred architecture of the cathedrals. When the lodges of speculative Freemasonry were founded in the seventeenth and eighteenth centuries from these operative medieval guilds, this knowledge was transformed into the symbolism, which today forms the basis of Masonic ritual.

Medieval associations of masons could involve up to seven hundred members who made contracts with the Church to build cathedrals and monasteries. It is believed that one particular masonic building association originated in Cologne in the thirteenth century and utilized initiation ceremonies that granted entry to its members who were called free masons. Eventually these operative masonic lodges accepted outsiders, provided they could prove themselves to be men of learning or ones who held high social position. By the end of the sixteenth century, the lodges of working masons had largely dispersed and were replaced by those of speculative Freemasonry, with its emphasis on the esoteric symbolism of the Craft as a metaphor for spiritual progress and enlightenment.

Although the medieval masons were down-to-earth artisans, they also possessed a mythical framework to explain the origins of their trade. The operative masons divided all available knowledge into seven liberal arts and sciences. These were classified as grammar or correct speech, rhetoric or the application of grammar, dialectics or distinguishing truth from falsehood, arithmetic or accurate reckoning, geometry or the measurement of the earth, music, and astronomy. Of all these arts and sciences, the stonemasons regarded geometry as the most important.

According to their beliefs, geometry had been taught by a pre-Flood patriarch named Lamech. He had three sons: One invented geometry, another was the first mason, and the third was a blacksmith who was the first human to work with precious metals. In common with Noah, Lamech was warned by Jehovah of the impending flood caused by the wickedness of humanity and the interference in world affairs by the Watchers or Fallen Angels. Lamech and his sons decided

to preserve their knowledge in two stone pillars so that future generations would discover it.

One of these pillars was discovered by Hermes Trismegistus, or
Thrice Greatest, known to the Greeks as the god Hermes and to the
ancient Egyptians as the ibis-headed scribe of the god Thoth (pro-
nounced Tehuti). The so-called Emerald Tablet of Hermes is said to
contain the essence of the lost wisdom from before the days of the biblical Flood. According to occult sources, this tablet was discovered in a
cave by the mystic Apollonius of Tyana, who was regarded by the early
Church as a rival to Jesus. The first published version of the Emerald
Tablet dates from an Arabic source of the eighth century CE, and it
was not translated into Latin in Europe until the thirteenth century.

Yet the myth of Hermetic wisdom had a profound effect on the
gnostics, who were heretical Christians in direct conflict with the early
Church for attempting to fuse paganism with the new faith. They also
claimed to possess the secret teachings of Jesus, which he divulged
only to his inner circle of disciples. These teachings had been censored
from the authorized version of the Christian scriptures approved by
the Church councils, which met to decide the structure and dogma
of early Christianity. Gnostic philosophy emerged in a different form
in medieval Europe in the rise of the heretical Christian movement
of the Cathars and the chivalric Order of the Knights Templar. The
Hermetic tradition provided the spiritual inspiration for many secret
societies in the Middle Ages, and its influence can be discerned in
both speculative Freemasonry and Rosicrucianism.

In the Masonic tradition, it is said that stonemasons were first
organized into a corporate body during the building of the Tower of
Babel. According to Genesis 11:4–6, the concept of this tower was to
reach up to heaven and contact God. The fall of the Tower of Babel
destroyed the common language spoken by humanity and ended the
second Golden Age that followed the Flood. The architect of the
tower was King Nimrod of Babylon, who was a stonemason and who
is described in the Bible as "a mighty hunter." He provided his cousin,
the king of Ninevah, with sixty masons to assist in the construction of

his cities. On their departure from Nimrod's land, they were told to remain steadfastly true to each other, avoid dissensions at any cost, live in harmony, and serve their lord as their master on earth. According to popular belief, the Hebrews received their knowledge of masonry from the Babylonians and introduced it to Egypt when they were taken into slavery. In Egypt this knowledge was influenced by the mysteries and the occult traditions of the pyramid builders, who were versed in the techniques of sacred geometry.

The key to the pagan origins of Freemasonry lies in the symbolic story related to candidates for initiation into the three degrees of Masonry, known as Entered Apprentice, Fellow Craftsman, and Master Mason. In Masonic lore, the basis of this legend is the semimythical story of the construction of King Solomon's temple in Jerusalem. This building was regarded as the repository of ancient occult wisdom and symbolism by both the Freemasons and the Order of the Knights Templar.

King David initiated the building of the temple at Jerusalem, and after his death, his son Solomon completed the task. To build the edifice, King Solomon imported stonemasons, artists, and craftsmen from neighboring countries. Specifically, he sent a message to the king of Tyre asking if he could hire the services of the king's master builder, Hiram Abiff, who was skilled in geometry. Hiram was a widow's son who had trained as a craftsman working in brass. Because of Hiram's artistic talents, Solomon appointed him chief architect and master mason of the temple to be built in Jerusalem.

Hiram completed the temple in a period of seven years (this number is especially significant in occult tradition and Masonry), but this achievement was overshadowed by his mysterious and violent death. At noon one day, as the other stonemasons were resting on their midday break, Hiram visited the temple to check on the progress of the work, which was nearly finished. As he entered the porch of the temple, passing through the entrance flanked by the two pillars at the gateway, Hiram was approached by one of his fellow workers, who demanded from Hiram the secret of the master mason's word. Hiram refused to provide this secret information, telling the worker that he would receive it in good time once he had progressed further in his career. The mason was not satisfied with this answer and struck Hiram a blow that made him stumble, dazed and bleeding, to the second gate of the temple. There he was accosted by a second mason who asked the same question, and when no answer was forthcoming this man also hit him. Hiram staggered to the third (western) entrance of the temple, where another mason lay in wait. The process was repeated, and this time the chief architect died from the third blow.

The three renegade masons carried Hiram's body from the temple to the top of a nearby hill, where they dug a shallow grave and buried him. They marked the grave with an acacia tree, and in the afternoon returned to work as normal. When Hiram was found to be missing, a search party was organized, but it was fifteen days before his corpse was discovered. Solomon was informed and ordered that Hiram's body should be exhumed and reburied with a full religious ceremony and the honors due a craftsman of his rank. The three assassins were eventually exposed, tried, and put to death for their crime.

If this legend is examined in relation to the religious circumstances during the reign of Solomon, some interesting facts arise that provide insights into the hidden pagan symbolism of Freemasonry. First, during the time Solomon was on the throne of Israel, Tyre was renowned as a center of goddess worship. Although Solomon is generally seen as a leading devotee of Yahweh (or Jehovah), he had a lengthy correspondence with the pagan king of Tyre and requested that that this king send his master builder, who must have been engaged in erecting temples dedicated to the worship of the great goddess, to help him design and build his temple to Yahweh.

A careful reading of the Herbrew scriptures reveals that when the Hebrews resettled in Canaan after their escape from slavery in Egypt, the worship of their tribal god, Yahweh, was strongly resisted by the indigenous inhabitants, who revered the fertility goddess Aserah, or Astarte, and her male consort. The situation when the worship of Jehovah was introduced into Canaan can be compared to the early medieval period in Europe, when the Roman missionaries tried to convert the heathen tribes, and to nineteenth-century Africa, when white settlers forced Christianity on the natives. It is also obvious from discrepancies in the Hebrew Creation myth recorded in Genesis that early Judaism was heavily influenced by the pagan beliefs of the nomadic tribes, who were the ancestors of the Israelites. In establishing the religion of Yahweh, the patriarchs of the Hebrew scriptures drew upon the rich structure of mythology that existed in neighboring countries, including Sumeria and Babylon. In particular, the myths of the Garden of Eden and the Flood can be identified as foreign imports grafted onto the Judaic belief system.

It was only through the militant campaigns of a small elite of patriarchal priests, who, for the most part, but not always, were supported by the monarchy and the ruling class, that Yahwehism became the dominant religion of ancient Israel. It was resisted by the common people, who were supported by heretic members of the establishment. The conflict that this caused can still be detected in Orthodox Judaism in which the Supreme Creator is represented as neither male nor female. One medieval Jewish philosopher stated, "God is not a body nor can bodily attributes be ascribed to him [sic] and He has no likeness at all." Despite this attempt to present Divinity as an abstract entity, the majority of Jewish rabbis regarded Yahweh as masculine in nature. His alternative title of Adonai, which is translated as "Lord," confirms this belief.

It is only in the secret teachings of the mystical system known as the kabbalah, which is the esoteric doctrine of the Judaic religion, that the ancient concept of an androgynous deity survives in the feminine image of the Shekinah, or "bride of God." In Jewish synagogues, the Shekinah is welcomed at sunset on a Friday evening in prayers to celebrate the beginning of the Sabbath. In these prayers, the Shekinah is welcomed as the bride of God. The kabbalists teach that only through her can Creation be manifested. This idea is reinforced by the folk belief that the Shekinah materializes unseen over the marriage bed on the wedding night. This suggests a relic of ancient fertility rites performed in honor of a goddess.

Ancient memories of goddess worship also survive in the Jewish myth of the she-demon Lilith, who inspired sexual desires in men by sending them erotic dreams. In kabbalistic teachings, Lilith was the first wife of Adam, before Eve, and taught him the arts of magical enchantment. From their illicit union was spawned the elemental realm of elves, fairies, and gnomes according to occult lore. She abandoned the first man after he refused to allow her to take the dominant position when they made love. Lilith was not originally a demonic figure but can be traced back to a Sumerian goddess called the Lady of Beasts, who was depicted in the form of an owl. Lilith symbolizes the dark aspect of the great goddess of the old pagan religions in her femme fatale or enchantress form. This aspect of the feminine has always been rejected by patriarchal cultures whose sexual puritanism transformed it into a demonic symbol because they were incapable of handling the potent erotic energies associated with it.

Initially, the worship of the fertility deities of Canaan was an integral part of Judaic religion. The goddess Aserah, or Astarte, her consort El, and their son Baal—meaning "lord"—were widely venerated. Effigies of the goddess were erected all over Israel as described in the Hebrew scriptures books of Kings, Chronicles, Judges, Deuteronomy, Exodus, and Micah. Gideon is recorded as having destroyed an altar to Baal on the command of an angel (Judges 6:25–31) and there are references to the worship of a fertility god and goddess at altars erected in the temple at Jerusalem.

How does Solomon feature in this tradition of goddess worship? During the Middle Ages, the Hebrew king gained an infamous reputation as a master magician who could raise elemental spirits. In fact, several grimoires, or magical workbooks, were either named after him (e.g., *The Key of Solomon*) or credited to his authorship. He was generally regarded as a powerful magus, healer, and exorcist. Today, some born-again Christians denounce him as a devil-worshipper who led the Israelites away from the true God. In the apocryphal Book of Wisdom, written in the first century BCE, Solomon is quoted as saying, "God gave me true knowledge of things as they are; an understanding of the structure of the world and the way in which the elements work, the beginning and the end of eras and what lies between . . . the cycles of the year and the constellations . . . the thoughts of men . . . the power of spirits . . . the virtues of roots . . . I learned it all, secret and manifest."

In addition to his magical attributes and occult powers, Solomon is regarded by some authorities as a secret worshipper of the goddess. The king's conversion to paganism and his worship of strange gods are blamed on his marriages to foreign princesses, who introduced their religious customs to his court (1 Kings 11:1–8). There is also speculation that the legendary queen of Sheba introduced the heretic king to the occult doctrines of her land (situated either in East Africa or Arabia). She not only brought camels loaded with spices, gold, and precious stones when she visited Solomon but also included in her entourage priests who allegedly initiated the Jewish monarch into the mysteries of her pagan religion based on sun worship.

In the Hebrew scriptures (1 Kings 3:3) it is said of Solomon that "he sacrificed and burned incense in high places." These were the sites of shrines dedicated to the worship of the great goddess. The available evidence suggests that during the 370-year history of the original temple at Jerusalem, the structure was wholly or partly used for goddess worship for two hundred years. When one of Yahweh's prophets denounced Solomon's waywardness and rejected him in favor of a young man called Jeroboam, who became the new king (1 Kings 11:29–40), the worship of pagan gods briefly abated. In 1 Kings 23:4–7 it is recorded that the high priest Hilkaih destroyed the shrines to the goddess Astarte that the old king had erected all over Israel.

Unfortunately for the Yahwehists, the choice of Jeroboam to be the new religious leader of Israel was a miscalculation. The young man soon reverted to the worship of the pagan bull god (1 Kings 12:33) and was disgraced. The cult of goddess worship was further reinforced by the arrival in Israel of Princess Jezebel, the original "scarlet woman" who was the daughter of the king of Sidon and a priestess of the old pagan faith. Jezebel's image as a shameless hussy evidently stems from the explicit sexuality of the rites she performed to the goddess, which horrified the puritanical priests of Yahweh. Under the influence of

Jezebel, her husband, King Ahab of Israel, built an altar to Baal and a sacred grove to the goddess (1 Kings 16:30–33). It is said that 850 priests of Baal and Astarte were entertained at a lavish banquet organized by the new queen, who worshipped Astarte. In the streets of Jerusalem sacred fires were lit, spiced honey cakes were baked, libations of wine were poured on the ground, and incense was burned as a sacrificial offering to the fertility goddess. Eventually, Jezebel was overthrown by the worshippers of Yahweh because of her erotic excesses, and she was killed. Goddess worship survived for many years, however, and when Josiah began his crusade to restore Yahwehism, he first had to destroy the shrines and altars erected by the common people to the old gods (2 Kings 23:4–15).

The goddess-worshipping Solomon had sent to Tyre, a center of pagan worship, for Hiram Abiff, the master builder, to become his chief architect for the temple in Jerusalem. Hiram, however, was murdered at the conclusion of the building work, as described earlier, which suggests a ritual killing or human sacrifice. Because Hiram was the designer of pagan temples, it seems probable that he incorporated elements of pagan symbolism into the architecture of Solomon's temple. In fact, the building was constructed in a pagan style that was used widely in the Middle East for sacred shrines; it included a vestibule, a nave, and an inner sanctuary with two pillars guarding its entrance.

The main entrance of the temple was of primary symbolic importance, for it was flanked by two pillars, historically known as Jachin and Boaz. They formed the framework to the outer court or porch of the temple where, according to legend, the stonemasons who built the edifice gathered to hold their meetings. It has been suggested that these two pillars were placed there to imitate the obelisks that were erected at the gateways of Egyptian temples. The most famous of these were erected on the orders of Pharaoh Thothmes III at Heliopolis, or the City of the Sun, in the fifteenth century BCE. These pillars, called Cleopatra's Needles for some unknown reason, can be found today on the embankment of the River Thames in

London and in Central Park in New York. The symbols on the base of the American obelisk have been tentatively identified as masonic signs. Thothmes III is regarded by some modern occultists as the legendary founder of the Order of the Rosy Cross.

The twin pillars in front of Solomon's temple also have similarities to traditional Canaanite fertility symbols. The temples dedicated to the goddess in Tyre are said to have featured stone pillars of phallic design at their entrances. These pillars were the focus of fertility rites performed in honor of Astarte at her special festivals. Connections have also been made between these pillars and the monoliths used by Lamech and his sons to preserve their ancient knowledge in the hieroglyphic symbols carved on their surfaces. Kabbalists identify them as symbols of the masculine and feminine principles by which the universe came into manifestation, as expressed by the twin pillars of the Tree of Life symbol. It is also agreed by both occultists and Freemasons that these two pillars represent the male and female energies that are the basis of Creation. Their position on either side of the entrance to the temple, which was dedicated to the goddess, suggests that this gateway may represent the female labia. In ancient religious belief the temples of the goddess—whether Astarte, Ishtar, or Isis—were designed to be symbolic of the female body and this was reflected in their sacred architecture.

The most important part of Solomon's temple was the inner sanctum or holy of holies. This symbolized the womb of the goddess and was the repository of the Ark of the Covenant, which contained the sacred laws of the Hebrew race given to Moses on Mount Sinai by Yahweh. Only the high priests were allowed to enter the inner sanctum, where the Ark, made of gold and shittimwood, was kept. The lid of the Ark was a gold plate on which knelt effigies of the mythical guardians of the Covenant known as the cherubim. They faced each other and had large wings that arched over the Ark. This was the mercy seat upon which the God of Israel allegedly descended to communicate with his high priest.

According to Professor Raphael Ktav in his book *The Hebrew*

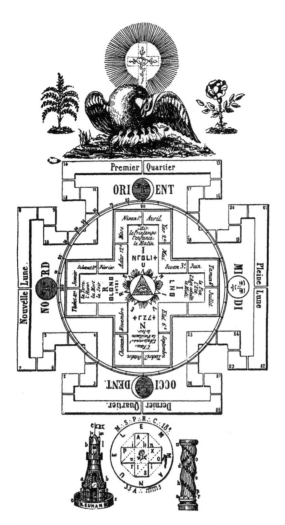

Solomon's temple (a nineteenth-century illustration from a Rosicrucian source)

Goddess, the cherubim who guarded the Ark of the Covenant in the temple were in the shape of naked female figures with wings. The word *cherubim* means "messenger" and in Hebrew mythology refers to an intermediary of divine origin who acts as a go-between for humanity and God. The two cherubim in the holy of holies were described by the Jewish mystic Philo, writing in the first century CE, as symbols of the dual nature of God and the male and female principles of Creation. Philo regarded the deity worshipped by the ancient Hebrews as androgynous—that is, having both male and female characteristics. According to one account, one of the cherubim was male and the other was female.

If Hiram Abiff was a pagan worshipper of the goddess and was responsible for designing her temples in Tyre, what was the significance of his ritual murder at the hands of his fellow masons in Jerusalem? In the ancient rites of the goddess, the ritual death or sacrifice of her consort or a priest representing him features prominently. This sacrificial element in goddess worship was widespread in the Middle East and would have been well known to the Israelites. With this sacrificial aspect is also found the myth of the resurrection of the dying god, which is present in the legend of Hiram Abiff in his burial and exhumation. The best-known example of this myth, in a pagan religious context, is the story of Isis and Osiris in ancient Egypt, which had a profound effect on the development of the pagan mysteries in the classical world and it also influenced early Christianity.

In Egyptian mythology, Isis and Osiris are represented as the earliest rulers of the Nile delta in primeval times. During their reign, Egypt flourished because the two deities civilized the land and its people, who had previously been savage barbarians addicted to cannibalism and perverted sexual practices. Isis and Osiris introduced a legal code, agriculture, the arts and crafts, temples, and the correct worship of the gods. Because of these deeds, the Egyptian people adored their rulers and worshipped them as divine beings.

Osiris, however, had a rival and enemy, his twin brother Set (or Typhon, meaning "insolence" or "pride" in Greek). Set wanted to rule the country and constantly plotted against the royal family. While Osiris was abroad and Isis ruled alone, Set plotted with seventy-two fellow conspirators to kill the king on his return. He had secretly measured Osiris's body and made a special chest that fit the king perfectly. When Osiris returned, Set invited the king to a welcoming feast. Isis warned her husband not to go, but Osiris only laughed and said he had nothing to fear from his weak brother.

At the feast, everyone present admired the jeweled chest made by

Set. He said that he would give it as a present to the person whose body fit it. One after another the guests tried, but they were the wrong size. Finally, Osiris climbed into the chest and Set and his co-plotters slammed down the lid, nailed it shut, and sealed it with molten lead. Then they threw the casket into the Nile.

When Isis heard the news of her husband's murder, she was grief stricken. According to Egyptian beliefs, the body of a dead person had to be buried with the correct funeral rites or else the soul would wander the earth for eternity. Isis set out on a quest to find the body of Osiris, and she traveled up and down the Nile, asking everyone she met if they had seen the chest. Eventually, some children told her they had seen the coffin at the mouth of the river, floating out to sea. The queen discovered that it had been washed up on the shores of Byblos in Syria, where it had become entangled in the branches of a tamarisk tree. The king of Byblos cut down the tree, not realizing that the coffin of Osiris was embedded in the trunk, and made a pillar from it to support the roof of his palace.

When Isis found out what had happened, she sailed to Byblos and by deception became a nurse in the royal household, serving the queen of the land who was named Astarte. This, of course, was also the name of the fertility goddess worshipped at Tyre, Sidon, and in Canaan by the Israelites. Through her friendship with the young queen, Isis persuaded the king to cut open the tree, which released the body of Osiris. She took the corpse of her husband back to Egypt, and the tamarisk tree pillar then became an object of worship in Byblos.

On her return to Egypt, Isis left the chest in a safe place while she went off to find her son, the hawk-headed solar god Horus. Set, however, had heard of the queen's return and, while out hunting, had discovered where the chest was hidden. In his rage he dismembered the body of Osiris and scattered it in fourteen pieces all over Egypt. When Isis was told of this further outrage, she traveled all over the land to retrieve the parts of Osiris, and every time she found a part of the body, she erected a shrine to mark the place. Each of these sacred sites was on a hill, and the burial spots were marked by a tree to signify that Osiris had risen from the dead. The fourteenth part of Osiris's body—his penis—was never found because it had been swallowed by a fish. Isis made a gold replica of her husband's organ and buried it at Mendes, where there was a temple dedicated to the worship of a ram or goat god. In medieval times, the devil was sometimes called the goat of Mendes because it was believed that at his temple bizarre rituals were performed involving naked priestesses undertaking the sex act with goats. In addition, in the medieval witch trials it was alleged that women had intercourse with the devil, who appeared in the shape of a ram or goat.

Osiris became the focus of the cult of resurrection in dynastic Egypt, and his devotees believed that by worshipping him they would attain eternal life. Because Osiris had introduced barley and corn to Egypt, his major religious festival coincided with the gathering of the harvest and he became recognized as a god of vegetation who died in the autumn and was reborn in the spring. His myth therefore has similarities to that of other Middle Eastern fertility gods such as Adonis, Attis, and Dionysius.

Osiris was also credited with introducing the vine and grapes into Egypt. Likewise, in the Greek mysteries Dionysius, or Bacchus, was worshipped as the patron god of the vineyard, and he was often depicted simply as a bearded face carved on a tree or represented by a pillar decorated with a bearded mask surrounded by leaves. These representations are similar to the foliate masks said to represent the English folklore character Jack-in-the-Green or the Green Man that can be seen in pre-Reformation churches. We can also compare these images to those in the story of Osiris's body entangled in the branches of a tree that is later worshipped as a sacred cult object.

Dionysius and Osiris both have links to the cult of Adonis, whose worship was widespread throughout the Middle East in ancient times. Adonis was revered by the Semitic peoples of Babylonia and Syria and was originally known as Tammuz, but this name was changed to Adonis, which means "lord" and has obvious linguistic connections to the Jewish Adonai used to describe one of the aspects of Yahweh.

According to legend, Adonis or Tammuz was born at midnight on December 24 and burst into life from the trunk of a tree. Both these events suggest parallels to Osiris, Jesus, and the Green Man. Tammuz was a boy-god and the consort of the Babylonian goddess of love and war, Ishtar, who was revered by the Sumerians as Nanna and by the Canaanites as Astarte. Ishtar was identified with the moon and the "morning star," Venus (the symbol associated with the rebel angel Lucifer in the Judeo-Christian Bible, who was later misidentified as Satan or the devil), and she features in the Babylonian myth of the Flood borrowed by the Hebrews.

In the myth of Tammuz and Ishtar, the young god is Ishtar's lover and he is killed by a wild boar and transported to the underworld. Mourning her loss, the goddess travels to the land of the dead in an attempt to recover her lost consort. While she is away, the crops fail, the cattle become sterile, and men and women lose the ability to make love. At each of the seven gates of the underworld, the goddess is forced to remove an item of clothing until, naked and defenseless, she finally enters the realm of the dead. As a result of her plea to the rulers of the underworld, Tammuz is reborn. Ishtar returns to earth and the fertility of the land is restored.

The worship of the fertility god Tammuz as practiced in the vicinity of the temple in Jerusalem is mentioned by Ezekiel, the prophet of the Hebrew scriptures. Describing a vision given to him by Yahweh, the prophet says in Ezekiel 8:14, "Then He brought me to the door of the gate of the Lord's house [Solomon's temple] which was toward the north; and behold there sat women weeping for Tammuz." He then goes on to describe a group of men standing within the temple precincts facing the east and worshipping the sun in the manner of the pagans.

The myths of Osiris, Dionysius, and Adonis-Tammuz contain the key elements of death, rebirth, and fertility. These elements, together with the role of each of the men as a consort of the great mother goddess, are central to any understanding of the legend of Hiram Abiff, the pagan origins of Freemasonry, and the Utopian vision that forms the political ideal of those occult fraternities that are based on

Masonic ideals. According to ancient accounts, the ruler of Tyre was also called Hiram and was said to have been a priest-king of the cult of Adonis. In accordance with the religious beliefs of the time, this priest-king was sacrificed to the goddess when he became too old to represent Tammuz in the annual festival dedicated to the god. On his death, the king's soul allegedly passed into the body of his son or the chosen replacement, who then ruled as the priest-king in his place. Is it possible that Hiram Abiff was the son of the priest-king of Tammuz? He is certainly referred to as the son of the widow (the mourning goddess), and this title was adopted by medieval masons to describe themselves.

In the kabbalistic traditions describing the building of Solomon's temple, it is said that the craftsmen who came from Tyre were paid in corn, wine, and oil. These were the sacrificial offerings associated with the fertility cults of the dying gods such as Osiris and Adonis. The same traditions relate how Solomon carried King Hiram of Tyre off to hell by evoking a demon. When the king returned, he told Solomon all that he had seen and learned in the infernal kingdom. The rabbis suggest this was the true source of Solomon's wisdom. It is possible that this story means that the Hebrew king became a pupil of Hiram and was instructed by him in the mysteries of the goddess Ishtar or Astarte and her descent into the underworld. There are references in the lengthy correspondence between the two kings consisting of riddles Solomon had to solve. This suggests that some secret information or esoteric knowledge was being transferred to the Hebrew monarch in a coded form.

Early Masonic historians regarded Hiram Abiff as a symbolic representative of Osiris, the god of death and rebirth. Hiram is slain at the west gate of the temple, which is where the sun sets. In Egyptian mythology, the underworld, or Halls of Amenti ruled by Osiris as the lord of the dead, is situated beyond the western ocean. Traditionally, the god rises from the dead in the north, and in Egyptian mythology this direction is ruled astrologically by the zodiac sign of Leo the lion. In the third degree of Freemasonry, the candidate representing Hiram

Abiff is symbolically raised from the dead by a special Masonic handshake known as the lion's grip.

In both the Masonic and Egyptian mysteries, the resurrected "god" is buried on a hill in a tomb marked by a tree. Osiris was also called the Lord of the Acacia Tree—and this was the same tree planted on the grave of Hiram Abiff by his three assassins. In Canaan the worship of the goddess Astarte involved trees and pillars erected in sacred groves and on hills as symbols of her divinity. In Royal Arch Masonry the candidate for initiation is informed that the sacred name of God is really Jebalon. This name has been deciphered as a coded reference to the two major gods of the Middle Eastern fertility cults—Osiris and Baal—combined with the Hebrew tribal god Jehovah. In Masonry, God is also referred to as the Great Architect of the Universe, which signifies the importance of sacred geometry in the design of sacred buildings based on the Hermetic axiom of "As above, so below." This axiom imparts the ancient philosophy that the material plane of existence is a mirror reflection of the spiritual realm.

The political aspirations of Freemasonry, revealed in their influence on the revolutionary movements and protosocialism of eighteenth- and nineteenth-century Europe, can be traced back to the myth of the Golden Age in predynastic Egypt during the reign of Osiris and Isis and, before the Flood, to the Babylonian and Hebrew myths of Creation. In the legend of Osiris, the god-king is a civilizing influence in a land inhabited by primitive savages who had no concept of morality or law. The priesthood of Osiris was the heir to a political Utopia expressed through spiritual symbols. It is this vision that was shared by the secret societies of medieval Europe, which were associated with the rise of Freemasonry and the political doctrine that was at its center.

Occult tradition alleges that Hiram Abiff was secretly a member of an ancient society known as the Dionysian Artificers, who first appeared around 1000 BCE, when the temple in Jerusalem was being erected. They took their name from the Greek god, possessed secret signs and passwords by which they recognized each other, were divided into chapters or lodges ruled by a master, and were dedicated to helping the poor. They established lodges in all the Mediterranean lands and their influence spread as far east as India. With the rise of the Roman Empire, Dionysian lodges were founded in central and western Europe, including the British Isles.

The Artificers were also connected with another secret society known as the Ionians. Members of this society had settled in Asia Minor and were dedicated to the spread of civilization, especially in its Greek form, to what they regarded as the barbarian world. Allegedly, the Ionians were responsible for the famous temple of the goddess Diana at Ephesus. Architects from this society traveled from Tyre with members of the Dionysian Artificers to work on Solomon's temple. Later, the Artificers called themselves the Sons of Solomon and used as their trademark Solomon's magical seal: two interlaced triangles representing the union of the male and female energies. The Artificers who settled in Israel founded the Cassidens, who were a guild of craftsmen skilled in the repair of religious buildings. This new sect was allegedly instrumental in the foundation of the mystical Jewish group known as the Essenes, who have become famous through the modern discovery of the Dead Sea Scrolls. In the esoteric tradition, Jesus of Nazareth is said to have been an Essene and there are allegedly connections between this group and the medieval Knights Templar.

The Dionysian Artificers believed that the temples they built had to be constructed by the principles of sacred geometry reflecting the divine plan of God. By the use of symmetry, measurement, and proportion the Artificers constructed religious buildings to represent the human body as a symbol of the universe. Their theory of architecture was based on Hermetic philosophy and the pantheistic belief in the holistic unity between the universe and God. They also promoted the political ideal of a Utopia on earth expressed in symbolic form. Humanity was the ashlar, or crude block of stone, that the master mason or Grand Architect (God) was constantly molding and polishing to transform it into an object of perfection. The hammer and chisel of the mason became symbolic of the cosmic forces that shaped the spiritual destiny of humankind. In eighteenth-century speculative

Masonry, the hammer or gavel was a symbol of divine power. It was used to measure the hallowed precincts of the lodge, which was as far as the grand master could throw the hammer in any direction.

The Roman architect and master builder Vitrivius, born in the first century CE, was influenced by the Dionysian Artificers. His theories formed the basis for much of the architecture of the Roman Empire, and, with the rediscovery of classical knowledge in the sixteenth century, they also had an impact on the greatest architects of the Renaissance. Vitrivius's concept of the magical theater, representing the microcosmos of the world as a symbol of the macrocosmos of the universe, was repeated in William Shakespeare's famous phrase "All the world's a stage, and all the men and women merely players . . ." and the naming of the Globe Theatre. It has been claimed that Shakespeare was a Rosicrucian initiate, and if he was, he would have been familiar with the ideas of Vitrivius and the Dionysian Artificers.

In the Masonic tradition, the emperor Caesar Augustus is named as the patron of the masons in ancient Rome and is said to have been grand master of the Roman College of Architects. This society was organized into guilds with symbols based on the tools of the mason's trade such as the plumb line, the square, compasses, and the level. The college had initiation rituals involving the pagan myth of death and rebirth that are familiar from the Egyptian and Greek mysteries. A temple built and used by the college was unearthed at Pompeii, which was destroyed by the volcanic eruption of Mount Vesuvius in 71 CE. Among the symbols discovered in the temple were the double triangle of Solomon, the black and white tracing board (first used by the Dionysian Artificers), the human skull, the plumb line, the pilgrim's staff, and the ragged robe. All these later emerged as significant symbols used in the lodges of medieval masonry and speculative Freemasonry.

The traditions of the Roman College of Architects appear to have been passed onto the Order of Comacine Masters, which flourished during the reign of the emperors Constantine and Theodosius in the fourth century CE, when Christianity was emerging as the dominant religion of the Roman Empire. According to its founding legend, the order was started by ex-members of the Roman College of Architects who were forced to flee from the barbarians when Rome was sacked. They set up their new headquarters on the island of Comacini in Lake Como, and in 643 CE, they were placed under the patronage of the king of Lombardy, who gave to the order control over all the masons and architects in Italy. The Comacine Order was divided into lodges ruled by grand masters and its members wore white aprons and gloves and recognized each other by secret signs and passwords.

The order was responsible for the Lombardic and Romanesque styles of architecture and can be seen as the link between the architects and masons who built the pagan temples and the master builders who erected the Gothic cathedrals of western Europe in the Christian Middle Ages. There is evidence that the Comacini masons traveled all over Europe and, according to the historian Bede, even reached Anglo-Saxon England, where they were responsible for building a church in Northumbria.

Although the masons who built the medieval churches and cathedrals were nominally Christian, the profusion of heathen symbols and images in these ancient buildings indicates many of them were still pagan at heart. Reference has been made earlier to the Green Man images found in old churches, but other pagan symbols can also be found, including the Sheela-na-gig, which are crude representations of the naked female form in the shape of women with their legs open to display their cunni. They have been identified as images of the pagan goddess of fertility worshipped in Celtic times and were believed to have been placed on churches to ward off evil spirits. Other carvings found in medieval churches depict monks and priests in sexual poses with wanton young girls, performing homosexual acts, or wearing the heads of animals.

Along with their pagan religious beliefs, the medieval masonic guilds also held radical political views advanced for their age, which they expressed freely and with some conviction. In common with their pagan antecedents, the masons were promoters of a Utopian vision of humanity's future. In a period when feudalism was just another name for slavery, the guilds of artisans organized themselves into mutual self-help groups that preached the virtues of democracy and the rights of the individual several hundred years before these goals would be achieved by the common people.

This public image of protective associations that used their powers to promote fair-trading and business ethics concealed the fact that the Freemasons were a secret society with pagan origins that promoted political opinions that were regarded as extreme. In accordance with the esoteric doctrine concealed in the symbolism surrounding the building of Solomon's temple, the Freemasons believed it was their spiritual duty to perfect the temple of the human body as a representation of the Divine. The occult initiates who were the real power behind the secret societies knew that to achieve their aim, they had to use the political system, and in the twelfth century they began to put their plan into operation.

2

THE CURSE
OF THE TEMPLARS

To understand the rise of the medieval secret societies, we first have to examine the background to the foundation of Christianity that formed the major influence on European politics in the Middle Ages. Orthodox histories of the early Church give the false impression that the new faith replaced the allegedly degenerate pagan religions within the space of a few hundred years and with only moderate resistance from the followers of the old gods. The deathbed conversion of Emperor Constantine to the new religion and his acceptance of it as the official faith of the Roman Empire, which was already in decline during his lifetime, provided the early Christians with an established power base. Yet they still faced strong and often violent opposition from the adherents of the pagan religions who were reluctant to accept the new faith—at least not in the form presented by the early Church, which had effectively suppressed the authentic teachings of Jesus of Nazareth.

When Jesus was preaching his radical message to his fellow Jews in Judaea, which was under Roman occupation, the priesthood of the established pagan religions had become corrupt and power-crazed. They were being challenged by the mystery cults that offered the occult path to spiritual enlightenment. These mystery cults were based on the ancient motifs of death, rebirth, and fertility expressed through the inner symbolism of the pagan religions of Egypt, Chaldea, Babylon, and Greece. They used elaborate initiation ceremonies, arcane symbolism, and theatrical rituals to provide the initiate with the revelation of the spiritual reality hidden behind the illusion of the material world. During initiation, the neophyte was placed in a trance and experienced contact with the gods through a symbolic journey to the underworld. He or she symbolically died and was then symbolically reborn as a perfected soul. The purpose behind these rituals was to prove to the candidate that the body in which he or she incarnated on the physical plane was an illusory object, that the spiritual realm was the only true reality, and that reincarnation on earth was a learning process for spiritual development. These pagan beliefs were to form the central mystery drama of the initiation rituals practiced in the lodges of speculative Freemasonry.

While the Church prohibited pagan doctrines such as reincarnation (which was condemned by the Council of Nicaea in 325 CE), rededicated pagan temples to Christian worship, and transformed the old pagan gods into saints, it soon discovered that it was impossible to eradicate paganism totally. Goddess worship was prevalent in the ancient world and the Roman Church's devotion to the Virgin Mary is one example of the feminine principle's influence on its early beliefs. The Virgin was given the title Queen of Heaven and was depicted wearing a blue robe decorated with stars and standing on a crescent moon. This image is almost identical to ancient representations of Ishtar, the goddess of love, as she was worshipped by the Babylonians. The statues of the Madonna holding the infant Jesus in her arms, which were erected in Catholic churches, are almost exact copies of the effigies of Isis suckling her baby son Horus, which are found in Egyptian temples.

During the period following the emergence of the mystery cults and the adoption of Christianity as the official religion of the Roman Empire, a new mystical movement arose in the Middle East that attempted to synthesize the best elements of the decaying paganism with new Christian beliefs. This movement was known as gnosticism, from the Greek *gnosis* meaning "knowledge." The gnostics believed, in common with the original disciples of Jesus, that direct contact could be made with God without the intercession of an established priesthood. They claimed to have preserved the real teachings of Jesus that they believed were suppressed by the ecclesiastical councils set up by the Church to produce a unified dogma for the new religion.

The gnostics derived their spiritual inspiration from a variety of sources, including the Greek and Roman mysteries, ancient Egyptian mythology, the Hermetic tradition, the dualistic doctrines of Zoroastrianism, Middle Eastern fertility cults, the Chaldean stellar religion, and esoteric Christianity. Gnosticism derived its central beliefs from the writings of the Persian spiritual teacher Zoroaster, who lived circa 1800 BCE. He was a priest of the Indo-Iranian religion that involved the worship of the elemental forces of water and fire. At the age of thirty, Zoroaster had a vision during which one of the Iranian gods, Ahura Mazda or Ormazd, appeared to him and said he was the supreme being. From this moment, Zoroaster broke away from the established religion and taught his own philosophy based on the universe as a cosmic battleground between the opposing forces of light and darkness in eternal conflict. According to Zoroastrianism, the enlightened person had to choose between one or the other of these principles.

Initiation for both genders into the Zoroastrian religion and its rites took place at the age of fifteen. The candidate for initiation was given a special cord that he or she wore as a girdle, passed three times around the waist and knotted in the front and at the back. Every day, the initiate untied the cord and then replaced it while reciting prayers in the fashion of a Catholic rosary. In fact, there are similarities between this cord and the one worn by the Brahmin priests in India, especially because it was worn over a white cotton shirt or tunic, which was a symbol of spiritual perfection.

In its later stages, Zoroastrianism became associated with the mystery cult of the bull god Mithras, which originated in Persia as an offshoot of the Zoroastrian religion, but swiftly spread westward, where it made many converts among the soldiers of imperial Rome who were attracted to its alpha male image. Mithras was a scholar god of light who, like Jesus, was born in a cave surrounded by animals and shepherds at the winter solstice in December. A famous statue of Mithras, which can be seen in the British Museum, depicts him sitting astride a bull and plunging a dagger into its throat. Blood pours from the wound and drips onto the earth to fertilize the land. Mithras wears a short tunic and cloak and on his head is the Phrygian cap, which was also associated with Adonis and Attis. This distinctive headgear was later adopted by both the medieval masons and the revolutionary guard during the French Revolution.

In Zoroastrianism and gnosticism, Mithras is the mediator between the cosmic opposites of Ormuzd and Ahriman, the gods who represented the forces of light and the powers of darkness, respectively. By understanding the role of Mithras, the gnostics taught that his human devotees could learn how to reconcile the good and evil aspects of their own nature. They realized that evil was only the shadow image of good and that both had to exist in an imperfect world. Mithras was also associated with another gnostic deity known as Aion, who represented endless time. The Zoroastrians viewed the universe as operating within a cyclic time scale. Aion was a god of both destruction and creation who was symbolized in human form with a lion's head and a serpent entwined around his body. He is often depicted as ithyphallic and stands on a globe of the world surrounded by the starry circle of the zodiac. A statue of Aion unearthed from a Roman villa of the first century CE and now preserved in the Vatican shows him winged and naked except for a Masonic-type apron.

The candidate for initiation into the Mithraic mysteries participated in a rite of death and rebirth that can be compared to Masonic ceremony. He was told to lie on the ground and act as if he was dead. The high priest of the cult then grasped the "dead" initiate by the right hand and raised him up in a symbolic act of rebirth. After the initiation, the members of the cult shared a ritual meal of bread and wine. During this symbolic communion, they believed they were eating the flesh of the young sun god and drinking his blood.

As stated earlier, the gnostics also derived some of their lore from the stellar religion practiced by the Chaldean astrologers. They adopted the seven planetary spirits or gods of their pagan pantheon, which were also represented by the classical gods of Roman and Greek mythology: Mercury (Hermes), Venus (Aphrodite), Mars (Ares), Jupiter (Zeus), Saturn (Chronos), Sol, and Luna. In gnostic belief, these gods were transformed into archangels who then became the central focus of medieval magic and the Hermetic tradition.

The gnostics attempted to unite both paganism and Christianity and, as a result, produced a hybrid version of the new faith based on the heretical texts that circulated after the death of Jesus. It is well known that the gospels were written many years after the Crucifixion and that their authors were not direct witnesses to the events they describe, even though these authors used the names of the disciples of Jesus. The early councils of the Church decided which gospels were to be included in the authorized Christian scriptures and rejected those that did not fit into their version of the Christian faith.

In the orthodox version of the Christian scriptures, Jesus is alluded to as the offspring of the royal house of David, which means he was descended from the magician Solomon, who built a temple in Jerusalem for the worship of the goddess. The gnostics noted references in the heretical gospels to Jesus having brothers and also the fact that he was called the son of the widow because his human father, Joseph, died before Jesus began his preaching crusade. The son of the widow was a symbolic title that was also given to Hiram Abiff, the Egyptian god Horus, and Mithras.

Gnostic belief stated that Jesus was an ordinary man who had been overshadowed by the spirit of God and became the Christ—from the Greek *kristos* meaning "anointed one." This advent happened when he was baptized in the River Jordan by his fellow Essene, John the Baptist. The physical death of Jesus on the cross, the gnostics argued, could be truly explained only if the Christ force left him before the crucifixion. Alternatively, Jesus could have survived death on the cross by substituting a scapegoat who died in his place, or if he was taken down from the cross while still alive, was revived, and was smuggled out of the country.

If Jesus did not die on the cross, what happened to him? Various speculative theories have him leading a monastic life in an Essene community on the shores of the Dead Sea after the crucifixion; dying of old age in Kashmir; being killed by the Romans at Masada during the Jewish revolt; or even traveling to Europe with his wife, Mary Magdalene, to sire the future French royal dynasty.

Whatever they believed about the death of Jesus, the majority of gnostics rejected the symbol of the cross. They believed it was totally wrong to worship an instrument of death and torture. Other gnostics adopted the more extreme view that the god of the Hebrew scriptures, Jehovah, was Satan and that the Supreme Creator of the universe had sent Christ to incarnate in the body of Jesus to save humanity from Satan's evil clutches. According to this view, the Romans and the Jewish priests were acting as agents of Satan-Jehovah and they conspired to have Jesus murdered, so to honor the cross was to worship a symbol of satanic evil.

This belief was also held by the Manicheans, who took their name from their founder Mani, who was born in Persia in the third century CE. Mani had been converted to gnosticism through the teachings of Zoroaster and he preached the philosophy of dualism, according to which the universe was symbolically divided between God and Satan, who were eternally battling for the souls of humankind in a cosmic chess game. The Manicheans had strict religious beliefs, including a rule of celibacy for their priesthood—both men and women, a vegetarian diet, and a total prohibition on the consumption of alcohol and drugs. Mani's teachings spread rapidly through the Middle East and the Roman Empire, and at one stage the Manicheans were seriously competing for converts with the emergent Christian cult. Manicheanism also spread eastward from Persia, and in China and India it gained many converts during the early centuries of the Christian era.

Mani's heresy seems to have been a contributing factor in the rise of the Cathars, or Albigensi, in southern France in the eleventh and twelfth centuries CE. The origins of the Cathars are obscure, but it is known that dualistic heretics had established groups in the Middle East and eastern Europe in the tenth century. In Bulgaria, one sect known as the Bogomils was ruthlessly persecuted by the Church, which accused them of unnatural sexual practices. It is from this sect that we owe the origin of the modern slang word *buggery*, meaning anal intercourse, although there is no evidence that members of this cult ever indulged in this practice outside the imagination of their accusers.

From Bulgaria and Yugoslavia the Cathars (from the Greek *cathari*, meaning "pure ones") established communities in northern Italy, the Alpine regions, and southern France. As in most gnostic philosophies, the Cathars taught the dualistic belief in the opposing powers of light and darkness. Yet they also taught the pagan belief in reincarnation and they identified the material world as the plane of illusion. The Cathars believed that humankind could be saved only by leading a moral life and, in common with the gnostics, they rejected the cross as an evil symbol. They refused to accept the Roman Church as the true guardian of the teachings of Jesus, taught that all men and women were equal, and founded hospitals and schools for the poor. Within their priesthood, the Cathars had an inner circle marked by seven degrees of initiation, representing the stages to spiritual perfection. Ceremonies for these stages were performed out of doors, in caves and in the woods, and the Cathar initiates wore white tunics tied with a cord.

Faced with the Cathar threat, the Church reacted in the traditional manner: It charged the heretics with devil worship, human sacrifice, cannibalism, incest, homosexuality, and celebrating the Black Mass. The last charge was based on the Cathar practice of the *agape*, or love feast, a ritual that had been inherited from the pagan mysteries. In 1209, the Church launched a crusade against the Cathars and thousands of them were killed. When asked by his men whom they should put to the sword and whom they should spare in the towns they attacked, one knight who led the crusade replied with the immortal words: "Kill them all. God will know his own."

The Cathars did not meekly accept their persecution by the Church but fought back with all the resources at their disposal. Final defeat came, however, at Montségur, a stronghold in the foothills of the Pyrenees, where, in March 1244, more than two hundred Cathar priests were massacred by Christian forces. Shortly before the stronghold was overwhelmed by the crusaders, it is claimed that a secret treasure was removed from the castle and hidden somewhere in the surrounding countryside. Speculation has been rife over the centuries as to the nature of this treasure. Some occultists have even claimed that the Cathars were the guardians of the Holy Grail—the cup used by Jesus at the Last Supper—which the Cathars did not want captured by the Roman Church because they regarded the pope as the puppet of Satan. Other theories claim the mysterious treasure was a hoard of esoteric writings on the hidden teachings of the Cathars that were derived from pre-Christian sources, which does seem more likely than the Grail theory.

Historians who have studied the Cathars have pointed out that the area around Montségur has many pagan connections. A few miles from the castle is the site of a druidic altar dating from Celtic times and a Christian cross carved with pagan symbols. In nearby caves there is evidence of the worship of Mithras, and the site of Montségur itself was reputed to have been a center of solar worship thousands of years before the arrival of the Cathars.

As we have seen, the Cathars had links to Middle Eastern dualism, the mystery cults, and the gnostics, and it is through these connections that they can be linked to Islamic secret societies such as the Sufis and the Assassins, who in turn influenced the Christian Order of the Knights Templar. Traditionally, the Sufis are followers of the esoteric tradition concealed within the orthodox practices and beliefs of Islam. Today, the religion founded by the prophet Muhammad is essentially patriarchal, but the original religion of Arabia was centered on the worship of the feminine principle. The city of Mecca, the holy center of Islamic belief, was originally the site of a pagan temple. It is believed that the mysterious black stone revered by modern Muslims, which was allegedly given to Abraham by the archangel Gabriel in Islamic lore, was in fact the cult object of a pre-Islamic center of goddess worship.

According to Islamic belief, Friday is a sacred day. In the classical world, this day was dedicated to the goddess of love, Venus. The traditional color of Muhammad is green, which is associated with the great mother goddess in her Egyptian aspect as Isis, the Lady of Nature. The Islamic symbols of the scimitar and the crescent and star have been identified as connected to the moon or Venus. It is possible that the prophet Muhammad had contacts with the gnostic belief system. He was certainly taught by Christian monks and acknowledged their contribution in the founding of his new religion. Although Islam and Christianity were political rivals in the Middle Ages, there were several connections between the two religions: Both were monotheistic and patriarchal and derived their spiritual inspiration from a common Semitic source. The followers of Islam recognized Jesus as a great spiritual teacher, although they did not accept his divinity, and they also revered many of the patriarchs of the Hebrew scriptures.

While the Sufi tradition allegedly originated within Islam, it has been suggested that its beliefs were far older. In his posthumous book *The Masters of Wisdom,* J. G. Bennett describes how the Russian mystic Gregori Gurdjieff took him to see the prehistoric cave paintings at Lascaux. Gurdjieff showed Bennett the wall drawings of herds of reindeer crossing a river and explained this was a symbolic depiction of an ancient initiation ritual. According to Gurdjieff, the number of antlers on the deer represented the level of spirituality reached by the initiates, who considered the deer totemic emblems. Gurdjieff confided in Bennett that these ancient mystery schools dated back thirty thousand to forty thousand years and that he had learned about them while studying cave drawings in the Caucasian mountains and Turkestan. The Russian mystic had received initiation from Sufi masters, so when, in the same passage of the book, Bennett reveals that there is a tradition in Sufism that it originated in central Asia forty thousand years ago, we do not need to guess the source for this startling information.

The introduction of Islam was resisted by those Arabs who still practiced the worship of pagan gods. Following the death of the prophet Muhammad, several heretical sects arose promoting alternative forms of Islam, and secret societies were founded based on these philosophies. These sects included the Ismailis, the Batimis, the Karmathites, the Fatimites, and the Druses. Several of these heretical sects were inspired by gnostic and Manichean ideas and some claimed to preserve the pre-Islamic Arabian occult tradition.

The most powerful and well-documented Islamic secret society operating in the Middle East was the sect known popularly as the Assassins. Their origins are shrouded in mystery, but they seem to have been loosely connected to gnosticism. In the eleventh century CE, a mystic named Abdullah appeared in Persia with the mission to establish a pantheistic religion to replace Islam. He founded a secret society to propagate his beliefs, which were derived from a mixture of Hinduism and the teachings of the Persian heretic Mani. Initiates into this society were offered nine degrees of illumination that were similar to the initiation rites of the Eleusian mysteries practiced in ancient Greece.

The initiates were taught the mystical significance of the number seven, which in the esoteric tradition was the number of planes of existence from the material to the spiritual. They were also taught that God had sent seven great teachers into the world to lead humanity to spiritual perfection: Adam, the first man; Noah, survivor of the Flood; Abraham, the Chaldean founder of the religion of Yahweh; Moses, the Egyptian initiate and founder of the kabbalah; Jesus; Muhammad; and Ishmael. Members of the society were also taught the Greek philosophies of Plato and Aristotle and were indoctrinated with the esoteric teachings of the Sufis.

Abdullah's secret society spread throughout the Middle East, gathering in small groups to conspire against Islam until it was suppressed in 1123. One of its initiates was Hasan-i-sabbah, who organized an off-shoot branch of Abdullah's secret society in 1093 called the Order of the Devoted. It renounced the mystical pantheism of the original society in favor of the positive virtues of the Qur'an. It was this Order of the Devoted that developed into the feared sect known as the Assassins. It is alleged that the Assassins derived their title from the Arabic *hashishmar,* or "eater of hashish," which was the hemp plant used for ritual purposes. Other authorities claim that it is derived from the Arabic *hass,* meaning "to destroy" or *asana,* which means "to lay snares." Hasan took the traditional title of Sheikh al-Jebal, or Mountain Chief, hence his popular title Old Man of the Mountain. He and his followers established a castle at Alamut, or the Eagle's Nest, in Persia. Perched six hundred feet above a valley gorge and surrounded by hostile mountains, it was virtually impregnable. From this lofty fortress, the Assassins waged an international war of terrorism against anyone who opposed them.

Hasan died in 1124, but his society of trained killers lived on as hired mercenaries who were willing to murder anyone at a price. Several well-known European Crusaders used the Assassins, including the English king Richard the Lionheart and Frederick II of Sicily, who was excommunicated by the pope for hiring members of the sect to murder the duke of Bavaria.

The Assassin stronghold was finally overrun by the Mongols in 1256, and the members of the order were subsequently scattered all over the Middle East. As late as 1754, however, the British consul at Aleppo claimed that the Order of Assassins still survived in Persia, Syria, and India. It is also alleged they had taught their murderous skills to the Hindu cult of the Thuggee, or Thugs, who worshipped the goddess of destruction Kali and practiced human sacrifice during the days of the British Raj. In 1866, the Assassins were mentioned in a court case in Bombay featuring a Persian prince who claimed to be a direct descendant of the original grand master of the order.

Some authorities have attempted to provide concrete links between the Assassins and the Sufis, who have been identified as goddess worshippers because of their use of the double-ax symbol (associated with ancient goddess worship) and the shamanic nature of their rituals involving dancing and chanting. Pottery painted with the pentagram or five-pointed star and the *vesica piscis,* an abstract symbol of the female vulva, have been unearthed from the ruins of the Assassins' mountain stronghold. They also wore white tunics and a red sash, symbolizing innocence and blood, which is similar to the costume adopted by the Zoroastrians, the Sufis, the Cathars, and the Templars.

In the period when the Assassins were operating, the Roman Church launched its first Crusades to extend its political power into the Middle East and reclaim the Holy Land from the Saracens. The beginning of the Crusades can be dated from the 1060s, when Pope Alexander II granted indulgences to the knights who had fought the Moorish invaders in Spain. In 1096, an eccentric monk, Peter the Hermit, led a Peasants' Crusade, consisting of several thousand men, women, and children across Europe, to liberate Jerusalem from the Arabs. The majority of these unfortunates were massacred en route by bands of outlaws and by the armies of the Byzantine Empire, which included the modern countries of Bulgaria, Yugoslavia, Greece, and Turkey. This early, disastrous Crusade was followed by others that were better organized and led by trained knights. These achieved considerable military success and, in the early twelfth century, finally established a Christian kingdom in Jerusalem.

Despite the establishment of a Christian army of occupation in the Holy Land, European pilgrims traveling to the sacred sites still faced many dangers. On Easter 1119, a group of 309 pilgrims traveling from Jerusalem to Jordan were attacked and killed by the Saracens. King Baldwin II of Jerusalem was so shocked by this atrocity that he took steps to prevent it from ever happening again. Baldwin had in his employment a Frankish knight named Sir Hugh de Payens, who had spent three years fighting in the Holy Land. The king suggested to de Payens that he organize a chivalric order of knights to defend the pilgrim routes and he granted part of his palace as the headquarters for the new organization. The palace was inside the enclosure of a mosque, which stood on the site of Solomon's original temple, and for this reason Sir Hugh called his new order the Templi Militia, or Soldiers of the Temple. He later changed this name to the grander sounding Poor Knights of the Temple of Solomon in Jerusalem.

Baldwin initially funded the Knights Templar, but de Payens decided to travel to Europe and seek patronage himself, for he knew

Seal of the Order of the Temple

that if the order was to succeed, it needed support from the Church. He had already decided that the Templars would be warrior monks and he accepted the patronage of St. Bernard of Clairvaux, founder of the Cistercian monks. Bernard wrote the monastic rules for the order and interceded on its behalf with the pope, who granted his approval.

With the religious patronage of St. Bernard, the Templars took oaths of poverty, chastity, and obedience to Christian principles and declared their intention to protect the pilgrim routes to the Holy Land. They dedicated themselves to the Mère de Dieu, or Mother of God (Virgin Mary), swearing to "consecrate their swords and their lives to the defense of the mysteries of the Christian faith." Considering the history and later downfall of the order, this vow was very significant.

Although this account is the generally accepted version of the foundation of the Templars, controversy still surrounds the order's origins. In their best-selling book *Holy Blood, Holy Grail* (1982) Henry Lincoln, Michael Baigent, and Richard Leigh claim that the order was an offshoot of an even older secret society called the Priory of Sion. This organization was dedicated to the reestablishment of the old

Merovingian dynasty in France, which allegedly descended from the offspring of Jesus and Mary Magdalene, and it was the éminence grise behind the Order of the Rosy Cross.

The foundation of the Priory of Sion can allegedly be traced back to the gnostic adept Ormus, who lived in the first century CE. He was converted to the heretical version of the Christian message by Mark, a disciple of Jesus of Nazareth, and he formed a secret society uniting esoteric Christianity with the teachings of the pagan mystery schools. Ormus adopted as his symbol a cross surmounted by a rose to signify the synthesis of the new and old religions. The red cross was later adopted by the Templars, while the rose cross was the sigil used by the medieval Rosicrucians to identify themselves.

Whatever the origins of the order, with the support of St. Bernard, the Templars seem to have gone from strength to strength. Pope Honorius gave them his papal blessing and the order adopted a white

A Knight Templar

mantle with a red equal-armed cross as their uniform. At first, the Templars adhered strictly to their vows of chastity and poverty, but shortly after the foundation of the order, they began to acquire political aspirations. The Templar tradition was firmly based on the revival of the chivalric ideal of knighthood that had been severely weakened by the Crusades, in which women and children had been massacred. Knights who had left Europe with a strict moral code of warfare had been brutalized by the battles with the Saracens and had indulged in an orgy of bloody slaughter, raping, and looting. The Templars wanted to restore the principles of knighthood and establish a new golden age of chivalry. On a political level, their ultimate aim was a united Europe ruled by Christian principles, although their version of Christianity differed greatly from that promoted by the Vatican.

Inspired by the grand masters of the order who had followed Sir Hugh de Payens, the Templars acquired both political and material power. Even while de Payens was alive, the order had become internationally established. In 1129, de Payens visited both England and Scotland and there contacted wealthy patrons who donated land and money to his cause. The order had also established itself in France and Spain, and in the Holy Land it had built a network of castles to defend the pilgrim routes and the sacred places of Christendom.

By the beginning of the thirteenth century, the Templars had become the international bankers of Europe, and the order was appointed the treasurer to the French royal family and to the Vatican. The grand masters of the military orders of warrior monks, which included the Templars, the Knights of St. John (the Hospitallers), and the Teutonic Knights, had gained considerable political power. By the thirteenth century, they controlled 40 percent of the frontiers of Europe. Ships owned by the Templars and the other military orders not only carried fighting men to the Middle East but also ferried wealthy pilgrims as paying passengers. On their return trips, the ships brought back cargoes that included spices, perfumes, and silk, which were then sold to merchants at high prices.

In January 1162, Pope Alexander III issued a special papal bull granting the Templars extraordinary powers. They were released from all spiritual obedience except to the pope himself, were allowed to have their own chaplains and burial grounds, and were freed from paying tithes but could instead collect them. In addition, the pope stated that once a knight became a Templar, he was forbidden to leave the order unless he transferred to another military order. This papal bull strengthened even more the political power of the order, and the grand master is reputed to have told Henry II of England, "You shall be king as long as you are just," suggesting that he had the power to topple the king from his throne.

The money-making schemes of the Templars were legendary. It is said that a group of knights was sent to a convent near Damascus where a miracle had taken place: A statue of the Virgin Mary had become clothed in flesh and from her nipples there spurted a rich liquid that allegedly had the power to heal the sick and wash away sin. The Templars, it is told, returned from the convent with a large supply of the liquid from the Virgin's breasts, which they bottled and sold to gullible pilgrims.

Yet rumors of misconduct by the members of the order were beginning to circulate. As early as 1208, the pope had censured the grand master because he claimed that, though the knights wore the Christian cross on their tunics, few followed the teachings of Jesus. He alleged that many of the men admitted to the order were known sinners and were guilty of adultery and other unspecified sexual offenses. The activities of the Templars based in Palestine also received adverse criticism from those who considered them disloyal to the Christian cause.

In 1219, the Templars professed their obedience to a papal legate when he headed an expeditionary force against Damascus. Yet the knights then disobeyed his orders and acted on their own. When King Frederick II of Sicily undertook his first Crusade to Egypt, the Templars conspired with the sultan so that the king's campaign was a failure. Frederick retaliated by seizing the Templar estates in Italy and Sicily, and they duly responded by dispossessing the Teutonic Knights, founded by Frederick, of their large estates in Syria.

It became generally believed that the Templars were forming secret pacts with the Saracens. This rumor seems to have been confirmed when the order entered into an alliance with the emir of Damascus against the Hospitallers (Knights of St. John). In 1259, relations between the two orders had degenerated to such an extent that open warfare broke out and a battle was fought between them. There were frequent examples of the Templars forging alliances with the Saracens, and they even had contacts with the Order of Assassins in a plot to give the Templars rule of Tyre, the ancient center of goddess worship and birthplace of Hiram Abiff.

Because the Templars were so powerful, few would openly challenge them, but events took place that would lead to a weakening of their political power with fateful consequences for the future of the order. These events coincided with the loss of their headquarters on the site of Solomon's temple in Jerusalem and the expulsion of the order from the Holy Land in 1291, when it was recaptured by the Saracens. In 1307, King Philip of France faced bankruptcy and he owed the Templars a considerable amount of money. Phillip heard that accusations were being made against the order by two renegade members, Roffo Dei and the prior of Montfaucan, who had been imprisoned by the Templars for unknown crimes. The two men had managed to escape and they sought the protection of the French king, which he freely offered in exchange for incriminating evidence of the secret activities of the knights.

Phillip IV passed the information on to Pope Clement V, and the king and the pontiff conspired to lure the grand master of the order, Jacques de Molay, into a trap on French soil. The pope requested that the grand master visit Paris from his headquarters in Cyprus to discuss a new Crusade in the Holy Land to recover Jerusalem from the Arabs. De Molay left Cyprus accompanied by his personal bodyguard of knights, one hundred fifty thousand gold florins, and six packhorses loaded with silver. He deposited this treasure in the Templar chapter house in Paris.

To provide de Molay with a false sense of security, Philip made the grand master the godfather of his son and invited him to attend the coming funeral of his sister-in-law as a pallbearer. In reality, the wily king was plotting the downfall of the Templars and the death of de Molay. The knights were staying at the Templar citadel in Paris, and on October 13, 1307, the king executed his plan. Troops surrounded the building and everyone inside was placed under arrest. Within forty-eight hours warrants had been issued ordering the detaining of every Templar in France, even though this was technically illegal because the order answered only to the pope and not to civil laws. On November 22, however, the pope issued a bull to all the Christian rulers in western Europe ordering them to arrest any member of the order residing in their countries. The fate of the Templars was sealed.

The list of charges against the order was a familiar one, for it had also been used against the Cathars in southern France, but there were some interesting new elements. Specifically, the Templars were accused of denying the tenets of the Christian faith, spitting or urinating on the crucifix during secret rites of initiation, worshipping in a dark cave a human skull or head called the Baphomet, anointing this head with

Jacques de Molay, last grand master of the Order of the Temple

blood or the fat of unbaptized babies, worshipping the devil in the shape of a black cat, and committing acts of sodomy and bestiality.

Other lesser charges alleged that the Templars swore allegiance only to the order, made secret pacts with the Saracens and carried out Islamic practices, and murdered anyone who opposed their aims and buried them secretly in unconsecrated ground. The Templars broke their vows of chastity and procured abortions for their female lovers, and the grand master of the order heard the knights' confessions and absolved them of all sins they performed in the name of the Templars.

What basis, if any, do these charges have in fact? It is easy to see the sensational allegations, which were supported by confessions extracted under torture, as a pretense concocted by a bankrupt king to allow him legally to take the order's wealth. The pope supported the plan because he had become fearful of the Templars political power, which was creating a church within the Church, threatening his own position as the anointed head of Christendom. In addition, the Templars had spent many years in the Middle East and the order had been founded on the site of King Solomon's temple. Two important Templar citadels were located at the ports of Tyre and Sidon, which were ancient centers of goddess worship associated with the pagan origins of Freemasonry. The Templars' uniform of red and white was also worn by the Assassins, with whom the knights had allegedly made pacts. One of the charges made against the Templars was that they wore a magical girdle or cord given to each member at his initiation ceremony. This suggests possible connections to the Zoroastrians, the Cathars, and the Sufis.

In their confessions made under torture, the knights said that Templar initiation ceremonies took place at night in candlelit chapels. Initiates were forced to renounce their Christian faith as a sign of their loyalty to the order and to spit, urinate, or trample on a crucifix. Blasphemous as this may seem, it is possible the initiate was told to perform this act because, like the Cathars, the Templars rejected the crucifix as an evil symbol of suffering and death. Some initiates confessed that they had been told by their superiors in the order that Jesus was a false prophet and that they should not respect the crucifix because it was "too young." This suggests elements of both gnostic dualism and paganism.

Candidates entering the order also had to kiss their initiator on the mouth, the navel, the penis, and at "the base of the spine." These kisses were regarded by critics of the order as proof of the members' perverted sexual activities, but in the occult tradition the naval, sexual organs, and perineum are the physical locations of the psychic centers of the human body, known in the East as the chakras. The perineum marks the Kundalini chakra, which is the psychic source of sexual energy in the body. Various techniques can be practiced that liberate this energy so that it travels up the spinal cord to spiritually illuminate the brain. It is possible that during their sojourn in the Middle East, members of the order contacted adepts from the Arab mystery schools, who taught them the secrets of sex magic. This theory is supported by the confessions of Templars who said that at the climax of the ceremony the initiate indulged in an act of sodomy with the chaplain.

Speculation has always been rife as to the exact nature of the cult object venerated by the Templars. This was an image in the shape of a skull or head and was called the Baphomet, which is a word of unknown derivation. It has been variously described as an androgynous deity with two faces and a long white beard and a human skull that uttered oracular prophecies and guided the destiny of the order. Some writers on the Templars have even speculated that this object was the Turin Shroud—allegedly the actual one used to wrap the body of Jesus after his death.

The nineteenth-century occultist Alphonse Constant, a former Roman Catholic priest who took the Jewish pseudonym Eliphas Levi, wrote extensively about the deity of the Templars when he took up the magical path. Levi regarded the Baphomet as a magical and pantheistic figure representing the absolute in a symbolic form. He reproduced an illustration of the Baphomet that seems to be based on an effigy of the deity found on the commandery of Saint-Bris-le-Vineux, a building owned by the order. The gargoyle is in the form of a bearded horned figure with pendulous female breasts, wings, and cloven feet. It sits in a cross-legged position resembling statues of the Celtic stag god, Cernunnos, or the Horned One, worshipped in Gaul (France) before the Roman occupation.

In Levi's illustration, the Baphomet is a goat-headed figure with androgynous features sitting on a cube. A torch blazes between the goat's horns, representing cosmic intelligence and spiritual illumination. In occult tradition, Lucifer—who is regarded by the Church as the devil—is called the light bringer because he grants his disciples spiritual illumination through incarnation on the physical plane. The two-horned cult in north Africa also worshipped a goat god with a torch blazing between his horns. It has been claimed this cult was imported to Moorish Spain and southern France, where it infiltrated the medieval witch cult. According to Levi, the head of the Baphomet combines the characteristics of a dog, a bull, and a goat and therefore it represents the three sources of the pagan mystery tradition: Egypt (the jackal god Anubis was the guide of the dead to the underworld and is identified with the Greek Hermes); India (the sacred bull may be the origin of Mithras); and Judaea (the scapegoat Azazel—the leader of the Fallen Angels—was sacrificed in the wilderness to cleanse the sins of the tribe).

On the forehead of the Baphomet, marking the physical site of the pineal gland or third eye, is the magical sign of the pentagram or five-pointed star representing humankind in its unperfected state. It is also a symbol of the morning star, Venus, which was associated with Ishtar and Astarte. The Lord of the Morning Star was also a title given to Lucifer, describing his fall from heaven in the Bible.

The androgynous figure of the Baphomet has female breasts and the lower part of its body is veiled, portraying the mysteries of generation. The phallic nature of the goat god, however, is symbolized by the caduceus, or wand entwined with two serpents, which was carried by Hermes. This symbol hides the erect penis of the Baphomet figure. Its belly is covered with scales representing the reptilian origin of the human race in the evolutionary process.

The Baphomet's androgynous nature is emphasized by the fact that one arm is masculine while the other is rounded and feminine. In addition, one hand points upward and the other downward, representing the Hermetic axiom "As above, so below." The hands also point to one black and one white crescent moon, signifying the waxing and waning lunar phases. These symbolize both the duality of human nature and the male and female principles, whose union brought the universe into physical manifestation, and the powers of light and darkness.

What does the word *baphomet* represent? The late Montague Summers, who wrote several books on witchcraft and demonology from an extreme Catholic viewpoint, derived the word from the Greek *baphmetis,* meaning "the baptism of wisdom," which referred to a secret ritual known only to the grand master of the Templars. The late Madeline Montalban, a well-known occultist and founder of the Order of the Morning Star, translated *baphomet* to read *bfmaat,* a word derived from the primeval Enochian language, which she claimed was spoken before the fall of the Tower of Babal and on the lost continent of Atlantis. The word eventually became known more widely by the magical researches of the Elizabethan astrologer and magician Dr. John Dee. In Enochian the word *baphomet* or *bfmaat* can be translated, according to Montalban, as "the opener of the door." She further interpreted the Baphomet figure as a glyph of the zodiac sign of Capricorn, which symbolized the material ambitions and political aspirations of the Templars. On an esoteric level, the goatish emblem of Capricorn is regarded as a symbol for the occult initiate who climbs the celestial mountain to achieve oneness with the Divine.

The late Idries Shah, a Muslim writer and Sufi master, claimed that *baphomet* comes from the Arabic word *abufihamat,* which can be translated as "the father of understanding" or "the source of wisdom and knowledge," and is a title used to describe a Sufi teacher. It is quite possible that the Templars were exposed both to the beliefs of Sufism and to the gnostic dualist philosophy during their period in the Holy Land. Many of the Templars were Middle Eastern by birth, including the grand master Philip of Nablus, elected in 1167, who was Syrian.

Eliphas Levi alleged in his writings that if the letters of the word *baphomet* were reversed they would read TEM OHP ABI. When this anagram is extended and translated into Latin it becomes *Templi omnium hominum pacis abbas,* or "the father of the temple of peace of all men." Levi regarded this as a reference to the temple built by Solomon, whose esoteric purpose was to bring peace to the world.

It has also been alleged that the Templars were secret goddess worshippers, and it has been noted that their patron was the Virgin Mary. One of the objects found in the Templar chapter house in Paris was the silver image of a female figure. Inside this figurine were some human bones wrapped in red and white linen. Dr. Hugh Schonfield, an expert on the Dead Sea Scrolls, has claimed there is a link between the Templars and the Essenes. He states that the word *baphomet* can be translated, by reference to a secret Essenic code, to read *sophia.* This is the Greek word for "wisdom" and is the name of the goddess worshipped in the gnostic religion. In addition, the mysterious black cat allegedly worshipped by the order has been identified by some occultists as an image of the Egyptian cat goddess Bast or the lion-headed goddess Sekhmet.

The accounts of the worship of the Baphomet were largely derived from confessions extracted under torture during which several members of the order died. Many members, however, confessed without recourse to torture and they confirmed the stories that were told by the agents of King Phillip, who infiltrated the order. On October 22, 1307, the grand master of the order, Jacques de Molay, confessed before an assembly of academics at the University of Paris that the charges made against the Templars were true. He wrote to his fellow members in an open letter, instructing them to confess freely the evil practices in which they had indulged. As a result of this letter, one of the leading members of the order who confessed was the grand treasurer, Hugh de Pairaud. He said that he had been responsible for initiating many knights into the order and had seen the Templars' god, who granted them their worldly wealth, made the land fertile, and caused the death of their enemies.

The investigation of the Templars' crimes was thorough and it lasted several years. In fact, it was not until 1312 that the pope officially disbanded the order. Many of the Templars who were found innocent of the charges or who had submitted to the Church were freed and granted pensions. Those who refused to recant were burned at the stake. King Philip obtained sizeable parts of the Templar estates and revenues, and the balance was shared by the Knights of St. John.

In March 1314, after several delays caused by the inability of the pope to accept fully the guilt of the Templars, de Molay was offered the chance to submit to the Church. When he refused, he was sentenced to death. The pyre was lit on a small island in the Seine between the gardens of the royal palace and the Church of the Hermit Brethren. Just before he died, de Molay announced that he was innocent and cursed the French king and the pope. He said that Philip would be summoned to his maker within twelve months and the pope before forty days. Clement died on April 20 and Philip died on November 29.

Although the Templar Order was decimated in France, it did not suffer as much in other European countries. In England, King Edward II reacted slowly to the papal bull condemning the Templars. He did place its members under arrest, but the English master of the Temple was allowed to draw a pension. Within a month of the arrests, however, Edward confiscated all the Templars' property in the country and used their financial resources to swell his own coffers. Although one Templar priest confessed to denying Jesus at his initiation, no action was taken against him. Members of the order freely submitted to the Church to avoid any further punishment and were pardoned.

In Germany, Portugal, Switzerland, and Aragon the Templars were declared innocent, and in Cyprus, where the order had its headquarters, all the knights were acquitted of the charges brought by King Philip. Before his execution, de Molay had nominated a trusted knight named Larmenuis as his successor and told him to reorganize the order secretly and gather together its scattered knights. It is at this point in history that the Templars effectively disappeared from public view. They emerged in the following centuries as a clandestine organization working underground promoting Freemasonry, the occult tradition, and subversive politics.

THE ROSICRUCIAN
CONNECTION

After the suppression of the Templars, rumors were circulating in Europe that the secret tradition that they had followed was still being practiced. In the late Middle Ages the influence of the masonic guilds was still considerable, and rumor connected them to the Templar Order. It was said that during the Crusades a small group of Syriac Christians who claimed descent from the Essene sect were rescued from the Saracens by the Knights Templar and were placed under their military protection. These Christians were initiated into the innermost circle of the order and were taught all its occult mysteries. When the Syriac Christians left the Holy Land, they traveled across Europe and eventually settled in Scotland. In their new homeland they founded a chapter of the Templar Order that later merged with a lodge of speculative Freemasonry.

Following the destruction of the Templar Order, the masonic guilds attracted into their fold many men of learning who were non-masons—that is, they were not members of the building trade. It is through the influence of these newcomers, including occult initiates, that the esoteric symbolism of the masonic lodges was revived and speculative Freemasonry was established as a metaphysical system teaching the perfection of the human spirit through the symbols of the operative mason's working tools. Many Crusaders had made contact with the Sons of the Widow and Sufi philosophy while living in the Middle East, and on their return to Europe, they were instrumental in reviving the spiritual aspects of the masonic craft.

The Templar tradition seems to have gone underground at the beginning of the fifteenth century due to the Church's holy crusade directed at the practitioners of witchcraft. The medieval witch hunt, which lasted from the end of the fifteenth century to the beginning of the eighteenth century, claimed nearly a million innocent lives and was instigated by the publication in 1484 of the *Malleus Malefiracum (Hammer of Witches)*. This evil book was written by two Dominican monks, Heinrich Kramer and James Sprenger, who were members of the Inquisition set up in 1215 to root out and kill heretics.

Before the publication of the infamous *Malleus Malefiracum,* the medieval Church had dismissed witches as ignorant peasants suffering from delusions leading them to worship pagan gods, but the Dominican monks changed this view. In their opinion, witchcraft was a diabolical heresy that conspired to overthrow the Church and establish the kingdom of Satan on earth. Pope Innocent VIII agreed with their diagnosis and, in 1486, issued a papal bull condemning witches, which plunged Christian Europe into an orgy of bloody persecution that lasted nearly two hundred fifty years.

In this dark atmosphere of bigotry, anyone who professed magical powers or claimed to follow occult beliefs did not dare proclaim them in public. The occult tradition went underground and surfaced only briefly in the next few decades, usually within the establishment whose members were exempt from the persecution that decimated the lower classes who dabbled in the magical arts and witchcraft.

Vague references to the Templars were made in the available occult literature, although in the context of the paranoia that surrounded the witch hunt, the knights of the order were largely misrepresented as black magicians and Satanists. In his book *De Occulta Philosophia,* written in 1530, the German occultist and magician Henry Cornelius Agrippa mentioned the Templars in connection with the gnostics and the worship of the pagan fertility god Priapus, whose symbol was a huge erect penis, and the Greek goat-footed god Pan. He identified the order with the survival of paganism, suggesting that as a practicing occultist he had some special insight into the sensational allegations that led to its downfall. It is claimed that Agrippa was a member of a secret society that claimed descent from the Templars and that he wrote his description of their occult practices from inside information.

The fifteenth and early sixteenth centuries were very important with respect to the growth of the underground occult tradition. The Moors, who had invaded Spain from north Africa in the tenth and eleventh centuries and had even penetrated areas of southern France until they were driven back by the Christian kings, had introduced into Europe both the secret teachings of the Arab mystery schools and the Jewish mystical system known as the kabbalah. By the beginning of the 1500s, there had been a revival of interest in the gnostics, and Hermetic philosophy was also well known to the educated student of the occult sciences.

In 1460 a Greek manuscript consisting of an almost complete copy of the *Corpus Hermeticum,* the standard textbook on Hermeticism, had come into the hands of a monk hired by the de Medici family in Italy to locate rare manuscripts. The monk's patron, Cosmo de Medici, arranged for the manuscript to be translated, and it was published in 1463, marking the great occult revival of the period, which culminated in the flowering of the Renaissance, when artists, writers, and poets, inspired by classical paganism, produced the great works of art and literature that are so highly valued today as the spiritual and material treasures of European culture.

It was also during this important cultural period in Western history that the existence of one of the most influential secret societies in the esoteric tradition was revealed to the outside world. This society had as its ultimate aim the reestablishment of the ancient mysteries in a form that, unlike the Manichean heresy and the Templar Order, would be publicly acceptable. The earliest writings about this society, which was known as the Order of the Rosy Cross, began to circulate in Europe around the year 1605. They were contained in a manuscript called

The Restoration of the Decayed Temple of Pallas and provide the earliest known constitution of the order. A history of the Rosicrucians was written by an unknown author in 1610 but did not appear in print until four years later. It was entitled the *Fama Fraternitatis* and provided a legendary history stating that the order had been founded as early as the 1300s by a German mystic who was born into an aristocratic family.

This mystic, known only by the pseudonym Christian Rosenkreuz, had been placed in a monastery by his parents while he was still a young boy. He rebelled against the stifling authority of the clerical life, however, and took the chance offered to him by an older monk to accompany him to the Middle East. His companion died en route in Cyprus, but the young man traveled on to Damascus. There he became the student of a group of kabbalistic adepts who lived in the city. Rosenkreuz eventually returned to Europe, stopping first in north Africa, where he studied with Arabian occultists in Fez and Moorish Spain. During his studies in Fez, the young monk was taught the magical art of conjuring elemental spirits and was tutored in the secrets of alchemy, or the transformation of lead into gold.

The fact that Rosenkreuz traveled extensively in the Middle East, studying with Arabian occult adepts, suggests strongly that the Rosicrucians were familiar with the teachings of Sufism. Indries Shah has compared them to a Sufi secret society founded in Baghdad in the twelfth century called the Path of the Rose. It was founded by a Sufi master, Abdelkadir Gilani, whose personal symbol was a red rose. This Sufi group, like the Rosicrucians, practiced alchemy as a metaphor for spiritual transformation from matter to spirit.

When Rosenkreuz returned to Germany, he continued his occult studies, locking himself away for five years while he conducted magical rituals and alchemical operations. At the end of this period of isolation, he decided to inform the world of his newfound knowledge. Rosenkreuz possessed political ambitions and believed that the arts and sciences in Europe were in a state of decay. He believed that only by an injection of spiritual inspiration could European culture be saved from total moral degradation. To this end, Rosenkreuz attempted to spread his message

Fama Fraternitas, 1614

to his fellow Europeans but met only hostility, ridicule, or indifference. Realizing that an open approach was doomed to failure, Rosenkreuz decided to conceal his political and cultural reforms behind the mask of a secret society. This group would work clandestinely behind the scenes, influencing in a subtle way important people who could bring about the social changes about which Rosenkreuz dreamed.

Rosenkreuz revisited the monastery where he had been a novice monk before leaving for the Middle East. He persuaded three of its senior members, known in Rosicrucian literature as the Three Wise Men, to leave their monastic orders and join his venture. He asked them to swear an oath not to violate the secrets he was to give them and then revealed, over a period of several months, the occult knowledge he had received from his Arab masters. Rosenkreuz provided each of his students with a secret cipher to use to pass coded messages to each other. He also helped them build a house, which became the repository for the thousands of volumes of esoteric wisdom he had collected over the years.

Four other monks were introduced to the group, and these eight scholars were the nucleus of the Order of the Rosy Cross. As soon as the order had been safely established, seven of its members set out across Europe, secretly spreading its occult doctrines and leaving Rosenkreuz in Germany to continue his arcane researches. The members of the brotherhood decided not to reveal their true identities to outsiders and agreed on six rules of conduct, which all of them would follow without question: They would heal the sick without charge; they would wear no special garment that revealed their occult beliefs; every year on an allocated day, they would meet at the headquarters of the order to report their progress; each member would nominate a worthy candidate to replace him when he died; they would use the initials "RC" as their identifying mark; and the existence of the order would remain secret for at least a hundred years.

It was agreed by the early brethren of the Rosy Cross that when they died, their bodies would be buried secretly and without ceremony. Therefore, when Rosenkreuz himself died none of the other members knew where he was buried until his secret tomb was discovered by accident some one hundred twenty years after his death. It was in the form of a seven-sided vault illuminated by a perpetual light whose source none of the brethren could discern. Rosenkreuz's body was perfectly preserved inside the tomb despite the length of time that had passed since his death.

Although this is the generally accepted legend of the foundation of the Rosicrucians, some authorities claim that the order's true origins date back several thousand years. It has been alleged that the original Order of the Rosy Cross was founded by the pharaoh Thothmes III in the fifteenth century BCE. He gathered together all the learned scholars, priests, and philosophers of his time and formed them into a secret brotherhood of initiates who met to practice their rites in a temple on the banks of the Nile. In modern Rosicrucianism, the cartouche or personal seal of Thothmes is used as one of the symbols of the order in both private and public documents. The purpose behind the foundation of the order in ancient Egypt was to exert a civilizing influence on the ancient world and preserve the wisdom teachings of the mysteries.

Thothmes III was one of the most significant Egyptian rulers during the eighteenth dynasty (1587–1375 BCE). As a young man he was co-regent to Queen Hatshepsut, his sister, and when she died in 1480 BCE, Thothmes—whose name means "born of Thoth," the ibis-headed god of wisdom who was the Egyptian equivalent of Hermes—ruled on his own as supreme pharaoh. There were rumors that the young man had murdered his sister to gain the crown, but there is no proof to support this allegation.

Following Hatshepsut's death, Thothmes began a campaign of military expansion, which transformed Egypt into a world power. He invaded Palestine, Syria, and Nubia and extended Egyptian influence as far north as the Euphrates. The fear of Egypt's military might during his reign prevented attacks from outsiders and allowed the Nile civilization to develop in peace. The pharaoh's court received tribute from Egypt's conquered enemies, including gifts of precious stones, perfumes, spices, and gold, which swelled the royal coffers. With the guidance of the new pharaoh, Egypt became the wealthiest and most politically powerful nation in the Mediterranean area.

Thothmes was renowned for his hot temper and impetuous personality, but he was also widely respected as a general and a statesman. He was feared by his enemies but was deeply loved by his people. He never killed the rulers of the countries he conquered but deposed them and replaced their rule with Egyptian governors. At home, the pharaoh was responsible for establishing a legal system that insisted on the impartiality of the judges and treated all men and women as equals, showing no favors to members of the establishment. Thothmes was a cultivated man who was interested in the arts and sciences. He arranged for many rare plants, trees, and animals to be brought back to Egypt from the countries occupied by the army and is credited with being the first founder of a zoo and a botanical garden in the ancient world.

When Thothmes died, he was described by poets as "a circling comet which shoots out flames and gives forth its substance in fire." It was written about him that "there was nothing he did not know; he was Thoth in everything. There was no affair he did not complete." Special references were made to the great temple the warrior mystic built at Karnak in cooperation with his son, who ruled Egypt after his death as Amenhotep II.

According to the mythical history of the order, Rosicrucianism survived the demise of the old pagan religions and the rise of Christianity. It is even claimed that the three Magi who traveled from the east to pay their respects to the infant Jesus at Bethlehem were initiates of the order. The emperor Charlemagne of the Holy Roman Empire, who was an early patron of the masons who built the Gothic cathedrals, is said to have founded a Rosicrucian lodge at Toulouse in the ninth century CE. In 898 CE a second lodge was established in France, and in the year 1000 a group of heretical Roman Catholic monks founded the first Rosicrucian college, which flourished in secret from the eleventh to the sixteenth centuries.

Some of the notable grand masters of the Rosicrucian Order have allegedly included such famous historical personalities as Raymond VI, the count of Toulouse; the Italian writer, poet, and philosopher Dante; the German magician Cornelius Agrippa, who wrote about the Templars; the mystic and healer Paracelsus; the Elizabethan astrologer Dr. John Dee; the Hermetic philosopher Giordana Bruno, who was burned at the stake as a heretic by the Inquisition; Sir Francis Bacon, chancellor of England in the reign of King James; the philosopher Spinoza; the English scientist Robert Boyle; Sir Christopher Wren, who designed St. Paul's cathedral in London; Benjamin Franklin, who was actively involved in the American Revolution of 1776; the occultist and founder of Egyptian Freemasonry Comte Cagliostro; and Thomas Jefferson, president of the United States. In more recent years, the alleged grand masters of the order have included the English writer and statesman Lord Bulwer Lytton and the composer Claude Debussy.

Some modern Rosicrucians regard the legend of Christian Rosenkreuz as a symbolic fable published to reveal the existence and teachings of the order to the general public. The order itself had been operating in secret for at least fifteen hundred years since its foundation in ancient Egypt. As with the Templars, the source of the esoteric knowledge possessed by Rosy Cross initiates was the Middle East, specifically Egypt and the mystery schools of Arabia. The Rosicrucians' political manifesto included the establishment of a social system, which treated all people equally within a democratic framework. The three political aims of the order were initially the abolition of the monarchy and its replacement by a government composed of wise rulers, the radical reformation of the sciences and philosophy in accordance with spiritual principles, and the discovery of a universal medicine or elixir of life that would cure all illnesses and diseases. When this manifesto was published in the seventeenth century, the medieval system of feudalism was only slowly being replaced by more democratic forms of government. It would be nearly two hundred years before any major attempt was made to democratize the European systems of government (in the French Revolution) and in the colonies of North America. The English Civil War in 1640 laid the foundation for both these revolutions when the divine right of the monarch to rule without consulting the people was challenged in a bloody conflict, which ended in the death of the king.

Many writers on the Order of the Rosy Cross have alleged that the fraternity was founded by ex-members of the Templar Order after its suppression by Pope Clement. It is claimed that before the Crusades, members of the Rosicrucian Order secretly worked in the Holy Land for the common good of humanity. Certainly, both the Templars and the Rosicrucians used the symbol of the rosy or red cross and were dedicated to political and religious reform. Both groups, while nominally Christian, seem to have been secretly engaged in occult and pagan practices under the cover of orthodoxy.

The medieval Rosicrucians were popularly credited with possessing a wide range of magical powers, including the ability to prolong youth using occult techniques, knowledge of summoning spirits, the ability to make themselves invisible, and the ability to create precious stones from thin air and transform lead into gold. The term *rosy cross* was said to derive from the Latin *ros,* meaning "dew," and *crux,* or "cross," which refers to the chemical sign for light. According to this translation, the rosy cross is an occult symbol of the alchemical operation of transforming matter into spirit, represented by the transformation of lead into gold.

Like that of Freemasonry, the occult symbolism of the Order of the Rosy Cross represented the evolution of humanity from materialism to spiritual perfection. This symbolism colored the order's political aims, which involved, as we have seen, the restoration of the sciences of the ancient world destroyed by Christianity, the promotion of medical care for the poor, social reform, and the universal establishment of democracy. The Rosicrucians were linked to Freemasonry at an early date. As far as is known, the earliest written reference to speculative Masonry is a poem written in 1638, which refers to both the Masons and the Rosicrucians in the following words: "For what we pressage is not in grosse, for we be brethen of the Rosie Crosse, we have the Mason's Word and second sight, things to come we can foretell aright. . . ." From this we can deduce that the Rosicrucians knew the inner secrets of Freemasonry and possessed the psychic power to predict the future.

Because it used the Rosy Cross in its symbolism, the Order of the Garter has been linked with the Rosicrucians. It was founded in 1348 by King Edward III of England and was dedicated to the Virgin Mary, the Christianized version of the pagan great mother goddess. Edward was a student of the Arthurian legends, and meetings of the order took place in a special chamber in Windsor Castle around a table modeled on the one used by King Arthur's Fellowship of the Round Table.

The insignia of a knight of the Order of the Garter consisted of a jeweled collar composed of gold and red roses with five petals contained

The Rosy Cross symbol

within tiny garters. These roses alternated with twenty-six gold knots, each representing a member of the order. Hanging from the collar is a representation of St. George, the patron saint of England, killing the dragon, which is enameled with gold and set with diamonds. In addition to this magnificent collar, the knights wore a velvet garter with enameled red and white letters spelling out the order's motto, *Honi soit qui mal y pense,* or "Evil be to he who evil thinks." This was apparently the comment made by Edward when he picked up the garter dropped by the countess of Salisbury while they were dancing, and, according to legend, it was this event, which persuaded the king to found the premier chivalric order in English history.

The association of the Order of the Garter and the Rosicrucians may not be as fanciful as it seems at first glance. It is recorded that the son of Edward III had connections with a group of knights who had fought in the Holy Land and had been inducted into the Templar tradition. On their return to England, these knights founded an esoteric lodge that practiced the occult arts. It is also true that many famous men who were either Rosicrucians or Masons have, over the centuries, been knighted as members of the Order of the Garter, a privilege that can be granted only as the personal gift of the reigning monarch.

Connections between royalty and the Rosicrucians, despite the order's aim to abolish the monarchy, were even closer in Elizabethan England. One of the alleged grand masters of the order, Dr. John Dee (1527–1608), became the confidant of Elizabeth I and was involved in many of the political intrigues of the sixteenth century. Along with being a practicing astrologer, Dee was also renowned as a mathematician, navigator, cartographer, magician, Hermeticist, and natural scientist. He studied at Cambridge University and traveled extensively all over Europe, studying occult doctrines from leading kabbalists, mystics, and philosophers. He spent some time in Bohemia with Emperor Rudolf II of the Habsburg dynasty, who was a practicing occultist, and he was a well-known figure at many European royal courts.

On his return to England, Dee was invited to cast the horoscope of Mary Tudor and the young Princess Elizabeth. Unfortunately, in May 1555, a warrant for his arrest was issued following an accusation that he had bewitched the queen. Dee spent several months incarcerated in prison before the charge was declared false and he was released.

It is popularly believed that Dee was a charlatan and a sorcerer, but his library at Mortlake indicates he was well versed in ancient religious ideas, especially the pre-Christian teachings of Hermes Trismegistus, Zoroaster, and the gnostics. He owned a copy of the *Corpus Hermeticum* and had made a deep study of the pagan mysteries and the mythology of ancient Egypt. It is therefore not surprising that the Rosicrucians should claim this learned occultist as one of the leading members of their secret society.

Despite his brief spell of imprisonment during the reign of Queen Mary, Dee seems to have received the royal patronage of Elizabeth when she ascended the throne. It is recorded that the queen often rode out to Dee's house in Mortlake, on the River Thames, to discuss affairs of state with her favorite astrologer. Dee's advice was highly regarded by the queen, and in 1592, when he requested a living in rural Hampshire to pursue his occult studies, Elizabeth refused the request because she wanted to keep him close at hand.

Politically, Dee was an imperialist who wanted to see England take her rightful place in world history as a maritime power. In 1577, he wrote his *Treatise on Naval Defense,* which provided the blueprint for an imperial fleet that would rule the waves and form the bodyguard of a future British Empire. It seems that Dee's imperialistic vision was shared by others in Elizabeth's court whose influence on the queen was even greater than that of the Mortlake astrologer.

When he was not writing about politics, Dee took an active role in diplomatic and intelligence matters that helped further the imperialist aims of Elizabethan England. Dee was closely associated with one of the queen's most trusted advisors, Sir Francis Walsingham, who is credited with founding the British secret service. Walsingham was a wily character who had risen from obscurity to become one of the queen's favorites, and he served her loyally until his death.

Walsingham was first employed at court as a personal bodyguard to the queen, with the task of searching her apartments for signs of poisons. Elizabeth was the proposed victim of several assassination plots during her reign, including one conspiracy organized by the Jesuits. He soon developed a natural ability to acquire information through clandestine means and swiftly established an intelligence network, which extended beyond the shores of England to the Continent. It was rumored that, like Dee, Walsingham was a student of occultism and that he used the underground organization of witch covens in Tudor England to gather material for his intelligence service. The risk he took at a time when the practice of witchcraft was a capital offense cannot be overestimated, but, as for intelligence officers ever since, Walsingham took the risk of indulging in illegal activities because he regarded the defense of the realm as more important than his personal safety.

Walsingham's embryonic secret service was initially involved in counterespionage and the threat to national security presented by the assassination plots directed toward Elizabeth. Although she was a popular queen, she could boast a cult of personality that bordered on her being worshipped as the personification of the virgin goddess Diana, so Elizabeth was always in danger from her enemies. The Spanish were the leading contenders in the assassination stakes, and Walsingham and his agents played an important role in exposing the activities of foreign spies sent to England to infiltrate the court and high society.

In 1570, Walsingham was appointed ambassador to France, and while in this position, he extended his spy network across Europe. Dee was useful to the spymaster because during his European travels, the astrologer had made many important contacts in aristocratic and royal circles, including contacts with high-placed occultists who were members of secret societies. He passed information on to Walsingham about these people, and the head of the secret service was able to contact them and seek recruits for his network of agents on the Continent.

While Walsingham was in Paris, he became involved in the negotiations for the proposed marriage between Queen Elizabeth and the duke of Anjou and worked to undermine it at every stage, believing it would be disastrous for the future of England. Frustrated by the lack of progress in the negotiations, Elizabeth instructed John Dee to visit Walsingham in Paris and find out what was going on. Dee was asked to cast a horoscope based on the suitability of the proposed marriage between the English queen and the French prince. He reported to Elizabeth that the stars did not predict a happy union and he advised against it.

In common with most intelligence agents, Walsingham was fascinated by secret codes and ciphers. In consultation with Dee, the spymaster formulated a series of codes, which were used by his agents to spread messages. He also employed skilled code breakers, who were used to translate the codes used by England's enemies. In 1562, Dee had discovered a book on cryptography written by the abbot of Spanheim. He utilized the ideas in this book to write his occult volume called *The Monad*. This book has always been regarded purely as a study of esoteric symbolism, but Sir William Cecil, a leading member of Elizabeth's government, stated quite clearly that it was a work that had been of great value to the security of the realm. This suggests that Dee wrote it so that it could be of use both to occultists and secret agents. It has even been claimed that the records of the conversations in the Enochian language received by Dr. Dee from the angels through the mediumship of Edward Kelly were also used to conceal secret communications relating to the magician's work for the intelligence service.

Dee was not the only Rosicrucian openly involved in political work. Following the publication of the *Fama Fraternitatis,* several lodges of the order were founded, and the members of these groups claimed that the Rosicrucians had been active in the events that surrounded the Reformation and rise to the Lutheran movement in Germany and Switzerland. The order had good political reasons for initially supporting the Protestant cause. On the surface, as heirs to the pre-Christian Ancient Wisdom, secret societies would have gained little from religious reform. Yet by supporting the Protestant dissidents, they helped to weaken the political power of the Roman Catholic Church, the traditional enemy of the Cathars, the Templars, and the Freemasons. At first, the Rosicrucians believed that the religious reformers behind the Protestant movement would be the creators of spiritual tolerance; thus they gave them their support. In practice, Protestantism became as spiritually bankrupt as the Roman version of Christianity and in fact exorcized from the faith those elements of paganism that gave it some substance of esoteric credibility.

In Austria, the Rosicrucian influence on the Reformation was centered around Johann Valentin Andrea, a Lutheran clergyman born in 1586 who had visited Switzerland and been impressed by the social reforms carried out in that country. When he returned to Austria, the cleric set up a mutually protective association on Swiss lines among the workmen of his local cloth factory. In 1620, Andrea also made contact with several liberal Austrian noblemen and with their help founded several Rosicrucian lodges in the country. At one stage he was credited with the authorship of the *Fama Fraternitatis,* although he always denied writing it. He certainly propagated Rosicrucian tenets, including the foundation of a college of wise men and women who would act as social reformers, and he was a close friend and supporter of Martin Luther. It was noted that Luther used as his personal seal the symbol of a rose and a cross, but whether he was a Rosicrucian initiate is debatable.

The new Protestant version of Christianity proved to be no more tolerant of alternative spiritual beliefs than the Catholic brand. Religious intolerance is a pernicious evil that has permeated esoteric Christianity since the days of the early Church. The Protestants reacted savagely to what they regarded as the paganism inherent in the Roman belief system and promoted a puritanical form of religious worship. During the English Reformation instigated by Henry VIII, the destruction of churches and cathedrals can hardly be justified, even by the corruption of the clerical establishment at that time. The Protestants also devalued the role of the feminine principle in the Christian faith by rejecting the Virgin Mary, leaving a spiritual vacuum that was only partly filled in the eighteenth and nineteenth centuries by the rise of Anglo-Catholicism within the Church of England, which restored some of the old mysteries to the Protestant religion.

Many people in high places who had positions of power and influence were attracted by the Utopian ideals of the Rosicrucians. One of these was the antiquarian Elias Ashmole (1617–1692), who was a close friend of Charles II, a knight of the Order of the Garter, founder of the famous Ashmolean museum and library at Oxford, and a speculative Freemason. Ashmole was also a friend of the astrologer William Lilly and was involved in the formation of the Royal Society, which was based on Rosicrucian concepts. In 1652, Ashmole revealed his connection to the Rose Cross by stating that one of the first members of the order was an Englishman who cured of leprosy the duke of Norfolk, grand marshal of England. Ashmole could only have known this as a member.

In 1650, Ashmole published a book called *Fasciculus Chemicus*, written by Arthur Dee, who was the son of the Elizabethan astrologer. Dee was the personal physician to Czar Ivan the Terrible from 1621 to 1644.

Johann Valentin Andrea

On the death of Ivan, the *boyars* (members of the highest rank of feudal aristocracy) plotted to replace him with a non-Russian ruler, but with the help of Dee, the Romanov dynasty was established on the throne. Like his father and Ashmole, Dee may have been a Rosicrucian initiate, but he was certainly also an agent for the English secret service.

Ashmole and William Lilly founded a Rosicrucian lodge in London in 1646 based on the Utopian ideal of the creation of a new Atlantis, which symbolized the golden age before the Fall when humanity was spiritually perfect, and the rebuilding of Solomon's temple as revered in the Templar tradition. Ashmole and Lilly may have been influenced by the beliefs of Sir Francis Bacon, who was the viscount of St. Albans and wrote *The New Atlantis,* which promoted the Rosicrucian manifesto.

The position of the Freemasons and the Rosicrucians during the English Civil War and the Commonwealth is confused. The social reforms and attacks on the religious establishment that characterized the activities of Oliver Cromwell during the 1640s would suggest that secret societies supported his cause. Many Rosicrucians and Masons, however, were aristocrats whose natural inclinations, despite their liberal beliefs, would have been to support the royalist cause. Although the original Rosicrucian manifesto advocated the abolition of the monarchy, this aspect of the order's beliefs seems to have been diluted considerably.

It is claimed that after the Restoration the more progressive Puritans, including possibly some members of groups such as the Levellers and the Diggers, who had been persecuted by Cromwell, infiltrated the Masonic lodges. It is possible that some of these elements were associated with the foundation of the Royal Society in 1660. The society was formed to reform science, religion, and the arts and was based on the Rosicrucian concept of the invisible college. Several of the leading members of the Royal Society were either Masons or Rosicrucians.

By the late 1640s, the neo-Rosicrucian Order had become firmly established throughout Europe. Although threatened by clerical persecution, the order had formed lodges in Nuremburg, Hamburg, Paris, and Amsterdam. At the beginning of the eighteenth century, the lodges of speculative Masonry were also coming out into the open. One of the most important Masonic personalities of this period was the chevalier Andrew Ramsay, a supporter of the Jacobite cause to bring the Stuart dynasty back onto the British throne. Ramsey lived for a long time in France, and, in 1736, he addressed a gathering of French Masons and referred to the Templar tradition. He revealed that Masonry was the heir to the secrets of the Templars, who in turn had inherited the Ancient Wisdom of the pagan mysteries.

Freemasonry had been introduced into France by English aristocrats who supported the Stuarts. They were members of the Society of Legitimists, who campaigned on behalf of the Scottish prince's claims to the British crown. Lord Derwentwater founded the first lodge in France, at Dunkirk, in 1721, with a charter granted by the Grand Lodge of England. Many Frenchmen joined the new Masonic lodges, even though the government issued orders prohibiting membership; the king decreed that no member of the court should join a lodge, and those that did faced imprisonment in the Bastille. Innkeepers were threatened with fines of three thousand francs if they used their premises for Masonic meetings. Despite this official disapproval, Masonry flourished, and by the 1750s, numerous lodges practicing the Scottish rite, which had higher degrees than the English version of Freemasonry and seems to have been Rosicrucian-inspired, were established all over France.

In 1738, the Roman Catholic Church officially condemned Masonry, which was precipitated by the public declarations of the grand master of the French lodges, the duc d'Anton, who preached the revolutionary ideals of liberty, universal brotherhood, love, and equality. He was succeeded by the comte de Clement under whose grand mastership French Freemasonry split into several rival groups. On the comte's death in 1771, the duc de Chartres was elected as his replacement and was installed as the leader of the Grand Orient, the independent ruling body of French Freemasonry, which separated it from the Grand Lodge of England.

The Grand Orient had links to several other occult secret societies, including the Martinists, or followers of Martinez de Pasqually, who was a Rosicrucian adept. He passed his mantle to Louis Claude Saint-Martin, who had given up a promising career in the French army to follow the mystical path. Saint-Martin taught that humanity could achieve union with the godhead through direct contact with the Divine, as taught by the gnostics. He also believed that all men were kings and supported the political aims of equality and democracy for all.

One of the most political Masonic lodges of the eighteenth century was founded by Savalette de Lage, who formed a secret society called the Friends of Truth. The political philosophy of this group mapped out the ground plan of the social reformation, which was later to become the inspiration for the French Revolution. Another politically-orientated Masonic lodge called Neuf Soeurs (Nine Sisters) was founded in Paris and had links with de Lage. It had the task of creating an alternative education system, for the established one was firmly in the hands of the clerical authorities that used it to promote their own version of Christian education.

Public lectures on history, literature, chemistry, and medicine were given by members of the Neuf Soeurs lodge at an establishment called the College of Apollo (the Greek sun god). During the Revolution, this college changed its name to the Lycée Republican and its tutors addressed the students wearing the Phrygian cap of the revolutionary militia. Among the leading members of this radical lodge were the duc de la Rochafoucard, who translated the American Constitution into French; Captain Forster, who sailed with the explorer Cook to the Pacific; the philosopher Voltaire; the American politician and scientist Benjamin Franklin; and the revolutionary John Paul Jones.

It was in the eighteenth century that the Templar tradition, forced underground for nearly four hundred years, began to emerge as an influential factor in Masonic and Rosicrucian beliefs. Chevalier Andrew Ramsay had hinted at the Templar influence on Freemasonry, but it was Karl Gotthelf, the baron von Hund, who established it firmly within the Masonic tradition with his foundation of the Strict Observance Rite. Von Hund had been initiated into a Masonic lodge in Paris led by Lord Kilmarnock, the grand master of Scottish Freemasonry. This lodge claimed to be the guardian of the Templar tradition and may have been the inheritors of the Templar beliefs imported into Scotland by the Syriac Christians or descendants of the lodge founded by the son of Edward III in the fourteenth century. Alternatively, supporters of the Jacobite cause alleged that a Masonic lodge had been founded in Scotland in the early 1700s and drew its charter from a surviving Templar chapter in Bristol that had been operational for several hundred years.

At his initiation into Masonry, von Hund claimed he was introduced to a mysterious figure called the Knight of the Red Feather, whom he later identified as Prince Charles Stuart. This person gave von Hund permission to found a branch of the neo-Templars in Germany. According to von Hund's version of the founding, the original Scottish chapter of the Knights Templar had been founded by two English members of the order who were alchemists who had discovered the elixir of life.

The popular myth circulating in occult circles in the eighteenth century was that the Templars had been initiates of a gnostic teaching passed down by the Essenes, who had also initiated Jesus into its mysteries. Neo-Templarism was therefore an attempt to combine pagan wisdom and Christian ideals. In Freemasonry the influence of the Templars was felt in the myth current in the eighteenth century that compared the three renegade knights who betrayed the order to King Philip of France to the three fellow masons who murdered Hiram Abiff in Solomon's temple. Masonic references were also made to the assassination of a prominent Templar, Charles de Monte Carmel, who was ritually murdered shortly before the order was suppressed. His murderers concealed his body by burying it under a thorn bush, where it was discovered by other Templars. The eighteenth-century Masons regarded this event as a turning point in Templar history and as instrumental in its eventual downfall.

According to Masonic historians, the survival of the Templar tradition was masterminded by the last Templar grand master, Jacques de Molay, while he was in prison. On the night before his execution, de Molay sent a trusted confidant to the secret crypt in Paris, where the bodies of the order's past grand masters were entombed. This messenger took from the tomb various symbolic objects sacred to the order, including the crown of the king of Jerusalem, a seven-branched candlestick from Solomon's temple, and statues from the church marking the site of the alleged burial place of Jesus.

De Molay told his trusted aide that the two pillars that stood at the entrance of the Templar tomb were hollow and contained large sums of money. He was told to use this wealth and the symbolic objects to re-create the order so that its secrets would not be lost. The two pillars of the crypt's entrance were probably copies of the obelisks at the gateway of Solomon's temple. In addition to gold coins, the hollow pillars may also have contained manuscripts detailing the secret inner teachings of the Templar Order.

Along with von Hund, there was another claimant to the Templar revival in Germany: Johann Augustus Starck, who had encountered Masonic Templarism while teaching languages in St. Petersburg. He also made a separate contact with a surviving Templar tradition in southern France that practiced in the Cathar style. Starck believed that the original Templars had inherited their occult lore from Persia, Syria, and Egypt and that this had been passed on to them by an Essene secret society operating in the Middle East during the Crusades. His version of neo-Templarism received the patronage of European aristocrats, and membership of the new Masonic Templar lodges he founded included dukes, counts, and princes. In Sweden, Gustav III became the patron of neo-Templarism because he believed it had been founded by Prince Charles Stuart and he was a fervent supporter of the Scottish pretenders and the Jacobite cause.

In 1771, there was a grand convention of all the Masonic lodges claiming a mythical descent from the Templar Order. Starck's group was amalgamated with the lodges founded by baron von Hund, who, because he could offer no documentary evidence of the origins of his version of Templarism, was forced to retire and took only an honorary position in the new organization. At the time of the grand convention, which established neo-Templarism's place in the Masonic tradition, Prussia was ruled by the mystical Frederick the Great, who was both a Freemason and a student of the occult. In 1767, Frederick founded two neo-Masonic lodges called the Order of the Architects of Africa, devoted to the Manichean heresy, and the Knights of Light, which practiced the magical arts. Frederick was a financial supporter of orthodox Freemasonry and in 1768, he commissioned the building of a grand lodge for use by the Prussian brethren. One of the many titles used by the Masonic secret societies founded by Frederick was the Illuminati. A few years later this name was adopted by a group of occultists who, despite their short public exposure, are regarded as the key figures in the hidden political history of the subsequent two hundred years and are still revered by conspiracy theorists as the ultimate secret society.

More sensational nonsense has been written about the Illuminati than any other secret society, yet the real facts about this mysterious organization and its role in the revolutionary movements of eighteenth-century Europe are extraordinary. The Illuminati was founded in 1776, the year of the American Revolution, by a young professor at the Bavarian University of Ingoldstat, Adam Weishaupt. He was of Jewish descent, but as a young boy he had been educated by the Jesuits in the Catholic faith. When Weishaupt began to teach law at the university, however, he became an active supporter of the Protestant cause and was involved in a series of bitter arguments with prominent Catholic clergymen.

While an undergraduate, Weishaupt studied the ancient pagan religions and was familiar with the Eleusinian mysteries and the theories of the Greek mystic Pythagoras. As a student, he had drafted the constitution for a secret society modeled on the pagan mystery schools, but it was not until he was initiated into Freemasonry that Weishaupt's plan was spawned.

Weishaupt first made contact with a Masonic lodge in either Hanover or Munich in 1774 but was sadly disappointed by what he discovered. In his opinion, the other members of the lodge were ignorant of the occult significance of Freemasonry and they knew nothing about its pagan symbolism or origins. His contact with the Masonic tradition had, however, given Weishaupt an insight into the structure and organization of a secret society, and he used this experience to found his own clandestine fraternity.

On May 1, 1776, Weishaupt announced the foundation of the Order of Perfectibilists, which was later to become more widely known as the Illuminati. The new order's first meeting was attended by only five people, but it soon attracted the notice of influential members of Bavarian society who shared Weishaupt's egalitarian and socialist political ideas. Within a short period of time, the Illuminati had lodges all over Germany and Austria, and branches of the order were also founded in Italy, Hungary, France, and Switzerland. Weishaupt conducted a secret operation to infiltrate Masonic lodges and established a power base within Continental Freemasonry as part of his long-term plan to use his secret society for political change in Europe.

Weishaupt's political vision was of a Utopian superstate that abolished private property, social authority, and nationality. In this anarchistic state, human beings would live in harmony within a universal brotherhood based on free love, peace, spiritual wisdom, and equality. Speaking before the French Revolution, Weishaupt said, "Salvation does not lie where strong thrones are defended by swords, where the smoke of censers ascends to heaven, or where thousands of strong men pace the rich fields of harvest. The revolution which is about to break will be sterile. It is not complete." This suggests that Weishaupt's principal targets for reform were the monarchy, the Church, and the rich landowners who kept the European peasants in servitude.

The antiroyalist and anticlerical nature of the Illuminati was graphically illustrated by the mystical symbolism of the initiation ceremony into the highest grade of the order: The candidate was led into a room where, in front of an empty throne, there stood a table on which were

Adam Weishaupt

placed the traditional symbols of kingship—a scepter, a sword, and a crown. The initiate was invited to take up these objects but was told that if he did, he would be refused entry to the order. The initiate was then taken into a second room, draped in black. A curtain was pulled back to reveal an altar covered in a black cloth on which stood a plain cross and a red Phrygian cap as used in the Mithraic mysteries. This ritual cap was handed to the initiate with the words "Wear this—it means more than the crown of kings." This ritual is very similar to the initiation into Mithraism, when the neophyte is handed a sword and a crown and rejects them saying, "Mithras alone is my crown."

Adam Weishaupt established a network of Illuminati agents throughout Europe who had access to cardinals, princes, and kings. These agents reported back the gossip and intrigues of the courts to their grand master, which Weishaupt used for his own political purposes. Both men and women were initiated into the order, and

Weishaupt taught sexual equality. He came into conflict with the Church because he also taught his disciples that religious freedom was the right of everyone. He believed that once the masses had been freed from the shackles of religion, they would demand political freedom and the right to enjoy life without the moral straitjacket imposed by the puritanical teachings of the Church on sexual matters. Some writers on the Illuminati, especially those who present Weishaupt as a proto-communist, have described the order as ultramaterialistic. It is true that Weishaupt had an almost pathological hatred of established religion, but it cannot be denied that he was a spiritual person, although his spirituality would have horrified the clerics who opposed him.

He firmly believed in the redemption of humanity and the res-toration of human beings to the state of perfection that he believed existed in the halcyon days before the Fall. Like the Rosicrucians and the Freemasons, Weishaupt believed this redemption was possible by the application of the occult traditions preserved by the pagan mys-tery schools that were the guardians of the Ancient Wisdom. He also believed that the Church was a corrupt organization that had lost the original teachings of Jesus and was concerned only with holding on to power for materialistic reasons. The secret doctrine of Christianity, he believed, was still preserved by the Rosicrucian and Masonic tra-ditions. Where he differed from those two secret societies was in his determination to overthrow the existing political system, even if that could be achieved only through violent methods. It was the Illuminati attempt to overthrow the Habsburgs in 1784, exposed by police spies who had infiltrated the order, that led to the Bavarian government's ban on all secret societies and its efforts to drive underground the fol-lowers of Weishaupt.

The Illuminati participation in the events leading up to the French Revolution of 1789 has been the subject of considerable specula-tion and sensationalism. One of the founders of the Revolution, the comte de Mirabeau, is said to have been a prominent Illuminati. It is also reputed that the ground plan for the uprising was discussed at the Grand Masonic Convention in 1782 at Wilhelmsbad, which Mirabeau attended as an observer. Mirabeau allegedly confessed to other delegates at the Convention that he was a disciple of the Albigensian heresy. His aim was to bring down the French monarchy and destroy the Catholic Church so that a "religion of love" could be established in France.

When he returned to France, Mirabeau introduced the philosophy of Illuminism into his Masonic lodge, whose members included several political activists who became leading revolutionaries and later served under Napoleon. By 1788, nearly every lodge in the Grand Orient had been infiltrated by supporters of Weishaupt who were active in spreading the political policies of terrorism against the state, the abolition of the monarchy, religious freedom, sexual permissiveness, and social equality.

One of the most colorful figures who played an important role in the political intrigues that culminated in the French Revolution was Comte Cagliostro. His real name was Joseph Balsamo, and he had been born in Parlemo, Sicily, in 1743. As a young man, Cagliostro traveled around Europe and Asia as the disciple of an Armenian mystic named Althotas, who claimed to possess the philosopher's stone that could transform base metal into gold. In Rome, Cagliostro married a young noblewoman, Lorenza Felicioni. It was alleged that the comte controlled his new wife by using hypnotism, which had been taught to him by his fellow Mason Dr. Mesmer. It was Lorenza, obviously freed from her hypnotic spell, who later denounced her husband to the Inquisition for practicing heresy.

Cagliostro was inducted into Freemasonry in Germany and he was also an initiate of the Illuminati. On an esoteric level, his contribution to the occult tradition was the creation of Egyptian Freemasonry. This, he claimed, returned Masonic symbolism to its rightful position as the center point of the ancient Egyptian mysteries. In Germany, France, and England there were established lodges that practiced a combination of Egyptian Freemasonry, kabbalism, and ceremonial magic. Both men and women were initiated into these new lodges, and this fact, coupled with stories of strange magical practices in which the initiate was breathed upon in a mysterious manner by the grand master or mistress, led to rumors of sex orgies and perversions.

Politically, Cagliostro was involved with the Society of Jacobins, which supported the French Revolution. He had also attended the Grand Masonic Congress of 1785, when further plans were made by the Illuminati to create the atmosphere for mass uprisings in France against the monarchy. Cagliostro received funds from the Illuminati and traveled all over Europe as its agent, spreading the gospel of revolutionary politics. He lived in Paris for several years and set up an apartment on the rue St. Claude that was decorated with effigies of the gods and goddesses of ancient Egypt and an altar on which stood a stuffed monkey and a human skull. Cagliostro sold medallions of his own likeness as talismans and was mobbed by admirers in the street. He initiated members of Parisian high society into his Egyptian lodge and was even patronized by the royal family. Few knew of his real mission hidden behind this facade of occult mumbo jumbo.

In 1785, Cagliostro was the focal point of the Diamond Necklace Affair—an Illuminist plot to discredit the monarchy in the eyes of the French people. Cagliostro was asked by Cardinal de Rohan, a French priest who dabbled in the occult and had fallen in love with Marie Antoinette, to purchase a diamond necklace for the queen on the cardinal's behalf. De Rohan was under the impression that he had been corresponding with his royal love, but in fact his letters had been intercepted by the comtesse de la Molte, who had pretended to be the queen. Cagliostro purchased the jewels and handed them over to the cardinal, who duly delivered them to the palace, where they were received by the comtesse. She and her secretary broke up the necklace and sold the individual stones in Paris and London. Unfortunately, the fraud was discovered by the queen and King Louis XVI arrested the conspirators, including Cagliostro, throwing them into the Bastille.

Foolishly, the king decided to have the ringleaders of the plot tried by the parliament, which at that time was strongly antiroyalist and had been infiltrated by Illuminist and Masonic agents. Cagliostro was acquitted of all charges, although the comtesse de la Molta and her accomplice were found guilty. The resulting scandal inflicted severe damage on the reputation of the French royal family and the Church and planted the seeds of the public's simmering suspicions about the degenerate court life of the monarchy.

Following the court case, Cagliostro was forced into exile and fled to England. There he set up his headquarters at 50 Berkeley Square, which is today reputed to be the most haunted house in London. In 1787, while he was living in London, Cagliostro wrote to his friends in Paris, predicting the coming Revolution, the fall of the Bastille, the overthrow of the monarchy, the destruction of the Church, and the founding of a new religion based on love and reason. These accurate predictions were probably more based on his inside knowledge of the plans of the Illuminati than any psychic faculty he might have possessed.

Cagliostro's mentor was the legendary Comte de Saint-Germain. This mysterious occultist claimed Russian, Polish, and Italian blood and was an alchemist, spy, industrialist, diplomat, and Rosicrucian. Saint-Germain was active in Europe from 1710 to 1789, during which time he always had the appearance of a man in his early forties. It is said that the comte was introduced to the secret rites of Tantric sex magic while studying in the East and that it had provided him with a technique to prolong his youth. In 1743, he lived for several years in London, writing music, and he became a close friend of the Prince of Wales. He was forced to flee the city, though, after becoming entangled in a Jacobite plot to restore the Stuarts and being exposed as an agent of the French secret service. In 1755, he traveled to the Far East to become the pupil of occult adepts in Tibet, but he also found time to engage in spying operations against the British East India Company.

As the secret agent of the French royal family, the comte de Saint-Germain became involved in several political intrigues. He negotiated on behalf of the French king with Frederick the Great during the Seven Years' War and was responsible for the alliance between France and Prussia. He was also involved in the plot to overthrow Peter the Great in 1762 and replace the Russian czar with Catherine II. In gratitude for the comte's help in her rise to power, she allegedly placed the Masonic lodges in Russia under her personal protection. In 1770, Saint-Germain, this time acting as an agent for the French king, was involved in the partition of Poland and the Treaty of St. Petersburg, by which the Austro-Hungarian empire, Russia, and Prussia shared the spoils.

The comte founded two secret societies of his own called the Asiatic Brethren and the Knights of the Light and was allegedly a leading member of the Illuminati, although he does not seem to have shared that society's radical political ideals. He was heavily engaged in Masonic, Rosicrucian, and Templar activities with his patron, Prince Karl von Hesse-Kassel. As early as 1780, Saint-Germain warned Marie Antoinette that the French throne was in danger from an international conspiracy. The comte was supposed to have died in 1784 but was seen by several witnesses with Cagliostro and Mesmer at the 1785 Masonic Congress. In 1788, he appeared in Paris, warning aristocrats of the impending holocaust, and in 1789, he was in Sweden preventing an Illuminist plot against King Gustav III. Rumors continued to circulate for many years after his alleged death that Saint-Germain was still alive working behind the scenes in European politics or studying obscure occult doctrines in a Himalayan lamasery.

From 1785 to 1789, several of the Masonic lodges in France were working full-time to undermine the monarchy and the established government. Yet many French Masons remained loyal to the royalist cause during the Revolution; it was only a select few who took an active part in the radicalism of the period. Even within the ranks of the revolutionaries, there were indications that liberal elements were in opposition to the role played by the secret societies. In 1789, the marquis de Luchet who supported the Revolution, claimed, "There exists a conspiracy in favor of despotism against liberty, of incapacity against talent, of vice against virtue, of ignorance against enlightenment. This [secret] society aims to govern the world."

Whether prompted by Saint-Germain's warning, in June 1789, the French king tried to forestall the revolutionary elements by introducing a program of social reforms. Unfortunately, he also demanded that the monarchy be preserved, with the nobility having the power of veto on any modifications of policy. Within weeks of this announcement, the absolute power of the monarchy was challenged by popular revolts in towns all over France, which climaxed in the storming of the Bastille. This event led to the major political reforms of the Revolution, including the founding of a republic, the secularization of the Church, and eventually the mass executions of the aristocracy and the royal family during the Reign of Terror.

The overt influence of the Masonic-Illuminist tradition in the Revolution was notable. In revolutionary literature of the period, the Illuminist symbol of the eye in the triangle appears on book covers and the red Phrygian cap, borrowed from the mysteries of Mithras and the initiation rites of the Illuminati, was adopted as the headgear of the citizens' militia. Mirabeau allegedly said when the Bastille was stormed, "The idolatry of the monarchy has received a death blow from the sons and daughters of the Order of Templars." The Masonic tenets of equality, liberty, and fraternity became the rallying cry of the mob, while the red banner, a Masonic symbol of universal love, was openly carried in the streets by the revolutionaries. It is said that when the French king was executed, a voice cried out from the crowd "De Molay is avenged!"

In the early days of the Revolution, the anticlericism of the Illuminati was consciously adopted by the mob, as evidenced by attacks on the Church and the destruction of clerical property. A lithograph was published showing a naked man staring upward at heaven: He holds a mattock in one hand and stands on a tree that had been chopped down. In the branches of the tree are emblems of the state and the Church. In the background, a lightning flash illuminates the stormy sky and sets a crown ablaze. In this cartoon the archetypal man, symbolizing the common people, is himself addressing the Supreme Being. This suggests that despite their anticlerical stance, the revolutionaries still believed in a form of monotheistic spirituality. At the height of the political reforms, even the fanatical Robespierre attacked unenlightened people who supported the Revolution but preached materialism. He also condemned those intellectuals who could find no place in their theories of life for the concept of God. Another leading political activist of the time, Cemot, said, "To deny the Supreme Being is to deny Nature itself."

Within a year of the beginning of the Revolution, the land in France had been divided up among the peasants, slavery was eradicated from the French colonies, price controls were introduced to protect the living standards of the poor, and a democratic constitution was created. The Committee of Public Safety passed laws introducing free education, free medical services, and the guidelines for a welfare state. The price for these reforms, however, was high: The threat of foreign invasion and counterrevolution led to a centralized dictatorship of a new ruling class and to the Terror that destroyed all opposition to the alleged betrayal of the original aims of the Revolution. As with all radical political movements, those who advocated the replacement of the status quo were soon seduced by the power they had gained and became oppressors who were worse than the tyrants they replaced.

The role of the Illuminati and the Masons in the French Revolution was confused by the abandonment of the high ideals of the political movement that had instigated the original social reforms. The radicalism of the Masonic lodges before the Revolution had alienated their traditional following among the aristocratic classes in France. Even before 1789, the aristocrats had begun to resign from those lodges promoting socialism and, as a result, their organization was seriously weakened. By 1792, very few Masonic lodges were practicing and the movement was in a state of apathy. Those lodges that had survived faced hostility from the revolutionary government. At Versailles in 1792, the former grand master of a Masonic Templar lodge was lynched by an angry mob. Elsewhere, Masonry came under suspicion; those in power saw its role as a secret society as a cover for counterrevolution. Given that it was instrumental in the Revolution, it is ironic that within the space of a few years, French Freemasonry became the victim of the monster it had helped to create.

As early as 1791, allegations concerning the role of the Masons and the Illuminati were already beginning to circulate, based largely on the confessions of Cagliostro, who had been arrested by the Inquisition in 1789. In an attempt to save his life, the comte told his accusers about the international conspiracy by the Illuminati, the neo-Templars, and the Freemasons to start revolutions all over Europe. He revealed that their ultimate objective was to complete the work of the original Knights Templar by overthrowing the papacy or infiltrating agents into the College of Cardinals so that eventually an Illuminist would be elected pope.

In his confession, Cagliostro admitted that large sums of money had been placed by representatives of the Illuminati in banks in Holland, Italy, France, and England to finance future revolutions in those countries. He even claimed that the House of Rothschild, the international banking family founded in 1730, had supplied the funds to finance the French Revolution and that it was acting as secret agent for the Illuminists. No evidence to support this wild allegation has ever been uncovered and we can only presume it was a figment of Cagliostro's imagination or a deliberate libel for personal reasons that are unknown.

By 1796, the allegations of Masonic and Templar involvement in the French Revolution were becoming a cottage industry. It was pointed out that de Molay had been imprisoned in the Bastille and this was the first target of the Paris mob. Connections were made between the Templars and the Jesuits on the flimsy evidence that both groups were dedicated to the setting up of a "church within the Church." It was alleged that the duc d'Orleans, the grand master of French Freemasonry and a close friend of Mirabeau, was involved in an Illuminist plot against the French royal family. It was also said that he had practiced a secret, occult ritual and used relics belonging to de Molay in the process. Whether these were the sacred objects smuggled out of the Templar crypt in Paris on the eve of the grand master's death is unknown.

In 1796, *The Tomb of Jacques de Molay* was published, claiming that the French Revolution was the work of anarchists who traced their lineage back to the Templars and the Assassins. In 1797, a Jesuit priest, Father Bamuel, published his *Memoires pour serir de l'histoire du Jacobinisme* in which he traced the survival of the Manichean heresy through the Cathars, the Assassins, the Templars, and the Freemasons and said it was responsible for the French Revolution. He even claimed that the English Civil War had been a Templar conspiracy.

The exposure of the alleged Illuminist plot for universal revolution was greeted with shock by the other European royal families. They had seen what had happened in France and believed they were next in line. Before the French uprising, the police in Prussia and Austria had been placed on alert to counteract threats of subversion by secret societies. In 1790 the Bavarian government decreed membership in the Illuminati to be a capital offense. The fear of secret societies even extended to England, when Parliament debated the Unlawful Societies Act that would have prohibited Freemasonry. It failed because the English Craft had never dabbled in politics and was supported by both the aristocracy and the royal family.

With the rise of Napoleon in the postrevolutionary era, the Freemasons faced a bleak future. Bonaparte was aware of the Illuminist role in the Revolution, but he decided to use Freemasonry for his own political ends. He infiltrated the surviving lodges in Paris with his agents and installed his brothers Joseph and Lucien as successive grand masters of the Grand Orient. Their sponsorship attracted many leading members of the Napoleonic administration, and by the end of his reign, it could boast over twelve hundred lodges in France. By the early 1800s, Masonry was well established in the civil service at home and had also spread to the French colonies overseas. The tolerance of secret societies during the Napoleonic dynasty led to a revival of Templarism. In March 1808, a neo-Templar Order held a public requiem for Jacques de Molay in the Church of St. Paul in Paris and was presided over by Abbé Pierre Romains, the canon of Notre Dame who was the primate for the revived order. The Templars dressed in the medieval uniform of the knights and were escorted by a detachment of soldiers from the French army. The alleged bones and personal sidearms of de Molay were exhibited in the church and the piebald banner of the Templars was carried in procession through the streets to loud cheers from a crowd of onlookers.

In 1809, founded in France was a secret Masonic lodge modeled on the Illuminati and called the Sublimes Maitres Parfait (Sublime Perfect Masters), a title that also has overtones of Catharism. This new society professed extreme republican views and actively worked for socialist reforms, including abolition of the concept of private property. The Perfect Masters were opposed to Napoleon; they regarded him as a traitor who had betrayed the ideals of the Revolution. They sought to establish links to other European secret societies dedicated to political subversion and revolution. Exactly what the Perfect Masters achieved is unclear, for little is known of their activities after the 1820s, when the group's existence was revealed to the public, thus destroying its credibility as a secret society.

Meanwhile, the proroyalist Masonic lodges in France were secretly working behind the political scenes to restore the monarchy. They claimed success in 1814, when Napoleon abdicated in favor of King Louis XVII, and were allegedly behind the Paris revolt of 1830, which placed Louis Philippe on the throne. He placed the Freemasons under his personal protection and appointed his son, the duc d'Orleans, as the new grand master. On his death in 1842, the duc was succeeded by his brother, but at the Masonic convention that year in Strasbourg, the seeds of the 1848 Revolution were sown by radical elements in European Masonry. The convention was attended by both German and Italian republicans representing secret societies that preached and promoted anarchism and socialism. With the establishment of a provincial government in 1848, the French Masons began openly to demand liberty and political freedom, but this attempt at radicalizing political opinion in France ended with the restoration of the empire.

Napoleon III was hostile to Freemasonry and its dabbling in political matters. In 1850, he decreed that the Grand Orient and its lodges should not interfere with the politics of the country. Yet Masonry still received the private support of politicians, and, in 1852, the French president's cousin was elected grand master. He remained in office until 1861, when he was forced to resign for supporting the pope in a debate in the senate.

The Illuminati had apparently failed in its attempt to create an ideal social order in France, but its philosophy had influenced another revolution many thousands of miles away. In 1776 the American colonists had finally challenged the British in the War of Independence and the blueprint for a unique society based on democracy, religious freedom, and social equality had been drawn up in the New World. It originated in the founding of the first European colonies in North America in the seventeenth century by spiritual dissidents who included members of the Rosicrucian Order. The American Revolution provides an example of the most successful social experiment ever attempted by the secret societies in human history. Its political ramifications are still being experienced today in our modern world as the young nation seeks to justify its early spiritually inspired beginnings.

4

THE AMERICAN DREAM

Following the suppression of the Templars in the fourteenth century, the order in Portugal was exonerated of all guilt in an inquiry ordered by the king. Instead of disbanding, however, as the order was forced to do in most other European countries, the Knights Templar in Portugal was reformed, and the new order founded in its place took the name of the Knights of Christ and survived until at least the late sixteenth century. Its members included several famous navigators and explorers. It is said that the father-in-law of Christopher Columbus belonged to the order and that the discoverer of America inherited from his relative the charts and maps that made his voyage to the New World a success.

This historical curiosity is interesting because it offers an indication of the occult influences surrounding the foundation of America and its development into a world superpower. It has been suggested that Columbus's association with the Templar tradition may have been closer than simply marrying the daughter of a Knight of Christ. The explorer may in fact have been a member of a secret society with connections to the Templars and the Albigensian heresy.

Some historians claim that Columbus was an illiterate sailor who was educated by a guild of weavers based in the Italian city of Genoa. During this period, these craftsmen's guilds were often used as a cover by members of esoteric groups seeking to conceal their identities and true motives. Opposing this view, other historians see Columbus as a well-educated scholar, and the volumes of writings he composed during his lifetime tend to support this image of the explorer. Columbus was associated with a political group that hewed to the ideas of Dante, one of the alleged grand masters of the Order of the Rosy Cross who is known to have used codes and ciphers in his writings, a practice associated with membership in a secret society. Columbus's voyages of discovery were sponsored by Leonardo da Vinci and Lorenzo de Medici, both initiates of secret societies who found the explorer wealthy patrons among European royalty and aristocracy.

Whether Christopher Columbus was actually initiated into the Order of the Rosy Cross or any other secret society cannot be proved. He was certainly religious and believed he had a special mission in life, wearing a brown robe and girdle similar to the habits worn by Franciscan monks. He also heard spirit voices while in trance, and when he landed in America he believed God had led him to the New Jerusalem. The idea of America as the fulfillment of a biblical prophecy concerning the foundation of a spiritual Utopia on earth was a central belief in the Rosicrucian philosophy of the seventeenth century. In contrast to this religious piety, Columbus had an appalling attitude toward the Native Americans he came into contact with, whom he regarded as potential fodder for the slave market. These illiberal views would instantly disqualify him from membership of any Rosicrucian-inspired fraternity.

Columbus was the human instrument by which the New World was discovered—or perhaps *rediscovered* is the best word—but the next stage in the political development of America devised by the secret societies was to be the task of a true initiate of the occult tradition, Sir Francis Bacon (1561–1626), who was rumored to have been the illegitimate son of Queen Elizabeth I and the earl of Leicester. In his early career as a lawyer, Bacon became a member of a secret society called the Order of the Helmet, a group that worshipped the Greek goddess of wisdom, Pallas Athena, who is depicted wearing a helmet and carrying a spear. As a young man, he was also a student of

Hermetic, gnostic, and Neoplatonist philosophy and had studied the kabbalah.

Like many of his contemporaries, Bacon was a Utopian who received his inspiration from a belief in some ancient, half-forgotten Golden Age when humanity lived in harmony without war or violence. He projected this vision into the future, when, he hoped, enlightened religion, increased education, and the benefits of science would create the New Jerusalem. Unfortunately, many of the Utopians were hopeless romantics whose visions of the future seldom extended beyond the limits of their overworked imaginations. Bacon, on the other hand, had formulated a blueprint for the new Golden Age, which, although not published until after his death, provided the *raison d'être* for his life and political career.

His magnum opus was a novel called *The New Atlantis,* published in 1627, after the foundation of the English colonies in the Americas. It is the story of a family who is shipwrecked on a mysterious island ruled by philosopher-scientists who have flying machines and ships that can travel under the sea. In this fantasy novel, Bacon refers to America as the New Atlantis and describes the creation of a scientific institute along the lines of the invisible college advocated in Rosicrucian writings. This was later to provide the impetus for the Royal Society founded by the Order of the Rosy Cross in the reign of Charles II. Bacon's books often featured title pages with Masonic symbols, including the compass and the square, the two pillars of Solomon's temple, the blazing triangle, and the eye of God, indicating his association with the secret societies who supported his Utopian concepts.

Bacon's reason for supporting English colonization of the New World was the threat from the Spanish, who had already established a foothold in both North and South America. The Spanish fiercely resisted the religious reforms that swept Europe in the sixteenth century. Bacon was aware that the ships of the Spanish Armada had carried not only troops but also agents of the Inquisition who had planned to restore the Catholic faith in England by sword and fire. If Bacon's plans for the New World were to be realized, he knew that the Spanish had to be prevented from founding American colonies on a large scale.

The early attempts to colonize America spanned a period of nearly seventy years, although it is the epic voyage of the *Mayflower* in 1620, which is clearly remembered today. In fact, as early as 1550, the Spanish had colonized most of the Caribbean, Mexico, California, and South America. The French were busy colonizing Canada, and, in the 1580s, English colonies were settled in Newfoundland. The rapid colonization of the New World by English settlers did not really begin, however, until the reign of King James I in the 1600s.

In 1606, James set up the Virginia Company, which was granted his royal authority to begin settlements in the province of Virginia, named after Elizabeth I, who had been popularly called the Virgin Queen. The Union Jack first flew on American soil as a permanent fixture at Jamestown in Virginia in the spring of 1607, and in 1609, the first governor of the new colony was appointed. In that same year, James granted a charter to found the Bermuda colony, and three years later settlers from the original Virginia landing took up residence on the islands.

The early members of the Virginia Company were aristocrats who supported the Church of England and the monarchy. They included Lord Southampton, the earl of Pembroke, the earl of Montgomery, the earl of Salisbury, the earl of Northampton, and Sir Francis Bacon, who became a member in 1609. As chancellor of England, Bacon was able to persuade the king to issue the charters enabling the new colonies to proliferate in the New World.

As early as the 1600s, the seeds of the American Revolution in the following century were being sown. The English colonists were already divided into those who supported the monarch's right to rule from London and others who wanted the new colonies to be independent. Although Bacon's insistence on the founding of English colonies was prompted by the Spanish menace, his long-term political objectives were centered on the creation of a democratic society based on spiritual principles.

Bacon expressed his views on this subject several times, claiming, "This kingdom now first in His Majesty's [James I] time hath gotten a lot or portion in the New World by the plantation of Virginia and the Summerlands [Bermuda]. And certainly it is with the kingdom of earth as it is with the Kingdom of Heaven. Sometimes a grain of mustard seed provides a tree." He was more explicit in a speech to Parliament when he made a reference to the establishment of "Solomon's house" in the American colonies and mentioned his unpublished novel, *The New Atlantis,* as the blueprint for the development of the new country. In this clear reference to King Solomon's temple in Jerusalem, Bacon indicated that the founding of the colonies in Virginia was a spiritual as well as a political act.

The Virginia Company members who actually settled in America included several members of the Bacon family and friends of his who were initiates of the Rosy Cross. They were to be followed later by the Puritan faction, which embraced the Pilgrim Fathers who sailed on the *Mayflower,* escaping religious persecution in Europe to found the colonies in Massachusetts and the rest of New England. In addition to these religious separatists, it is claimed that as early as the 1620s, Masonic lodges had been formed in the American colonies, although speculative Freemasonry did not officially emerge in Europe until the beginning of the eighteenth century.

Along with the Puritans and Rosicrucians, there were other spiritual dissidents escaping persecution of a different type. One of these was Thomas Morton, an English lawyer who founded a colony that he called Merrymount in 1624 Massachusetts. Morton was a rebel who forged alliances with the local Indians, sold them muskets, and warned them of the genocidal tendencies of the Puritan colonists. In May 1628, Morton ordered that a maypole be erected in the center of his colony. Around this phallic symbol danced the members of his colony, local Indians, and refugees from the Puritan settlement who had rebelled against the strict code of the Pilgrim Fathers. The participants in this pagan revel wore stag antlers, bells, and clothes of many colors and elected a lord and lady to rule over their orgiastic celebrations.

On the evening of May Day, news of these erotic antics reached the ears of the Puritans, and an armed group raided the Merrymount colony to arrest Morton. The Indians were scattered into the woods by gunfire and the refugees from the Puritan faction were rounded up and marched back to the colony, where they were put in the stocks for defying their elders. The maypole was cut down and charges of practicing witchcraft were prepared against Morton. Due to insufficient evidence, the charges were dropped and Morton returned to the colony in 1629 and promptly erected another maypole. Following a year of threats and harassment, the Puritans arrested Morton again, burned down his house, and sentenced him to deportation.

On his return to England, Morton organized a political attack against the Puritans, using his knowledge of the law to challenge the legal validity of the charter granted to found the Massachusetts Company and accusing the colonists of religious hypocrisy and corruption. In England, Morton played down his pagan beliefs and presented himself as a dedicated Anglican who was resisting the Puritan excesses of the other colonists. His plan to dislodge the Puritans was nearly successful but was prevented by the outbreak of the English Civil War. In 1643, Morton returned to America, where he was again arrested and spent two years in prison. He was finally released in 1645, but his health had been affected by imprisonment and he died two years later.

By the 1650s, the Masonic influence was spreading in the colonies. A group of Dutch settlers who were third degree Freemasons arrived in Newport, Massachusetts, in 1658. They introduced Masonry to the colony and members of the Dutch immigrants operated a Masonic lodge in the area until 1742. In 1694, a mystic named Johannes Kelpius chartered an English ship to take himself and a group of followers to a colony in Pennsylvania. Kelpius was a German student of the kabbalah, a practicing magician, an astrologer, an alchemist, and a founder of the mystical Order of Pietists. This group based their beliefs on spiritual revelations received from spirit sources by psychic methods and they predicted the imminent Second Coming.

The modern American occultist and writer Manly Palmer Hall, has refuted claims made by nineteenth-century writers that the Pietists were a bona fide Rosicrucian group. Yet he does concede that the order introduced kabbalism, astrology, alchemy, and the Hermetic tradition to the new colonies. It is possible that contact was made among the Pietists, the Freemasons, and the Rosicrucians in the New World and that this led to a mutual exchange of esoteric knowledge.

It is difficult to imagine how the high ideals of the original colonists were broken by colonial rule, but it happened in a series of political mistakes made by the British crown and government. A set of circumstances arose in which the American colonists were forced to take a radical stand against British misrule, and from this defiance was born the political and spiritual impulse that led to independence and the creation of the United States of America. Arguments about the taxes levied on the American colonies by the British had been simmering for years, but they finally came to a head in 1773 with the passing of the Tea Act. The British government, attempting to save the East India Company from bankruptcy, arranged for the company to deliver its tea directly to the colonies. In revolt against the new tax they had to pay on tea, a group of Boston citizens disguised as Native Americans raided the East India Company's ships in the city harbor and threw their cargo overboard. The members of the Boston Tea Party were all Freemasons who belonged to the St. Andrews lodge in the city.

The British seem to have totally underestimated the strength of feeling in the American colonies over the Tea Act, hence perhaps the popular saying, "It's just a tempest in a tea cup." In March 1774, British leaders introduced a bill closing the Boston port until compensation was paid to the East India Company for the loss of its goods. Events quickly escalated, and when a small force of colony militia tried to seize an ammunition store at Concord and fired on the British redcoats, the American Revolution had effectively begun.

One of the most influential figures in the American Revolution was the writer, philosopher, and scientist Benjamin Franklin. He was a Quaker but had become a Freemason in 1731, when he joined the lodge of St. John in Philadelphia, which was the first recognized Masonic lodge in America. At the time he was inducted, Franklin was working as a journalist and wrote several pro-Masonic articles published in *The Pennsylvania Gazette*. In 1732, he helped draft the bylaws of his lodge and in 1734, he printed the *Constitutions*, which was the first Masonic book ever issued in America. He eventually rose to the rank of grand master of St. John's lodge and, in 1749, was elected grand master of the province. While living in France in the 1770s and working as a diplomat for the American colonies, Franklin was made grand master of the Neuf Sœurs lodge in Paris. Members of the lodge included Danton, who played a crucial role in the French Revolution, the marquis de Lafayette, and John Paul Jones, both of whom fought in the American War of Independence. While he was in Paris, Franklin used his Masonic contacts to raise funds to buy arms for the American rebels.

Benjamin Franklin's diplomatic activities in the years before the American Revolution brought him into contact with those in positions of power who shared his Masonic and occult interests. One of these was Sir Francis Dashwood, the English chancellor of the exchequer who was the founder of a secret society called the Friars of St. Francis of Wycombe, more popularly known in the coffee houses and brothels of London as the Hell Fire Club. Dashwood was the eldest son of a businessman and had married into the aristocracy. He sat in the House of Commons for more than twenty years and the House of Lords for nearly another twenty, served as chancellor from 1762 to 1763, and was a close friend of and political advisor to King George III. As a young man on the Grand Tour of Europe, Dashwood was initiated into a Masonic lodge in Florence. When he returned to England, he founded the Society of Dilettanti, which catered to the hard-drinking habits and debauched sexual activities of wealthy rakes. Dashwood also began to rebuild his ancestral home at West Wycombe, using ideas he had picked up in Italy. The ceilings were painted with murals depicting the Greek and Roman gods, and statues of these deities were scattered in the gardens. Dashwood also had a special lake created on the grounds where mock battles were staged for his guests using large-scale models of sailing ships.

In 1739, Sir Francis Dashwood returned to Italy and there made contact with several Continental Freemasons. He also visited Rome to witness the election of a new pope, even though he was anti-Catholic. The previous pontiff had prohibited the practice of Freemasonry in 1738 and excommunicated all Catholics known to be members of the Masonic lodges. The grand master of the Florence lodge, Lord Reynard, who was the son of the lord chief justice of England, had been forced to close down the lodge and destroy all its papers to avoid being arrested by the Inquisition.

On his return to England, Dashwood founded the Friars of St. Francis, and meetings were held in the mansion in a special room decorated as a Masonic temple. At this time, Dashwood was also a member of a neo-druidic order called An Ulieach Druidh Braithreachas, or the Druid Universal Bond. This organization had been founded in 1717 to revive the old Celtic pagan religion, and one of its chief druids from 1799 to 1827 was the visionary poet William Blake, who is also listed as a grand master of the Rosicrucian Order. Blake was involved with other secret societies at the time and had an interest in sex magic. Following rumors about sex orgies performed by the so-called Hell Fire Club at West Wycombe, in 1743, the Druid Universal Bond withdrew Dashwood's charter to practice druidism.

In 1751, Dashwood purchased Medmenham Abbey at Marlow on the River Thames and converted the thirteenth-century house, once owned by Cistercian monks, into a Gothic style folly. In the gardens he erected statues of classical gods and goddesses, including Venus, who is depicted bending over to extract a thorn from her foot—unsuspecting walkers, rounding a corner, are faced with her exposed buttocks. There was also a statue of the Roman god Priapus displaying his huge erect penis.

Exaggerated rumors and gossip about the activities at Medmenham Abbey carried out by Dashwood and his friends began to circulate in

London high society. It was whispered that prostitutes dressed as nuns attended orgies at the house. Satanic rites such as the Black Mass, involving prayers recited over the naked body of a woman as the altar, were allegedly practiced. In fact, the Medmenhamites were actually practicing a revival of the pagan old religion. According to one member of the Hell Fire Club, it was really dedicated to the worship of the Bonea Dea, or the great mother goddess, and the practice of the Eleusian mysteries. Some of its members may have indulged in pseudosatanic rites, although only as a prelude to the sexual antics that were an important aspect of the wild parties held after the meetings were finished.

In 1760, when King George III was crowned, several Hell Fire Club members were given high office: among them John Stuart, the earl of Bute, who was made secretary of state for the Northern Department, and Dashwood himself, who became chancellor of the exchequer. Among other important people who later joined the Hell Fire Club were the lord mayor of London, the son of the archbishop of Canterbury, the Prince of Wales, and Benjamin Franklin.

In 1758, Franklin visited England to seek support for the American colonists in their efforts to obtain more independence from the British crown. He stayed with Dashwood at West Wycombe, and the two Masons discussed ways in which the worsening relations between the colonies and the government in London could be improved. Franklin was worried that the situation was becoming dangerous and would eventually result in bloodshed. Dashwood seems to have worked for the American colonists as their representative in Britain, and in 1770, he put forward a plan to the British government for reconciliation between the two sides that would have led to American autonomy, but it was rejected.

Benjamin Franklin visited Britain again in 1773 and met again with Dashwood. He informed Dashwood that time was short and unless some compromise was found, the Americans would violently revolt against British rule and he wanted to avoid war. Franklin and Dashwood visited Oxford University and Sir Francis introduced his American friend to Lord North, the first lord of the treasury. The three men discussed the deteriorating relationship between Britain and the colonies and the possibility of a peaceful solution to the problem. Unfortunately, nothing came of this meeting and Franklin's attempt to negotiate a settlement failed.

Dashwood's influence in the matter was considerably weakened by the stories of sexual excesses at Medmenham. This gossip developed into a full-blown scandal with the revelations of a radical politician, John Wilkes, MP, who had been a member of the Hell Fire Club. Wilkes was a self-styled defender of democracy and liberty who supported the American colonists in their attempt to rid themselves of British imperialist rule. He claimed that the inner circle of the Hell Fire Club was made up of political conspirators plotting to deprive the Americans of their democratic rights. Considering Dashwood's involvement with Franklin and the fact that the two men were Freemasons, this seems very unlikely. It is obvious from the role played by Freemasonry in the creation of the new American nation that the Masonic fraternity supported freedom and independence for the colonies, but they wanted to see the new country born without the spilling of blood, while Wilkes obviously had his own reasons for demeaning the efforts of Dashwood and Franklin to avoid conflict.

With the outbreak of war between the British and the Americans, it was only to be expected that a man of destiny would arise who was capable of guiding the immediate fixture of the nation that arose from the ashes of the old order. The man who took this role in history was General George Washington, the descendant of a twelfth-century knight from the north of England who had served English royalty. The Washingtons were staunchly royalist; in fact, one of Washington's ancestors, a relative of the duke of Buckingham, had fought on the side of the Cavaliers in the English Civil War. With the triumph of Cromwell, two members of the family had emigrated to Virginia to escape Puritan persecution. They quickly established themselves as landowners, merchants, and local politicians and created the Washington dynasty of New Americans that was eventually to give birth to the first president of the United States on February 11, 1732.

Washington seemed set for a modest career as a farmer and land-owner, but with the death of his brother in 1752, he inherited property, a seat in the House of Burgesses, and, most important, as future events would show, a post as major in the colonial militia. Within two years, Washington was fighting the French, and with the encouragement of John Adams, who was both a Freemason and a member of the secret Order of the Dragon, he had begun a military career, which led him to become commander-in-chief of the rebel forces in the American Revolution.

George Washington was himself a high-ranking Mason. He had taken his first-degree initiation at a lodge in Fredericksburg, Virginia, in 1734. Among the fifty-six American rebels who signed the Declaration of Independence, only six were not members of the Masonic Order. The majority of the military commanders of the American revolutionary army fighting the British during the War of Independence were practicing Freemasons.

The secret influence of esoteric societies, both Masonic and Rosicrucian, in the American Revolution is illustrated by the occult symbolism in the American flag and the Great Seal, the national symbol of the country. The design for the Stars and Stripes was the result of a joint effort by a committee including Benjamin Franklin and George Washington, but it seems they were helped by the strange intervention of a mysterious person whose real name and identity is unknown.

Preparations for designing the flag took place in the house of a rebel leader in Cambridge, Massachusetts, in December 1775. At a dinner party attended by the flag committee, a stranger staying with the family of the house was introduced. He was referred to merely as the Professor and was described by those who met him as an elderly man who was very well read and extremely knowledgeable about the historical events of the previous century, as if he had actually witnessed them. He was a vegetarian, was accompanied by a large oak chest containing rare books and ancient manuscripts, and seemed to know Franklin. The stranger put forward several proposals about the design of the flag and these were eagerly accepted by the committee without any argument. When the dinner party broke up and the other committee members left for home, the Professor remained in conversation with Franklin and Washington for several hours. He allegedly told the two statesmen that America would soon take its rightful place as a new nation recognized by all the governments of the world and it was destined to be a future leader of civilization.

The designing of the Great Seal of America, which is the country's symbolic coat-of-arms, was also surrounded by occult significance and mystery. A committee was formed for the design on the afternoon of July 4, 1776, after Congress had formally signed the Declaration of Independence creating the new American nation: a resolution was passed requesting that Franklin, John Adams, and Thomas Jefferson design a device to be used as the official seal for the new country. Several of the colonies already had their own seals, but Congress wanted one that was universally recognized as representing the inspiration for the American Revolution and the destiny of the American people.

A French artist, Eugene du Simtière, was commissioned by the committee to create designs based on their ideas and, if necessary, to add his own. Each committee member proposed a different design for the seal. Franklin suggested Moses leading the Israelites across the Red Sea to escape the pharaoh's army. Jefferson selected a similar scene from the Bible, depicting the children of Israel marching through the wilderness toward the Promised Land. The exodus from Egypt to Canaan was symbolic both of the route taken by the Ancient Wisdom in the days of Moses and the emigration of the Masonic-Rosicrucian tradition from Europe to the New World in the seventeenth century.

John Adams, in contrast, took a theme from Greek mythology for his illustration for the Great Seal. He depicted the god Herakles, or Hercules, resting on his club and facing a choice between virtue and sloth, which can be interpreted as the twin choices facing the new nation. It should also be noted that in Plato's description of the mythical Utopia of Atlantis, he describes the land as situated beyond the

Pillars of Hercules in the Atlantic Ocean. Interestingly, Bacon's Utopian romance *The New Atlantis* was widely accepted as a blueprint for the new America and it would have been well known to people such as Adams and Franklin.

Du Simtière's design for the seal was more mundane but no less significant: Following tradition, he proposed a shield divided into six quarters, and on these were represented the heraldic devices of the six European countries that had provided settlers for the seventeenth-century colonies—the Tudor rose of England, the thistle of Scotland, the Celtic harp of Ireland, the fleur-de-lys of France, the eagle of Germany, and the lion of Holland. This shield was to be supported by twin goddesses personifying liberty and justice. It was surrounded by thirteen smaller ones representing the number of original colonies and also included the Illuminist-Masonic symbol of the eye of God in a triangle with the Latin saying *E pluribus unum,* or "one out of many."

Congress was not happy with any of the proposed designs, and in 1780, another committee was formed and additional work was carried out. In May 1792, a third group was appointed that submitted several designs, including a shield with thirteen pentagrams or five pointed stars—the occult symbol of humanity—representing the old colonies and thirteen red, white, and blue stripes. On the reverse of the seal was a truncated pyramid with thirteen steps surmounted by the eye of God surrounded by rays of light.

While Congress accepted the design on the reverse they were still not satisfied with the first side of the seal. They commissioned the secretary of Congress, Charles Thomson, to modify the design. Thomson had formerly been a teacher at a school in Philadelphia run by Benjamin Franklin and was a member of the American Philosophical Society. This organization had been founded by Franklin and other leading Masons to promote the arts and sciences in the colonies. It operated in the same tradition as the Royal Society in England and was based on the Rosicrucian concept of the invisible college.

The design of the Great Seal as it exists today is by Thomson and his colleague William Barton. On the front is the American bald eagle, which in astrological symbolism represents the zodiac sign of Scorpio, associated with death, rebirth, sexuality, and regeneration. The eagle holds in its talons a bundle of arrows and an olive branch. This represents the conflicting forces of war and peace, which have characterized the American nation over the years, and, in occult terms, symbolizes the dualistic concepts of good and evil, light and darkness, and the male and the female principles that the Masonic-Templar tradition inherited from the gnostics and the Manicheans.

On the chest of the eagle is a heraldic device in the form of a shield and above its head is a cloud containing thirteen pentagrams. In its mouth the eagle holds a scroll with the words *E pluribus unum* written on it. The general interpretation of this phrase here is that it refers to the creation of the new American nation from the original colonies, the many becoming one. This phrase also has an occult meaning, however, and is used by initiates to refer to the ancient belief that all the gods are one God. Even the most polytheistic of the old pagan religions recognized the existence of a Supreme Creator who ruled over all the other deities in the pantheon. This concept is to be found in Rosicrucian teachings, and in Freemasonry the phrase is used to refer to the one (God) in relation to the many (humanity).

The reverse side of the Great Seal designed by Thomson also reveals a wealth of occult symbolism: It shows the truncated pyramid with its steps representing the thirteen colonies. On the bottom step are the Roman numerals MDCCLXXVI—1776—the year of the Revolution. This was also the date of the founding of the Illuminati. Above the pyramid is the eye of God in a triangle surrounded by rays of light. This was the identifying symbol of Illuminism and it appeared on the covers of radical political texts published during the French Revolution by supporters of the Masonic tradition.

In occultism, the truncated pyramid represents the temporary loss of the Ancient Wisdom that occurred when the Christian Church achieved political power and began to repress the pagan religions, which were driven underground into secret societies. In ancient Egypt, when the pyramids were used as initiation chambers, each pyramid

OBVERSE

REVERSE

The Great Seal of the United States

had a special capstone made either from natural crystal or an alloy of precious metals. This capstone attracted cosmic rays and occult forces, creating the right conditions for the initiate inside the pyramid's inner chamber to experience spiritual illumination. Symbolically, on the Great Seal the eye in the triangle represents the missing capstone, which now exists only on a metaphysical level.

Above the eye in the triangle symbol is the motto *Annuit Coeptis,* which translates as "He favors our undertaking." This is a reference to the belief that the American Revolution was a divine event fulfilling a historic destiny for the future of the world. Washington was said to have been approached by an angel at Valley Forge who granted him a vision of the Utopian role America was to play in the centuries to come. As a God-fearing man, Washington believed that he had been chosen as the divine instrument that would bring this prophetic vision into reality. He was certainly an instrument for the Freemasons and Rosicrucians who planned the American Revolution and recognized in him the attributes needed for the first leader of the embryonic nation.

Below the pyramid, on the reverse side of the seal, is a scroll bearing the words *Novus Ordo Seclorum,* or the "New Order of the Ages." The colonists borrowed this motto from the works of the Roman philosopher Virgil. In its original form it is rendered *Magnus ab integro seclorum mascilir* and was inspired by a passage from the mysterious Sibyline books. These documents were said to contain the oracles of the sibyls and detailed the destiny of the Roman Empire. On an exoteric level, this plagiarism of a phrase from imperial Rome could easily be seen as an attempt to compare the new American republic to the glories of the ancient Roman Empire. On an esoteric level, for those Freemasons and Rosicrucians who were behind the creation of the new nation, the words *new order* could refer either to the replacing of monarchistic rule with republicanism or to the new Age of Aquarius. This coming new age replaces the old Piscean Age that began around the period when Jesus was preaching in Galilee. The occult conspirators believed that America would play an important role in the transition from the Piscean to the Aquarian Age, with this transition spanning a period of two hundred fifty years, from the time of the American Revolution of 1776 to the year 2025 CE.

The Masonic-Rosicrucian tradition had a profound influence on the formation of American democracy, but there was another European secret society with an important role in the early history of the nation. This fraternity was centered round the Adams family, which, as we have seen, was involved in the Revolution and provided the new republic with several presidents. In 1823, President John Adams ordered a tombstone to be erected to mark the grave of his ancestor Henry Adams, who had emigrated to the colonies from the southwest of England in the early 1600s. This gravestone records that Adams fled from the "Dragon persecution" in Somerset and founded a colony at Mount Walliston, which had been renamed Merrymount by the neo-pagan Thomas Morton.

It is claimed by the American writer Andrew E. Rothovius that Adams was not, as is generally assumed, a Puritan fleeing religious persecution, but a leader of a secret society called the Dragons whose members attempted to revive the old pagan religion in the reigns of Elizabeth I and James I. The Dragon title was a reference to the mysterious earth energy at sacred power centers and ley lines that link a network of ancient megalithic sites, such as standing stones and stone circles, across the British landscape.

The Dragons regarded King James's son Prince Henry as the only hope for the future of their country. James was a weak homosexual whose reign was overshadowed by attempts to remove him from the throne, including the infamous Gunpowder Plot of 1605. Henry had challenged his father's policies by seeking to instigate social reforms. He had even tried to persuade the king to abdicate once he was old enough to take over the reigns of power. This event was anticipated by the Dragons and they seemed to have regarded Prince Henry as a reincarnation of King Arthur who was destined to bring about their Utopian dream of a perfect society ruled by spiritual principles and laws. Disaster struck, however, on Henry's eighteenth birthday when he fell ill and died after a few days. Rumors circulated that he had been poisoned, either by his father or by conspirators within the court who objected to his liberal ideas. It was this tragedy that prompted many Dragon members to leave England and set sail for the New World. When they reached America, the Adams family, some of whose members were of the original Dragon colonists, concealed their pagan beliefs under a veneer of Puritanism. A few did have some contact with the pantheist Thomas Morton, but their long-term plan came to fruition with the American Revolution and the part John Adams took in its inception and aftermath.

In the early years after the Revolution, John Adams eagerly supported George Washington's key political ideas, which were based on geographical considerations. As an initiate of an occult tradition based on the sacred geometry used during the prehistoric megalithic culture, Adams found sense in Washington's theories. The first president wanted to construct a national capital combining the government with a center for national education. This capital would be at a central location in the country that was easily accessible to every citizen. A system of nationwide canals would be dug linking all the major cities of the new nation to the capital to form a communications network. In this way, the government would not be isolated from the people and anyone could have easy access to its political center. For various reasons, Washington did not pursue this ideal and instead became a disciple of the laissez-faire school of capitalism, which today has become the byword for the New Right in both the United States and many European countries with conservative governments.

John Adams was obviously disillusioned by Washington's abandonment of geopolitics, but in 1799, ten years after Washington's death, the new secretary of state revived the idea of the canal system and John Adams actively supported him, prompted by his idealistic vision of an egalitarian society as proposed by the original Dragons who had colonized America. Adams believed that by transforming the new canals, roads, and eventually railroads into a national transportation network, a nation could be created where all men and women were equal. Unfortunately, his grand plan was blocked by Congress, which voted against the supply of funds needed to finance it.

In 1824, John Adams's son John Quincy Adams became president and attempted to revive the national transportation system, but political events conspired against his success. Missouri had applied for statehood in 1820 and soon made clear that it and the other southern states that practiced slavery would not support the idea or any other policy that might assist the free passage of commercial goods or human beings across the south. In the north, the industrialists were also suspicious of any measure promising greater freedom for their workers and, in a strange alliance, they joined forces with the slave-owning southerners to create the new Democratic Party. They supported their own presidential candidate, Andrew Jackson, who was an advocate of slavery. In the election of 1824, Adams narrowly missed defeat, becoming president by only a slim majority. Although established in the White House, the new president spent much of his time in office fighting his political opponents, and thus his attempts at social reform were frustrated.

During his period in office, President Adams did try to pioneer the modern concepts of conservation and ecology. He attempted but failed to force Congress to prevent the destruction of the virgin forests in Florida that were owned by Andrew Jackson and his associates. He also attempted to introduce laws forcing factory owners to treat their workers more humanely. In 1828, the election was fought again between Jackson and Adams, with the former winning easily. The issue in the election was the contrasting personalities of the two candidates, with Adams satirized as an idealistic intellectual and Andrew Jackson projected as the bluff, no-nonsense war hero—a pattern that was to be repeated throughout American history. Adams left the White House embittered and disillusioned with the political process. He told friends that his spiritual vision of the new America had been destroyed by the alliance between the slave owners and the industrialists, both of whom had conspired to deprive him of reelection.

John Quincy Adams no longer held high political office, but his family was still influential in shaping radical ideas that had germinated in the Dragon tradition. His two grandsons, Henry and Brook Adams, wrote books offering an alternative vision of society based on spiritually derived values rather than the pursuit of wealth and materialism. Henry Adams visited the medieval cathedral of Chartres in France, which had been one of the greatest achievements of the masonic guilds. Chartres was built on the site of a druidic temple, and in Christian times the cathedral was dedicated to the Black Virgin, a version of the ancient pagan goddess. Following his visit to France, Adams wrote *Mont-Saint-Michel and Chartres*, published in 1913. In the book he pointed out that in the three centuries since 1600, the time of the beginning of American colonization by James I of England as influenced by the Rosicrucian grand master Sir Francis Bacon, humanity had developed more rapidly than ever before in history. Pessimistically, he predicted that in the period between 1915 and 1920 the human race would reach the zenith of its spiritual development and then rapidly descend into materialism and barbarity.

His brother, Brooks Adams, also assumed the role of a social prophet, publishing several important works on world affairs and the political role of America and its future destiny. A hundred years before the concept of the right and left sides of the brain (representing respectively intuitive and logical thinking processes) received scientific approval, Adams explained human history in terms of cyclic alternations of the domination of the calculative and imaginative mind. He believed that we had entered a historical cycle dominated by the logical, rational mind, with its emphasis on scientific progress, militarism, and the centralization of political power in a ruling elite. In the 1890s, when he wrote, he claimed that the seat of this centralized power structure was America and that it would replace the British empire as the leader of Western civilization. He predicted that the new century would see America taking an active role in a worldwide war that would establish the country as an imperial power ruled by a military-based government with a society devoid of spiritual or moral values and addicted to materialism. According to Adams's grim scenario, this situation would occur by 1920 and remain the dominant factor in American political and social life until the end of the twentieth century.

Although the spiritual vision of the Freemasons, Rosicrucians, and Dragons was betrayed in America, there have been several attempts in American history to revive the original ideals of the seventeenth-century colonists and return the country to the spiritual path. The presidency of Abraham Lincoln was a turning point in America's spiritual history. It was marked by the Civil War, and although thousands of lives were sacrificed, it led to a new spirit of freedom, the emancipation of the slaves, the modern concept of human rights, and the final union of the North and the South to create the modern United States of America.

Lincoln was known for his psychic interests and had become involved in the practice of spiritualism after the death of his son. Newspapers hostile to Lincoln's reforming campaigns often made sly references to his "progressive friends"—a coded reference to the inner circle of Quakers, spiritualists, and occultists to whom the president often turned for spiritual guidance. Lincoln himself possessed psychic powers, including clairvoyance and precognition and the ability to heal the sick.

The president was a close friend of a neo-Rosicrucian named Pascal Beverly Randolph. Born in 1825, Randolph had traveled in the East, where he had been taught the secrets of Tantric sex magic. He was of mixed blood and had fought for the Union during the Civil War, in which he led a Negro infantry company. After the war, Lincoln appointed him an educator of emancipated slaves in Louisiana. Randolph had begun his occult career in 1858, when he founded a Rosicrucian society called the Hermetic Brotherhood of the Light. The early Rosicrucians had been interested in the transformation of sexual energy into spiritual power and had used alchemical symbolism to conceal the process from outsiders. Randolph claimed to have been initiated into "the white magic of love" by a "dusky maiden of Arabic blood" in Jerusalem. This may refer to an actual sexual encounter in the East or it might have been a coded reference to the goddess worshipped in King Solomon's temple in Jerusalem.

Attempts have been made to dismiss Randolph as a charlatan who used occult practices for his own personal sexual gratification, but he was aware of the history of the Rosicrucian Order. He regarded Christian Rosenkreuz as the one who revived rather than founded the order and alleged that he, too, had been initiated into Tantric practices while studying in the Middle East. The aim of these practices was the creation of an elixir of life with the power to delay aging and prolong youth. Randolph claimed that this elixir was based on the mixed secretions of men and women produced at the height of sexual excitement. His belief that the sex act was a sacred ritual, which could be used to achieve spiritual enlightenment, led to his arrest in Boston for advocating free love. Although the prosecuting counsel described Randolph in court as "the most dangerous man in the world," he was acquitted.

Pascal Randolph was not the only Rosicrucian to announce his existence publicly in the nineteenth century. The formation of neo-Rosicrucian groups in England, which ultimately resulted in the Hermetic Order of the Golden Dawn, inspired a group of Freemasons in Pennsylvania to form a Masonic Rosicrucian order in 1879. This group, today known as the Societas Rosicruciana Civitatibus Foederatis, is open only to master Masons and, in 1980, had a total of 773 members. There is no evidence that Randolph was connected to these Masonic Rosicrucians, but links can be traced between his organization and the Ordo Templi Orientis, or OTO, which claimed to follow the Templar tradition. When R. Swinburne Clymer became the head of Randolph's group, he rejected the Tantric sex magic of its founder for more orthodox Rosicrucianism. Randolph, however, had already passed on his knowledge of Tantric practices to a group of French occultists, who in turn passed them to the German founder of the OTO.

The Ancient and Mystical Order Rosae Crucis (AMORC) was formally established in the United States by H. Spencer Lewis (1883–1939), who claimed that AMORC was directly descended from an early American Rosicrucian group that had formed a lodge in Philadelphia in 1624, but he also said he had received instruction in the occult mysteries from a Rosicrucian order in Toulouse, France, in 1909. According to Lewis, the authority to found AMORC was given to him by a member of the English branch of the order who had descended from Oliver Cromwell and had received her authority from the grand master of the order who lived in India.

The circumstances of Abraham Lincoln's assassination has some mysterious elements that have prompted some conspiracy theorists to represent it as an example of the workings of the secret societies in American history. The president's killer, John Wilkes Booth, was trapped in a burning barn after the murder and was shot dead by a soldier named Boston Corbett. Apparently, Corbett was a religious fanatic who had castrated himself for spiritual purposes. He was later committed to a mental hospital but escaped and was never seen again. It has been suggested that he was a secret member of the infamous Skoptsi sect that flourished in eighteenth- and nineteenth-century Russia. This weird cult traced its origins back to the pagan mysteries of the goddess Cybele, whose priests wore women's clothing and castrated themselves as a sacrificial offering at her altars. It is possible his sect may have been introduced into nineteenth-century America by Russian immigrants. Rumors persist that Booth escaped from the fire in the barn and lived until 1903 under an assumed name, financially supported by Lincoln's replacement in the White House.

AMORC symbol

Another intervention by the Masonic-Rosicrucian-Illuminati tradition in American history took place in the 1930s and coincided with the presidency of Franklin Delano Roosevelt, whose New Deal introduced a form of socialism into the American political system and led to allegations by his extreme right-wing enemies that he was a crypto-communist. Roosevelt was allegedly a member of a quasi-Masonic secret society called the Ancient Arabic Order of Nobles and Mystics and held the grade of a Knight of Pythias. This order claimed to be an offshoot of the Illuminati and included among its past members Mirabeau, Frederick the Great, Goethe, Spinoza, Kant, Sir Francis Bacon, and Garibaldi, but this list of notables suggests there was some confusion between it and the Order of the Rosy Cross.

Two nineteenth-century Freemasons, Walter Flemming and William Florence, were the co-founders of the American branch of the order. Florence had been initiated into a French lodge of the order in 1870 while staying in Marseilles. He was later inducted into another lodge in Algeria and returned to found the first American lodge in New York in 1871. Membership in the order was open only to Freemasons who had reached the thirty-second degree of the Ancient and Accepted Scottish Rite or who were members of Masonic Templar lodges.

The order's mythical origins date back to the seventh century CE or earlier and it was allegedly founded by a descendant of the prophet Muhammad. He in turn had derived the idea for the order from a politico-religious secret society in medieval Europe that taught spiritual tolerance and whose members included Arabs, Christians, and Jews. The symbol of the order is a crescent moon made from the claws of a Bengal tiger and engraved with a pyramid, an urn, and a pentagram. The crescent is suspended from a scimitar and in the order is a representation of the universal mother worshipped in ancient times as Isis. The horns of the crescent point downward to represent the setting moon of the old faith and the symbolic rising of the sun of the new religion of the brotherhood of humanity.

In 1945, President Roosevelt arranged for the reverse design of the Great Seal to be printed on the back of the dollar bill, an idea given to him by Henry Wallace, the secretary of agriculture, who was a practicing occultist. Wallace had suggested to the president that a new dollar coin should be minted showing the Great Seal design of the Egyptian pyramid and the eye of God. Roosevelt agreed with the idea in principle but suggested that it would be more practical to include the design on existing currency rather than create a new coin.

Wallace's idea originated with the Russian mystic and artist Nicholas Roerich, who acted as a guru to the secretary of agriculture. Roerich had worked with Stravinsky on his ballet *The Rite of Spring* and had designed scenery for Diaghilev's famous Russian ballets. He had spent many years traveling through Nepal and Tibet, studying with the lamas in the Buddhist monasteries of those countries and searching for the lost city of Shambhala, the legendary home of a fraternity of occult adepts or masters who had secretly influenced world affairs throughout history. These adepts were known variously in occult circles as the Secret Chiefs, the Hidden Masters, and the Great White Brotherhood and they were believed to be the éminences grises behind the formation of all of the important esoteric groups, including the Freemasons, the Sufis, the Knights Templars, the Rosicrucians, the Hermetic Order of the Golden Dawn, and the Theosophical Society.

Nicholas Roerich was a supporter of world peace and was associated with the new League of Nations founded after World War I to prepare for the establishment of a world government. In 1935, the same year the Illuminist symbol appeared on the dollar bill, Roerich was active in drawing up a pact signed by twenty-two countries that pledged themselves not to destroy cultural treasures. The symbol used to illustrate this pact was composed of three spheres symbolizing the trinity of love, power, and wisdom, enclosed within a larger circle representing the world.

The secretary of agriculture was well versed in occult knowledge. In a letter to his Russian guru, Wallace stated, "The search—whether it be for the lost word of Masonry or the Holy Chalice or the potentialities of the age to come—is the one supremely worthwhile objective. All else is karmic duty. But surely everyone is a potential Galahad? So may we strive for the Chalice and the flame above it." The chalice he refers to is the Holy Grail, regarded by the Rosicrucians as a feminine symbol for perfection, and "the age to come" is the dawning of the Aquarian Age. His relationship with the Russian mystic was to have serious political consequences for Wallace. Critics of the secretary of agriculture managed to obtain copies of the correspondence he had with his guru and they used it to expose his occult beliefs and to discredit his own bid for the presidency. Without any evidence apart from the fact that he was Russian, they also alleged that Roerich was a Communist sympathizer. In fact, Roerich was an internationalist and, while he may have supported the original democratic aims of the 1917 Revolution in Russia, he was an ardent critic of the excesses of Communism as practiced under Stalin in the 1930s. As a student of the esoteric tradition and an alleged agent of the so-called Great White Brotherhood, Roerich would have found the ultramaterialism of Communism less than attractive as a political ideology.

Wallace's reasons for wanting to introduce the reverse side of the Great Seal to American currency were based on his belief that

A portion of the U.S. dollar bill

America was reaching a turning point in her history and that great spiritual changes were imminent. He believed that the 1930s represented a time when a great spiritual awakening was going to take place and would precede the creation of a one-world state. According to Wallace's own account written in the 1950s, when he presented the idea of incorporating Great Seal symbolism into American currency, President Roosevelt was excited by the idea. In fact, the president was eager to have the Masonic symbol of the all-seeing eye on American currency because he said it was the sigil of the Grand Architect of the Universe. Before passing on the idea to the treasury, Roosevelt asked his cabinet colleague James Farley if the Catholics would object to the introduction of a Masonic symbol on the dollar bill. When he was told there would be no objections, Roosevelt instructed the treasury to start printing the new dollars.

Although Wallace failed in his attempt to become president, he continued his occult researches and studies. In later years, the ex-secretary of agriculture also became involved in psychic research. He supported the pioneering work of Dr. Andrija Puharich, a scientist who was responsible for fostering the psychic talents of a young Israeli man named Uri Geller and promoting him to the outside world through the media.

The strange incident of the dollar bill may represent one of the last attempts by the Masonic-Rosicrucian-Illuminati tradition to influence American politics openly. This tradition was rumored, however, to have worked secretly behind several political organizations in the United States since the days of Franklin Delano Roosevelt. The American Dream came to a tragic end on a November day in Dallas in 1963. This event was followed by a period of national suffering characterized by the Vietnam conflict, the civil rights struggle, Watergate, and the Iran-Contra scandal. It is very difficult to see the United States taking its predicted role today as the civilizing leader of the new age, although in the 1970s the new era of detente with the Soviet Union offered some hope for the future. In difficult time, history produces men and women of destiny and there was still time for the real American dream to be realized.

5

GERMAN NATIONALISM AND THE BOLSHEVIK REVOLUTION

In the years following the French and American Revolutions, events happening in Europe had a profound effect on the lives of millions of people generations later. New political alliances were formed, creating the conditions that allowed the rise of the three major European superpowers of the nineteenth century. These powers were personified by the dynamic families that were their hereditary rulers—the Romanovs of Russia, the Habsburgs of the Austro-Hungarian Empire, and the Hohenzollerns of Prussia who became the kaisers of Germany.

The bloody conflict that eventually ensued between these great European dynasties in the early twentieth century was to include the British and French empires and involve America in a European commitment lasting into modern times. Specifically, Russia and Germany were destined to dominate nineteenth-century politics in Europe, and the two countries gave birth to conflicting political ideologies that were instrumental in bringing about the holocausts of the two world wars in the last century. It would be too easy to dismiss these wars as isolated events, but the fact is that their causes date back to events in the nineteenth century and to political doctrines that had been germinating for several decades before the outbreak of World War I, 1914–1918.

On the surface, the motivation of the Romanovs, the Habsburgs, and the Hohenzollerns was purely territorial and political. Each family had imperial aspirations, especially the Habsburgs, who had been Holy Roman emperors by papal decree since medieval times. The tensions these aspirations created led to World War I, but at the beginning, the leaders of each nation were more interested in self-preservation than in conquering neighboring countries. The extra element in the unfolding historical tragedy was the influence of mysticism, the occult, and secret societies on the lives of the leading characters in this drama. Orthodox historians have chosen to ignore this aspect because they believe it has no real significance in politics. In fact, it is only through revealing this hidden conspiracy that the events of that time can be fully understood and placed in their true historical perspective.

In Russia the Romanov family came to power in the seventeenth century and ruled the country for three hundred years until they were deposed in the Bolshevik Revolution of 1917. The Romanovs emerged as the ruling dynasty during a period of anarchy and chaos, and the crowning of Mikhail Romanov, who allegedly ascended the throne with the help of the Rosicrucian Dr. Arthur Dee and the British secret service, established a dynasty under whose influence Russia would grow into a mighty empire with influence extending from eastern Europe to Asia.

Before their rise to power, the Romanovs were credited by their enemies with practicing witchcraft and possessing occult powers. In 1598, when Feodor Romanov plotted to seize the throne, he unfortunately placed his trust in Boris Gudonov, who also wanted to wear the Russian crown. Gudonov bribed the servants in the Romanov household and planted false evidence to prove that the family dabbled in the occult. The Romanovs were found guilty of practicing sorcery and spent many years in exile before Feodor's son, Mikhail, finally achieved the goal of the family and was crowned czar.

It was during the reign of Alexander I (1801–1825) that the secret societies exerted their greatest influence on the Russian court and the country's political objectives. The first Masonic lodge was officially founded in Poland in 1750, and within a few years Masonry had spread rapidly from there to mother Russia. By the end of the eighteenth century, Freemasonry, Rosicrucianism, and Martinism were flourishing in the spiritual hothouse climate of Russian society in which bizarre mystical cults and wandering holy men were accepted as a natural product of the orthodox religious experience.

In both Poland and Russia secret societies dabbled in radicalism, and their membership included activists engaged in socialist, revolutionary, and nationalist politics. One of the most active advocates of mixing radical politics with the occult was Count Thadeus Grabianka, who was under the mistaken impression that he had been divinely chosen as the king of Poland. He set up a court-in-exile at Avignon in France, one of the medieval haunts of the Cathars, and built a replica of Solomon's temple as a site for quasi-magical rites. In 1803, the count was forced to flee from France to avoid criminal charges for fraud. He found asylum in Russia and started a secret society in St. Petersburg that combined Rosicrucianism, Martinism, and radical politics.

The empress Catherine the Great, the wife of Czar Peter III, had ruled in Russia since 1762. She was an autocrat who was suspicious of anything resembling political reform that might weaken her power and was horrified by the outbreak of the French Revolution in 1789. When she was told of the execution of the French king, she became physically ill and was ordered to bed by her physicians. When she recovered, Catherine reacted by recalling all her subjects from Paris. She broke off diplomatic relations with France, ordered all French citizens to leave Russia or take an oath of loyalty to her, closed all Russian ports to French shipping, granted asylum to aristocrats fleeing the Terror, and provided funds to the royalist counterrevolutionaries. Her disquiet at the events in France was not helped by the revelation in 1794 of an alleged Illuminist plot to overthrow the Habsburg's Austro-Hungarian empire.

The young Alexander, who had been born in 1777, does not seem to have shared his grandmother's fears. In fact, he later expressed sympathy for the aims of those who started the French Revolution. Alexander stated his belief that all men and women should be equal under the law and have the right to freedom and liberty. He also expressed sadness at the destruction of the Polish nationalist movement, which had been ruthlessly crushed by his grandmother's armies.

Alexander had been named after St. Alexander Nevsky, a Russian national hero who had defeated the Swedish army and the Teutonic Knights. The new czar's religious education was in the hands of a Russian orthodox priest named André Samborsky, who was derided as a heretic by his clerical opponents. Samborsky had served as the official chaplain to the Russian legation in London and had married an English woman. His enemies claimed that Samborsky had become tainted with degenerate Western values while he was living in England. When he returned to Russia, he abandoned his clerical garb and wore an ordinary frock coat, shaved off his beard, and spoke with an English accent. The empress had deliberately selected this heretic priest to teach her grandson because she thought his open-minded attitude toward religion would help Alexander come to terms with spiritual matters in a more progressive way than his predecessors.

Grand Duke Alexander's father, Paul, was also a religious rebel who, as a young man, had known Freemasons and Martinists. He had opposed his mother's suppression of the Martinist Order, which had acquired several important converts in the Russian aristocracy, and supported a belief in a democratic society based on equality and liberty. Catherine had outlawed the Martinists in the wake of the French Revolution because she resented and feared their radicalism. Even before he ascended to the Russian throne, Paul expressed enlightened views. He had built new churches and schools, supported the rise of Lutheranism, financed new industrial enterprises, and promoted advanced agricultural techniques. He had even erected a hospital where peasants working on his country estate could get free medical treatment, and his image was therefore that of a social reformer who wanted to improve the living conditions of the Russian people.

In November 1796, Empress Catherine died of a heart attack and Paul became czar. His liberal supporters thought he would immediately begin a program of social reform and democracy. In fact, Paul's character had been slowly changing for several years, indicating that he was suffering from a progressive mental illness. His mother had been so concerned by his mental state that she had contemplated naming Alexander as her heir to prevent Paul from taking the throne after her death.

Paul had formed his own private army to rule his country estates and he had modeled it on the Prussian army corps. He had also surrounded himself with a group of brutish ex-Russian army officers who obeyed his every command without question. This obsession with military matters and a series of extramarital affairs led to tensions in his marriage, which were later to affect his rule. Soon after he became czar, Paul started to exhibit paranoid tendencies and imagined that secret cabals of conspirators were plotting to overthrow him. He withdrew his former patronage of the Martinists and the Freemasons and ostracized the aristocrats in his court who supported the secret societies and their political ideals.

The relationship between Paul and his son Alexander was virtually destroyed by a clash between Paul's rigid attitudes that bordered on dictatorship and the grand duke's desire to see social reform. As early as the autumn of 1797, Alexander wrote to liberal friends criticizing his father's regime and promoting his own destiny as an imperial reformer who would bring enlightenment to the Russian people. There was a mutual distrust between the two men bordering on hatred because Paul was aware that his mother had favored the grand duke and he suspected his son of a plot to replace him. Alexander had already drafted secret plans for reform, but he decided not to present these to his father because Paul's worsening mental condition caused him to act in an unpredictable manner.

By 1801, large sections of the Russian army were in open revolt against the czar's dictatorial style. Paul had hinted that he was planning to adopt a young German prince and name him as his new heir and threatened Alexander with death if he opposed the adoption. At this stage, a group of court officials conspired with the grand duke to force his father to abdicate in his favor. They believed if this did not happen soon, the people would rise up and the monarchy might be destroyed in a popular revolution.

On the night of March 11, 1801, the conspirators, assisted by rebel army officers who had pledged their troops to the coup, faced Czar Paul and demanded that he sign the document of abdication. When he refused, Paul was knocked to the floor and strangled. Grand Duke Alexander was informed of his father's violent death and was so horrified that he refused to accept the crown, which he said was stained with blood. He was quickly persuaded by the army officers, however, who told him that unless he accepted rule, the country would be plunged into a bloody revolution. Alexander reluctantly accepted and an announcement was made that the old czar had died of apoplexy during the night.

Early in his reign, Alexander lifted the prohibition on the Martinists and actively supported the role of secret societies in political life. The new regime was characterized by the formation of a group of advisors to the new czar who called themselves the Secret Committee. This group modeled itself on the Committee of Public Safety, which operated during the French Revolution, and consisted of radicals who admired the Cromwellian principle in English politics and the revolutionary government of France. Their ultimate aim was the creation of a democratic society in Russia, but they believed social reformation could happen only if the monarch was still in absolute control of the political process. For that reason, they rejected the republicanism of their French counterparts.

The new social reforms Czar Alexander planned were postponed by the war with Napoleon in 1805. Alexander seems to have regarded this war as a divine mission, and it is during the period of the military campaign that he first seems to have had difficulties discerning fact from fantasy. The idea of the divine mission was the result of predictions given to him by Madame von Kruderer, a famous psychic who was a student of the Swedish mystic Emmanuel Swedenborg. She acted as Alexander's spiritual guide and persuaded him that it was his holy duty to defeat the French emperor and restore the House of Bourbon to the throne in France. In 1815, while in Russian-occupied Paris, Alexander installed Madame von Kruderer in a hotel near the Elysée Palace and consulted her every day. She went into a trance and on one occasion informed the startled czar that he was the reincarnation of Jesus. Even Alexander could not accept this statement, and after this, the psychic's influence on his life began to wane.

Alexander's campaign against Napoleon had kindled in him new spiritual insights. Increasingly, he began to believe that his life destiny was to be the creator of an international brotherhood based on love and peace. He came under the spell of one of his courtiers, Koshelav, who had contacts with the Martinists, the Rosicrucians, the Pietists, the disciples of Swedenborg, and the Quakers and had been involved in the foundation of the Russian Bible Society that, despite its dull name, was a group of religious zealots who practiced a heretical form of mystical Christianity.

Koshelav offered the czar initiation into Freemasonry, but Alexander refused. He regarded himself as God's chosen instrument of divine power and as such he could not be initiated into a secret society. The czar did, however, accept tutelage from Koshelav in the secret teachings preserved in the Masonic lodges, which the occultist freely offered him. Koshelav was also associated with the Skoptsi, which practiced castration as a religious rite. The cult had first appeared in Russia in the 1750s among the Society of Flagellants, who were later known as the People of God. One critic described this extreme religious sect as practitioners of a mixture of folk Christianity and pagan rites.

The leader of the castration cult in the reign of Alexander was Kandvah Selivanov, who had attracted many disciples among Russian high society and the czar's court, although few made the final sacrifice required to enter the inner circle of the sect. Selivanov had delusions that he was the new messiah and called his home the House of God or the New Jerusalem. One of his female devotees, Catherine Tatarinova, also founded an occult society based on the practices of the whirling dervishes, who belonged to the Sufi brotherhood. She was a close friend of the leader of the castrator cult and through him was introduced to the czar. Alexander paid her an annual salary of six thousand rubles and consulted her about the esoteric meaning of the Bible.

Koshelav was the occult teacher who inspired the political dream that dominated the rest of Alexander's life: the creation of a united Europe where politics and religion would work hand in hand for the good of humanity. By 1815, however, Alexander had begun to question the legitimacy of secret societies and had become a convert to a mystical form of fundamentalist Christianity that rejected the paganism inherent in the Masonic and Rosicrucian teachings as primitive heathen superstition.

Alexander still pursued his grand idea of a politically united Europe, and to this end he proposed a Holy Alliance among Russia, Prussia, and the Austro-Hungarian empire. These allied powers would rule the new European federation in accordance with Christian values and morality. By this time, Alexander had identified the political forces working in Europe for radical change as the agents of the satanic powers of darkness, which had to be destroyed. Thus Grand Duke Alexander, the liberal reformer, had been transformed into Czar Alexander, the reactionary enemy of social progress. The shock of his father's violent death, which had brought him to power, and his mental conflict between autocratic power and championing reform, had finally caused him to completely lose touch with reality.

A pact to form the Holy Alliance was signed in September 1815 by Czar Alexander; Emperor Francis von Habsburg; and the kings of Prussia, Spain, France, and Sweden. The independent kingdoms of Naples and Sardinia were invited to join, but the Vatican and Britain refused to have anything to do with the new alliance. English aristocrats such as Lord Castlereagh and the duke of Wellington dismissed it as "mystical nonsense" and expressed amusement at a political treaty that united three kings dedicated to the Russian Orthodox, Catholic, and Protestant religions.

In 1820, Czar Alexander and the Habsburg emperor acted

together as members of the Holy Alliance to prevent a revolution in Italy. They believed that the new revolutionary fever in the country had been encouraged by a secret society known as the Carbonari, or Charcoal Burners. This sect had originated in Scotland at the time of Robert the Bruce and had spread to France, Germany, Poland, and Italy. Like Masonry, the Carbonari was a medieval guild organized by charcoal burners who traveled the country selling their wares. Although nominally Christian, the Charcoal Burners practiced rituals with pagan features and, in defiance of the pope, preached religious freedom and the ending of oppression and tyranny. Allegedly, the Carbonari also had connections with both the Freemasons and the Illuminati.

With over sixty thousand members in Italy, it was easy for the Carbonari to seize power in Naples and Piedmont. King Ferdinand was forced to take an oath of allegiance to the society and wear their symbol of the red, white, and blue tricolor. The Russian czar reacted to these developments in Italy with his usual melodramatic style by stating, "Our purpose [in invading Italy] is to counteract the empire of evil, which is spreading, by all the occult means at their disposal, the satanic spirit which directs it." Despite these fighting words, Alexander was facing mutiny among his own army officers who did not support his divine mission to rid Europe of secret societies. Although the Russian army stood in readiness, it was the Austrians who actually crossed into Italy, brutally put down the revolts in Naples and Piedmont, and drove the Carbonari underground.

Increasingly, Alexander became more and more under the malefic influence of extreme elements in the Russian Orthodox Church, who recognized in his sudden conversion to Christianity their chance to undermine the pervasive power of secret societies in Russian society. In 1822, Alexander issued an imperial edict outlawing Freemasonry and closing its lodges. It had been alleged by the Orthodox Church that the Masons were the archconspirators in an international plot with their English and Polish brethren to overthrow the czarist regime. Alexander's attack on the Freemasons was a disastrous move because, instead of reducing opposition to his autocratic rule, it increased the resistance and, as a result, many converts to the liberal political movement were recruited from the armed forces.

The czar himself seems to have suffered from some guilt, for in November 1824, when St. Petersburg was flooded and five hundred people died, he interpreted this disaster as a sign from God that he had failed in the divine mission to unite Europe. At the same time there was continuing unrest in the army and reports reached Alexander of plans to stage a military coup d'état. His health was suffering, and in the late autumn of 1825, having exiled himself from St. Petersburg on doctor's orders to recuperate in the Crimea, he died.

Russia was thrown into confusion by the czar's death. Many people did not even believe it. Stories circulated that Alexander had faked his own death and had become a wandering holy man or entered a monastery. Alexander had no sons or heirs, so his younger brother, Grand Duke Constantine, was destined to become the new ruler of Russia. Yet Constantine had married a Polish countess and therefore relinquished his right to the throne in favor of another brother, Grand Duke Nicholas. Unfortunately, Nicholas was unaware of the pact between Constantine and Alexander. When he heard of the czar's death Nicholas swore allegiance to his brother in Poland. Constantine, in the meantime, had pledged his loyalty to Nicholas from his home in Warsaw and had no intention of returning home to claim the Romanov crown. For a period of two weeks, Russia effectively had two czars until, on December 14, 1825, Nicholas finally accepted his brother's rejection of the throne and agreed to be Alexander's heir.

In the political chaos following Alexander's death, the liberal radicals decided to take advantage of the confused situation and revive the original aims of the late czar's regime. The Decembrist Movement, as it was later termed, was a group of intellectuals, writers, and army officers who had continued the Masonic tradition in secret since it had been driven underground in 1822. It included among its members the famous writer Count Pushkin, a confidant of the wife of Czar Paul. The leadership of the Decembrist group consisted of army officers who had fought with Alexander in the campaign against the French. These officers had made contact with the surviving Illuminist elements in French Freemasonry and had attempted to revive radicalism within the Russian aristocratic system. As the czar became more and more reactionary, they decided that the only way political change would occur in Russia was by a revolution. The confusion after the death of Alexander provided the Decembrists with the opportunity to stage a coup, seize control of the government, and set up a new liberal regime.

On the morning of December 14, 1825, the date set for the coronation, Nicholas had become aware of an army plot but strangely had decided to take no action. Stories swept the army barracks that Nicholas had usurped the throne and Constantine was the real czar. Contingents of the Moscow Guard and the Grenadiers assembled in the center of St. Petersburg, calling for Constantine to be crowned. Grand Duke Nicholas arrived in the square with the Horse Guards, who had remained loyal to him, and they charged the rebels. The ground was icy and several horses fell, blocking the progress of the charge, which was repulsed by heavy fire from the rebel forces. Nicholas then ordered the artillery to open fire on the rebel troops and a large crowd that had gathered to support them. The outcome was a massacre, which led Nicholas to comment sadly, "I am emperor, but at what price—the blood of my subjects." The coup had failed and the leaders of the Decembrists were arrested. Five were executed for their part in the failed rebellion.

Nicholas I ruled Russia for thirty years and was succeeded, in 1855, by his son Alexander II. During his reign, Czar Nicholas expressed a strong dislike for mystical matters, which was probably a result of the circumstances surrounding his rise to power and the crushing of the Decembrist plot. In contrast, Alexander II was a romantic who was not only very religious but also soon became involved in the new religion of spiritualism that was becoming popular in the salons of European high society. In 1841, Alexander married Princess Wilhelma Maria of Hesse, who shared his interest in occultism. In 1861, séances were held in the Winter Palace in St. Petersburg, attended by the czar and czarina, members of the royal court, and aristocrats. The royal family sat around a table while the Scottish medium D. D. Home, who was visiting Russia accompanied by the novelist Alexander Dumas, conducted séances to contact the spirits of the dead. Home later commented on the fact that the czar had a private library filled with thousands of books on the occult and spiritual matters.

Alexander was a reformer as well as an occultist and he knew that Russia had to be modernized. In 1856, he gave a speech vowing to abolish serfdom, but he found this task more difficult than he had imagined. One of the reforms the czar did achieve was to have great political consequences for the future: the transition from an army based on aristocratic privilege to a citizens' army. In common with his namesake, Alexander II tried to form a political and military alliance with the other great central European powers. In 1872, the czar, Emperor Franz Josef von Habsburg, and Kaiser Wilhelm I forged an alliance ratified in 1873 as the League of the Three Emperors. Political changes were taking place, however, that were soon to seal the doom of these three imperial powers, leading to World War I and marking the end of German imperialism, the Romanovs, and the Habsburgs.

In January 1871, through the political conspiring of Otto von Bismarck, King Wilhelm of Prussia was crowned kaiser, or emperor, of the Second German Reich. This event not only marked the birth of modern Germany but also inspired the rise of a pan-German nationalist movement that drew its spiritual strength from occultism and its ideology from the esoteric philosophies of secret societies. Within this new political movement lay not only the imperialist policies that formed the political background to the 1914–1918 war but also the extreme nationalist and racialist doctrines that in the 1920s spawned National Socialism, or Nazism.

As early as the 1850s, political movements had arisen whose aim was the union of all the German-speaking peoples of Europe. These movements were identified by their extreme nationalism and anti-Semitic, anticapitalist, and antiliberal views. By the 1870s, this political movement had established a mystical framework for its racial views heavily influenced by the esoteric teachings of the new Theosophical Society, founded in 1875 by a Russian medium, Madame Helene Blavatsky. Her aim was to synthesize Eastern forms of religion and occultism, such as Hinduism and Tantric yoga, with the western European occult tradition exemplified by Hermeticism, Freemasonry, Rosicrucianism, and the kabbalah. Madame Blavatsky claimed she was initiated into the occult mysteries while studying in India and Tibet. During her visits to these remote locations, she had contacted incarnated members of the Great White Brotherhood, including the comte de Saint-Germain and Master K. H., or Koot Hoomi, who was believed by some occultists to be the reincarnation of Thothmes III.

Madame Blavatsky had been influenced by the romantic novels written by the English statesman and occultist Lord Edward Bulwer Lytton (1803–1873). These occult novels had themes involving secret societies, mysterious initiations, and the existence of a clandestine tradition behind orthodox religion. Bulwer Lytton was a prolific writer whose novels were read not only in England but also in America and most European countries. It was widely rumored that he was a practicing member of the Rosicrucian Order and is often claimed as one of their grand masters. He had been elected as a Liberal member of Parliament in 1831 and played an important role in the passing of the Reform Bill. Lord Lytton's real interest, however, was in occultism, and it dominated his private life. He had an extensive library of books on the subject, including many rare treatises on medieval magic. He also allegedly operated a small group that practiced magical rituals such as the conjuration of elemental spirits and demons.

Bulwer Lytton's grandson claimed that his grandfather was a Rosicrucian and grand patron of the order. Evidence exists that does prove that he was proposed as honorary grand patron of the Societas Rosicruciana Anglia (SRIA), a neo-Rosicrucian order founded by Robert Wentworth Little in 1867. Wentworth, a clerk at Freemason's Hall in London, said he had access to secret documents in the archives showing a link between the medieval masonic guilds and the Rosicrucians. These documents had been discovered by William White, who was the grand secretary of English Freemasonry until 1857. He had been initiated into the Rosicrucian Order by the Venetian ambassador in London. In collaboration with the occultist Kenneth McKenzie, who belonged to the German Rosicrucian Order and had been granted a charter to found an English lodge, Wentworth Little founded the SRIA. In 1888, this new Rosicrucian society gave birth to the famous magical fraternity known as the Hermetic Order of the Golden Dawn, which was founded by two SRIA members, Dr. William Wynn Westcott and Samuel MacGregor Mathers, who said they had received their authorization from a German occult adept named Anna Sprengel, who lived in Bavaria, the home of the Illuminati.

MacGregor Mathers was a supporter of the Jacobite cause and was rumored to be a member of a political secret society known as the Jacobite Legitimists. This group claimed that the true heir to the Scottish throne was Princess Maria Theresa, the wife of Prince Ludwig of Bavaria. They demanded home rule for Scotland and supported Irish nationalism. In February 1893, the House of Commons was in an uproar when the banning of the society's official newspaper *The Jacobite* was debated. A Belfast MP said that unless the journal was banned, loyalists in Ulster would rise up in armed revolt against the British government. The Jacobite cause also had its supporters in the Theosophical Society, including Bishop C. W. Leadbeater, who was eventually disgraced in a homosexual scandal involving young boys.

Bulwer Lytton may have been a leading member of the SRIA, but there is no evidence that he attended any of its meetings. His honorary membership was granted because of the knowledge of Rosicrucian beliefs expressed in his best-selling novel *Zanoni*. In 1870, Bulwer Lytton was approached by the occultist Hargraves Jennings, the author of a lengthy treatise on the alleged sexual meaning of Rosicrucian and pagan symbols. Jennings sought the help of the politician to secure employment as a librarian because he was finding it hard to make a living writing on obscure occult subjects. Lord Lytton replied that he could not help him find suitable employment, but he did congratulate him on tracing the order's connection to ancient religions.

One of Bulwer Lytton's closest friends was the British prime minister Benjamin Disraeli, who shared his interest in the occult. In common with his aristocratic friend, Disraeli wrote several novels involving secret societies and political conspiracies. In 1856, Disraeli spoke out in the House of Commons against the threat posed by secret societies in Europe. He warned of the danger of supporting the revolutionary movements in Italy because of the influence secret societies had in them. He said, "The government of this country has not only to deal with governments, kings, and ministers but also with secret societies, elements which must be taken into account which at the last moment can bring all our plans to naught, which have agents everywhere, who incite assassinations and can if necessary lead a massacre."

Madame Blavatsky had also read Bulwer Lytton's novels and was very impressed by their occult content, especially *Zanoni* and *The Last Days of Pompeii*. The latter was published in 1834 and dealt with the time between the mysteries of Isis and early Christianity in first-century Italy. Blavatsky's esotericism was virulently anti-Christian, but this tendency was modified by her successor to leadership of the Theosophical Society, Annie Besant. She was a socialist, trade union organizer, and strike leader until she joined the Theosophical Society in 1889. Previously, she had been a member of the National Secular Society, the Fabian Society, the Social Democratic Federation, and the Free Thought and Radical Movement.

From 1874 to 1889, when she became a Theosophist, Annie Besant had campaigned on a wide range of reforms, including women's suffrage and sexual equality, antivivisection, penal reform, the organization of trade unions, the rights of ethnic peoples, and the right to freedom of speech. Her political work was modified after she joined the Theosophist Society, but in 1893 she attended the World Parliament of Religions in Chicago and was invited to visit India. As a result, she became involved in Indian nationalism and in 1916 founded the Home Rule League. Besant was interned for three months in 1917 by the British authorities because of her support for Indian independence.

In 1902 she was responsible for introducing Co-Freemasonry,

whose lodges admitted men and women on equal terms, from France to England. The Grand Lodge of England refused to accept Co-Masonry, which claims as its grand master the comte de Saint-Germain on the spiritual plane and which affiliated itself with the Grand Orient of France. There is no suggestion that Co-Masonry shares the French Freemasons' interest in radical politics. The lodges of Co-Masonry teach the inner wisdom of the Craft that has been lost to the orthodox Masonic Order in England. Many Co-Masons are also members of the Liberal Catholic Church and it promotes a form of esoteric Christianity through the Theosophical Society. In 1912, Annie Besant also founded a neo-Rosicrucian offshoot of Co-Masonry called the Order of the Temple of the Rose Cross, which was active until the end of World War I.

Bulwer Lytton's novels not only had an impact on the Theosophists but they also affected the mystical aspects of German nationalism. His occult novel *The Coming Race,* published in 1871, presented the fictional idea of a subterranean, matriarchal, socialist Utopia ruled by superior beings who had mastered the so-called *viril,* or life force. This was a mysterious energy manipulated by the adepts who ruled this underground world to perform healing and telepathy. It also had a destructive use as a death ray that was similar to the modern laser. One of the German mystico-political groups called itself the Viril Society and took its philosophy from Bulwer Lytton's novel. The Viril Society was originally founded as the Luminous Lodge, combining the political ideals of the Illuminati with Hindu mysticism, Theosophy, and the kabbalah. It was one of the first German nationalist groups to use the symbol of the swastika as an emblem linking Eastern and Western occultism.

The racial ideas of Madame Blavatsky concerning root races and the emergence of a spiritually developed type of human being in the Aquarian Age were avidly accepted by the nineteenth-century German nationalists, who mixed Theosophical occultism with anti-Semitism and the doctrine of the racial supremacy of the Aryan or Indo-European peoples. One of the leading occult societies of this type was the

Armanenschafft, founded by an Austrian esotericist Guido von List, who had spent a lifetime researching Teutonic mythology. List was a practitioner of the old pagan religion and was dedicated to reestablishing the ancient cult of Aryan sun worship and reviving the Norse priesthood of Wotan, or Odin, the one-eyed shaman god of the runes.

List based his society on the Masonic degree system of Entered Apprentice, Fellow Craft, and Master Mason. Initiates into the order were not only expected to learn the mystical meanings of the runic system but also were taught the secret history of the priesthood of Wotan. List claimed that when the Church suppressed paganism, its priesthood went underground and its traditions survived in the beliefs of the Templars, the alchemists, the Freemasons, and the Order of the Rosy Cross. He believed that the Templars and the Rosicrucians had inherited the spiritual and aristocratic aspects of the pagan priesthood, while the Freemasons, who were political radicals, adopted the democratic aspects of the occult tradition.

Guido von List had tenuous connections with two occult fraternities sharing his extreme, right-wing views and adhering to his idea of a pan-German empire based on spiritual principles derived from the pagan religion. The first of these groups was the aforementioned Ordo Templi Orientis (OTO), or the Order of the Temple in the East, founded between 1895 and 1900 by two high-ranking German Freemasons, Karl Kellner and Theodor Reuss. The OTO had been born from the Masonic Rites of Memphis and Mizraim created by John Yarker, who was an associate of the SRIA. Yarker had authorized the foundation of a German lodge of this Masonic rite by contact with Kellner, Reuss, and Dr. Franz Hartmann. The latter was a prominent occultist who had started the German Theosophical Society in 1896 and had links to various neo-Rosicrucian orders.

The OTO's official history taught that its unique Tantric doctrine had been given to its founders by three Eastern adepts and that the order possessed "the key which opens up all Hermetic and Masonic secrets, namely the teachings of sexual magic and all the secrets of Freemasonry and all systems of religion." When Kellner died in 1905, Reuss became the head of the OTO and, within a short time, branches of the order were founded outside Germany, including France, England, and Scandinavia.

Reuss was a complex character; as a young man he had worked as a spy for the Prussian secret service. He had lived in London, spying on socialist Germans in exile, including the family of Karl Marx. Reuss joined the Socialist League, whose members included Engels and the Utopian socialist William Morris, but he was exposed as an undercover agent and was quickly forced to resign from the organization.

There are some interesting connections between the OTO and the Hermetic Order of the Golden Dawn, whose membership list included the poet W. B. Yeats and his close friend Maud Gonne,

Seal of the Ordo Templi Orientis

both active in Irish nationalism. Reuss had founded several Masonic-Rosicrucian lodges in Germany with the authorization of William Westcott, who was one of the founders of the Golden Dawn. Another member of the Golden Dawn, Aleister Crowley, became the head of the OTO in England. Reuss had written to Crowley in 1912, accusing him of revealing the inner secrets of the OTO in his *Book of Lies,* which contained coded descriptions of various magico-sexual rites veiled in Rosicrucian symbolism. These rituals included one involving mutual oral sex as a form of occult meditation. Crowley told Reuss the story that the rituals had originated in documents belonging to Adam Weishaupt, the founder of the Illuminati.

Reuss eagerly accepted this tale because he believed that the OTO had links to the Illuminati. In fact, either Crowley or one of his disciples had written the rituals some years before. Crowley broke away from the Golden Dawn in 1900 following a leadership fight with MacGregor Mathers and because some of the other members had objected to his preoccupation with the use of sexual energy in magical workings. Crowley was delighted when Reuss appointed him head of the English branch of the OTO, and he took the magical name Baphomet from the idol worshipped by the Knights Templar.

Crowley also may have shared some of Reuss's political views as well as his interest in magical sex rites. When he was at Cambridge University, the young Crowley had belonged to a Jacobite legitimate society and had dabbled in extreme right-wing politics and may have been responsible for the various theories that soon began to circulate concerning the OTO's origins. It was claimed that the order had been founded in St. Petersburg many years earlier than 1895 by a mysterious count, that it was a direct descendent of the Order of Illuminati, or that it had been founded by a medieval Sufi saint who had taught the Templars the secret of sex magic.

The second occult fraternity was the Ordo Novi Templi, or the Order of New Templars (ONT), founded by Lanz von Liebenfels in 1907. Von Liebenfels was a romantic and had convinced himself he descended from medieval German aristocracy, even though he was the lowly son of a railway worker. He used his order to further extreme, right-wing racist views based on the Templar tradition. Von Liebenfels was a fantasist who claimed that Lord Kitchener, who died in mysterious circumstances when his ship sank off Archangel during the Allied campaign to defeat the Bolsheviks after World War I, was a secret supporter of the Order of New Templars. The ONT had established contact with several other radical right-wing groups with occult associations. It supported pro-Serbian nationalism, which played a crucial part in the events that led to the outbreak of hostilities in 1914, and assisted the Magyar nationalists in Hungary. During the 1920s, when Hitler and the Nazis were rising to power in Germany, the ONT acted as the international coordinator for European and American rightist groups. In the 1930s it acted as a front for the illegal National Socialist Party in Austria. This did not prevent the prohibition of the ONT by the Nazis in 1941 following the abortive peace mission by Rudolf Hess, which led to the widespread persecution of the occultists in the Third Reich.

An offshoot of the ONT and the Armanenschafft was the German Order, founded just before World War I. This anti-Semitic, racist, nationalist occult group used the swastika as its emblem and practiced rituals based on Masonry. Its philosophy was centered on the purity and supremacy of the Aryan race, the revival of the pagan traditions of ancient Germany, and the creation of a pan-German state. The German Order was the prototype of the Thule Society, which later influenced the embryonic National Socialist movement. With the rise of the Nazis, the mystical tradition of racial purity, neo-paganism, and theosophical occultism was dramatically projected into the public arena and become the political creed of the most powerful nation in Europe.

Before the rise of National Socialism, the agents of the secret societies were engaged in various activities that resulted in the end of the old European empires formed under the Holy Alliance of Czar Alexander I at the beginning of the nineteenth century. In Austria, the Habsburgs ruled with an iron fist. Any faint hope that the wave of liberalism would affect the Austro-Hungarian empire was destroyed in January 1889 at a

A page from Ostara, *the official magazine of the Order of New Templars*

hunting lodge in Mayerling. Crown Prince Rudolf von Habsburg alleg-edly shot dead his mistress, Maria Vetsera, and then committed suicide. Rumors circulated after the tragic deaths that the crown prince had been murdered by political enemies opposed to his ultraliberal ideas.

Prince Rudolf may have been a notorious womanizer, but he was also a philosopher who had studied the works of Descartes and Voltaire, the Masonic philosopher of the French Revolution. The crown prince was also a student of history, botany, physics, and soci-ology and had traveled widely in the Far East. Rudolf wrote a mas-sive twenty-four volume history of the Habsburg dynasty that is still regarded as the classic reference book on the subject.

The prince was an early supporter of the revolutionary concept of a world government, saying, "There will be wars until the people and nations have completed their development, until they at last unite themselves and mankind has become one family." He was in favor of a united Europe, secretly supported the independence of the Magyars, and recommended that the Austro-Hungarian empire should sever its ancient links to the Vatican. He spoke out against the corruption and excessive wealth of the Church and called on the aristocrats to pay taxes and for the land to be divided up between the peasants. In other words, he was the perfect target for assassination by those reactionary forces in European politics that resisted social change.

Rudolf's fault, apart from his obsessive sexual urges, was his idealistic naivete and faith in human nature. He truly believed that he could single-handedly stem the tide of anti-Semitism and extreme nationalism rising in the empire. As an internationalist, he believed that "the principle of nationalism is based on common animal principles. It is essentially the victory of fleshly sympathies and instincts over spiritual and cultural ideas." In 1882, he predicted, "Dark and ugly times await us. One can almost believe that old Europe is outdated and beginning to disintegrate. A great and thorough reaction has to set in, a social upheaval from which, after a long time, a whole new Europe may blossom."

In 1898, Rudolf's mother, Empress Elizabeth, fell victim to an assassin while staying in Switzerland. The empress was walking back to her hotel in Geneva with a lady-in-waiting when she was attacked by an Italian named Lucheni and stabbed through the heart. When questioned by the police, the assassin confessed he was an anarchist and said his original target had been the prince of Orleans, the pretender to the French throne, or King Umberto of Italy. He told the police that "other comrades" would later accomplish these murders. At his trial, when he was sentenced to life imprisonment, Lucheni shouted, "Long live anarchy! Death to the aristocrats!"

Lucheni was a disciple of the Russian anarchist and Freemason Mikhail Bakunin (1814–1873), the originator of the nihilist movement. He believed that degenerate western society could be saved only through atheism and anarchism. Bakunin's extreme anticlericalism led him to be denounced as a Satanist, and he is quoted as saying, "Satan was the first free thinker and the savior of the world. He freed Adam and impressed the seal of humanity and liberty on his forehead by making him disobedient." Bakunin was secretary general of the First International, a rainbow coalition of nihilists, anarchists, and Communists, and a political associate of Karl Marx and other revolutionary socialist leaders.

From 1900 to 1913 Europe was plunged into chaos as the revolutionary and nationalist movements attempted to force change violently on the old imperial powers. In 1905, the Greeks revolted against Turkish rule in Crete; the Russian Czar Nicholas II was forced to use troops to put down riots in St. Petersburg and a mutiny by sailors on the *Potemkin*. In 1908, both King Carlos I of Portugal and the crown prince were murdered. These assassinations were followed in 1910 by a revolution during which King Manuel II had to flee for his life. In 1912, Italy, Bulgaria, Turkey, and Serbia were at war. By 1913, Russia had declared war on Bulgaria and King George I of Greece had been murdered.

Against this backdrop of revolution, war, and assassination, the old alliances that had held together nineteenth-century Europe were crumbling. By the outbreak of World War I in August 1914, Russia and Germany were bitter enemies. The czar wanted a new alliance with Britain and France to prevent Germany from declaring war on Russia. He was confident that world peace could be achieved only by the creation of a triple entente of France, England, and Russia to combat the growing threat of German expansionism. The British, however, did not support this plan. Though they believed the public would rally to the defense of France if the Germans attacked it, they knew that they would not show the same eagerness if the kaiser invaded Russian soil. The British government was still hoping for some kind of reconciliation with the German kaiser so that Russia's imperial ambitions in Persia (modern-day Iran), Afghanistan, and India could be resisted. Meanwhile, the Germans negotiated with the ailing Emperor Franz Joseph of Austria to form an alliance to attack Russia. The Germans were also attempting to woo Romania and Serbia. This involvement with Serbia was to cost Franz Joseph the life of his nephew, Grand Duke Franz Ferdinand, and result in world war.

On June 28, 1914, Franz Ferdinand and his wife, Sophia, were in

Sarajevo on an official visit. As their car traveled through streets lined by cheering crowds, a group of assassins struck. For months they had been planning the death of the archduke and the duchess. One threw a bomb that hit the hood of the car, bounced off, and exploded in the road, wounding twenty bystanders. The bomb thrower fled the scene and tried to commit suicide by drinking a bottle of cyanide, but he was seized by the police before he could carry out the act.

Panic spread through the streets in the wake of the bomb attack, but the official convoy of cars continued on its route to the town hall. After making an official speech, the archduke decided to visit the local governor's adjutant, who had been injured in the bomb blast and taken to the hospital. It was a decision that was to cost him his life. Incredibly, the assassination squad was still in the streets. The car containing the archduke and his wife took a wrong turn, and in the confusion that followed, one of the assassins calmly walked up to the car and fired two shots from a Browning automatic pistol, killing the royal couple instantly.

The three principal assassins in Sarajevo were Gavrilo Princip and two of his friends, and they were all members of a nationalist group called the Order of the Black Hand, a secret society that had been founded in 1911 as the Union of Death to fight for Serbian liberation. The seal of the order was a clenched fist holding a skull and crossbones beside which there were a knife, a bomb, and a poison bottle. Members of the Black Hand included army officers, civil servants, lawyers, and university professors. Initiation ceremonies into the order were performed in a darkened room and involved neophytes holding a revolver in one hand and a knife in the other. They then repeated an oath to defend the Serbian cause "by the sun that warms, by the earth that feeds me, by the blood of my forefathers, by God, by my honor, and by my life."

All of the Sarajevo assassins were selected because they suffered from tuberculosis and did not have long to live. In accordance with the order's rules, they had agreed that if they failed in their mission, they would commit suicide by taking poison. The assassins were students with Bolshevik aspirations who previously had been involved in distributing socialist and anarchist pamphlets calling for worldwide revolution and the overthrow of the European monarchy. As much as the Habsburgs they murdered, the assassins themselves—especially Princip, who finally committed the murder and was filled with remorse afterward—were victims of an international conspiracy.

Although the Order of the Black Hand was dedicated to Serbian nationalism, there were those within its ranks who had wider political ambitions and saw the deaths in Sarajevo as a means to an end. The Russians were soon implicated in the plot when it became known that a secret payment of eight thousand rubles had been given to the leader of the Black Hand by the Russian military attaché in Belgrade. The order had apparently been accompanied by Czar Nicholas's assurance that he would support Serbia if war broke out between his country and the Austro-Hungarian empire.

It was also rumored that representatives of the Black Hand had met with several members of the French Grand Orient at the Hotel St. Jerome in Toulouse in January 1914. One of the items discussed at this meeting was allegedly the murder of the emperor Franz Joseph and the archduke Ferdinand. This indicated that the assassination was a complex plot organized by the Order of the Black Hand with the support of the Russian government and renegade elements of French Freemasonry. Their aim was to force Austria to invade Serbia and create the conditions for a major European war.

Following the assassinations in Sarajevo, the kaiser invited the Austro-Hungarian ambassador to lunch and told him that military action had to be taken swiftly to neutralize Serbia and offered him German support. The kaiser was obviously not aware at this stage of the Russian involvement in the deed because he told the Austrian diplomat that German intelligence reports suggested that the czar would not respond if the Habsburgs occupied Serbia. On July 28, 1914, four weeks after the assassinations, the Austro-Hungarian empire declared war on Serbia, even though the earliest its army could march into the country was mid-August. Russia responded by mobilizing her army in

Symbol of the Kabbalistic Order of the Rosy Cross

defense of Serbia, and on July 29, the kaiser informed the czar that unless his troops stood down, the German army would also mobilize. On July 31, the Germans demanded that Russia halt its mobilization, and when this demand was ignored, they declared war on August 1.

The French were formally asked by the Germans to remain neutral in the war, but they refused. The kaiser then falsely accused the French of violating his territory and he declared war on France. Meanwhile, the kaiser was negotiating with the British to insure their neutrality, but on the second day of August, Britain warned the Germans not to attack French shipping in the English Channel. On the third day of August, the German high command informed the British foreign office that their troops planned to march through neutral Belgium to attack the French. In a stern reply, the Germans were informed that if even one of their soldiers set foot on Belgian soil, Britain and Germany would be at war. World War I had effectively begun.

Sarajevo and its international repercussions caused the downfall of the Habsburgs and Hohenzollerns, but also the Romanov dynasty was swept away by the Bolshevik Revolution of 1917. In pre-war Russia, the royal family had been heavily involved in occult practices. Between 1900 and 1905, the French occultist Dr. Gerard Encausse visited Russia and held magical séances for the czar and czarina. Encausse was a member of the Kabbalistic Order of the Rosy Cross, founded in 1888 by two prominent French occultists, the marquis Stanilas de Guaita and Josephin Paladin, who came from an eccentric Catholic family that was made up of religious fanatics and extreme supporters of the monarchic system. His brother Adrien was a homeopathic doctor and kabbalist who claimed to have been initiated into an ancient Rosicrucian order in Toulouse in 1858. Encausse had also been initiated into the Golden Dawn lodge, founded by Samuel MacGregor Mathers in Paris, which practiced the mysteries of Isis.

At the magical séances held by Encausse, it is claimed that the French occultist conjured the spirit of Czar Nicholas's father, Alexander III. In 1905, Russia was on the brink of revolution: There was rioting in the streets. Strikes, and rumors of mutiny occurred in the armed forces. Nicholas asked the spirit of his father for advice and was told to resist the revolutionary forces. If he did not deal severely with this outbreak of unrest, the causes of the uprisings would return in a few years and his rule would be seriously threatened. Encausse seems to have stayed in contact with the czar after he returned to France, and the occultist and the monarch exchanged letters at regular intervals. The French magician, however, confided to friends that he thought Nicholas was relying too much on spiritual sources of advice to run the country and was ignoring his ministers.

Encausse was particularly concerned when he heard that the czar and czarina had come under the hypnotic influence of a mystic monk called Grigori Rasputin. He was a member of the Khlysty, or People of God, a neo-gnostic sect that practiced flagellation and sexual indulgence as a method of making contact with the Divine. Rasputin was a product of the spiritual revival that had swept Russia in the early 1900s. Interest in the occult was widespread at all levels of society and weird religious sects proliferated and sexual permissiveness was encouraged. Wandering holy men, occultists, and spiritualists attracted thousands of followers, including members of the aristocracy and the royal court.

Czarina Alexandria seems to have been infatuated with Rasputin and was in awe of his healing powers after he had allegedly saved the life of her son. Despite his dirty, unkempt appearance, he exerted a strange power over women. He was capable of withholding orgasm for long periods, and one titled lady who made love to him said that the experience was so sensual that she fainted from pleasure. Rasputin apparently believed that sexual domination could be used as a method of achieving spiritual enlightenment and told his many lovers that it was God's will that they surrender their bodies to him.

Rasputin's influence on the royal family was regarded as sinister by many court insiders and those who opposed czarist rule. Encausse warned Nicholas that the monk was an evil influence, claiming that, "kabbalistically speaking, Rasputin is a vessel like Pandora's box. He contains all the vices, crimes, and filth of the Russian people. Should this vessel be broken, its dreadful contents will spill across Russia." Rasputin's enemies claimed he was an agent of secret societies working to weaken the czar's rule and destroy the monarchy from within. They alleged that at a secret Masonic conference held in Brussels in 1905, representatives of various European secret societies had plotted to use Rasputin as the instrument to bring down the Romanovs.

Despite this claim, when war broke out in 1914, Rasputin advised the czar not to involve Russia in the fighting. He predicted that the country would suffer a terrible defeat and the monarchy would be destroyed in the bloodbath to follow. It would seem there were several political factions in Russia who were attempting to prevent Rasputin from exercising influence over the czar. In 1913 conspirators plotted to castrate and murder the holy man, but the wily monk heard of the plan and took evasive action.

In June 1914, coincidentally on the same day as the Sarajevo assassinations, a prostitute named Gusyeva attempted to murder Rasputin while he was on holiday at the Black Sea resort of Yalta. She stabbed the monk in the stomach, but although he lost a considerable amount of blood, he survived. She told police she had attempted to kill Rasputin because he was a heretic and a fornicator who had seduced a nun. Gusyeva was diagnosed as insane and was committed to a mental hospital.

Following the assassinations in Sarajevo, the czarina sent a stream of telegrams to Rasputin asking his advice on the serious international situation. Rasputin replied by sending a telegram to the czar telling him to keep Russia from being enticed into war. If it was drawn in, he predicted, "it will be the finish of all things." Rasputin was obviously not aware of Russian complicity in Sarajevo, and Nicholas ignored the monk's advice. Rasputin later claimed that if he had been well enough to have visited St. Petersburg in person, Russia would not have entered the war and the course of world history would have been changed.

As the war progressed, Rasputin's enemies used his antiwar sentiments to claim that the monk was pro-German, was in league with revolutionaries, and was a secret agent in the kaiser's intelligence service. Meanwhile, hostility to the Romanovs was growing among the ordinary Russian people and was aided by the activities of socialist agitators who wanted to replace czarism with a workers republic. Rasputin seems to have had a premonition of his impending doom and the consequences it would have for Russia and the Romanovs. In 1916, he wrote to Nicholas, saying, "If I am killed by common assassins, and especially if they are my brothers, the Russian peasants, you have nothing to fear. But if I am murdered by the boyars [the nobles], if they shed my blood, their hands will remain soiled with my blood. Brothers will kill brothers. They will kill each other. There will be no nobles in the country."

In December 1916, right-wing factions within the aristocracy conspired to rid Russia of Rasputin. They believed that if he were allowed to live, the army would rise in revolt against the Romanovs. The conspirators, led by Prince Felix Yusapov, enticed the monk into a trap. He was fed chocolate cakes and wine laced with cyanide, which apparently had little effect on him. He was then shot in the chest at close range. The monk fell to the floor as if dead, but a few moments later he revived long enough to attack his would-be assassins. Rasputin tried to escape but was shot twice more as he fled. His body was then bundled into a car, taken to the Petrovsky Bridge, and thrown into the river. Popular legend relates that he was still alive when he was thrown into the icy waters and actually died from drowning.

The Russian people reacted to Rasputin's death with indignation. He had been loved by the masses, and after his death, the mystic monk was treated as a martyr. The czar's court was regarded as the source of the conspiracy that had killed a popular hero. In the months following Rasputin's death, it was widely expected that a right-wing coup would oust the Romanovs from power. The czarist secret police therefore concentrated their efforts on infiltrating extreme rightist groups and secret societies, which, while supporting the monarchy, regarded Nicholas as a weak ruler. In fact the revolution, which finally toppled the unpopular Romanovs, was a product of the extreme left and began with the establishment of a liberal and democratic government.

In March 1917, food riots broke out in St. Petersburg, which was renamed Petrograd by the protestors, and the troops sent to quell the disturbances joined the revolt. With the breakdown of law and order, a right-wing provisional government was formed to run the country. On March 15, faced with mounting criticism of his policies, Czar Nicholas abdicated in favor of his younger brother, Mikhail, but the new czar soon realized he did not have the confidence or support of either the armed forces or the people and thus he also abdicated, handing over executive power to a provisional government. This move was widely welcomed by world leaders who believed that democracy was soon to be established in Russia.

The provisional regime ruled for eight months until November

(October by the old calendar still used in Russia at this time). During that period, it promoted democracy and promised freedom of religion, speech, assembly, and the press. In an attempt to disorganize the war effort, however, the kaiser arranged for the revolutionary Lenin to return to Russia, and Lenin called upon the peasants to take control of the farms and factories. In July 1917, with the government still trying to fight an unpopular war and with the country divided internally, radicalized soldiers, sailors, and Bolsheviks attempted to seize control of Petrograd. The revolt failed due to the intervention of regular army units in the city that still remained loyal to the provisional government.

On November (October) 7, 1917, the Bolsheviks finally came to power when soldiers of the Petrograd garrison, aided by sailors, the workers, militia, and the Red Guard, stormed the Winter Palace and arrested the members of the provisional government. The revolution was not bloodless, for in 1918, fighting broke out between the Bolsheviks and the White Russians, who still supported the monarchy. The Allies intervened in the resulting civil war and detachments of American, French, British, and Italian troops landed in Siberia to prevent the seizure by the Germans of war materials stored at the ports of Archangel and Murmansk. Allied forces blockaded the Russian coast from October 1919 to January 1920 and supplied the White Russians with military hardware, including British-made tanks. They could not, however, prevent the defeat of the White army or the relentless progress of the Bolshevik revolution that created the USSR.

Rasputin's prophecy of the downfall of the Romanov dynasty had come true, although he had not lived to see it. Even if he had survived the right-wing plots to kill him, it seems unlikely the mystic monk would have been tolerated for long in the new Soviet Union. One of the first acts by the Bolsheviks was to suppress the Russian Orthodox Church and outlaw the various religious sects that had flourished during the reign of the czars.

1894 poster by Albinet advertising the Salon Rose-Croix. It shows Hugh de Payens, first master of the Templars, represented as Dante, and Joseph of Arimathea, first grand master of the Grail, represented as Leonardo da Vinci. (Photograph by Michael Holford)

Membership certificate of the
Bristol Lodge of the Rosicrucians,
issued by W. G. Westcott,
Supreme Magus, May 19, 1984
(Collection of Gerald Yorke;
photograph by Michael Holford)

Savior of the World,
a figure common on
gnostic gems. French
Revolutionary period
(Collection of Gerald
Yorke; photograph by
Michael Holford)

*Washington as
a Freemason*
(Library of
Congress,
Washington, D.C.)

*Sir Francis Dashwood
(1708–1781),
chancellor of the
exchequer and founder
of the Hell Fire Club*
(Hulton Picture
Library)

Gregori Efimovitch Rasputin
(Hulton Picture Library)

Aleister Crowley
(Hulton Picture
Library)

*Crowley dressed as a
black magician* (Hulton
Picture Library)

Franz Ferdinand of Austria with his family
(Hulton Picture Library)

Comte de Saint-Germain (Bibliothèque Nationale)

Man as microcosm, the Universe in miniature, from Utriusque Cosmi Historia *by Robert Fludd, seventeenth-century mystical philosopher* (Ann Ronan Picture Library/ E. P. Goldschmidt and Co. Ltd.)

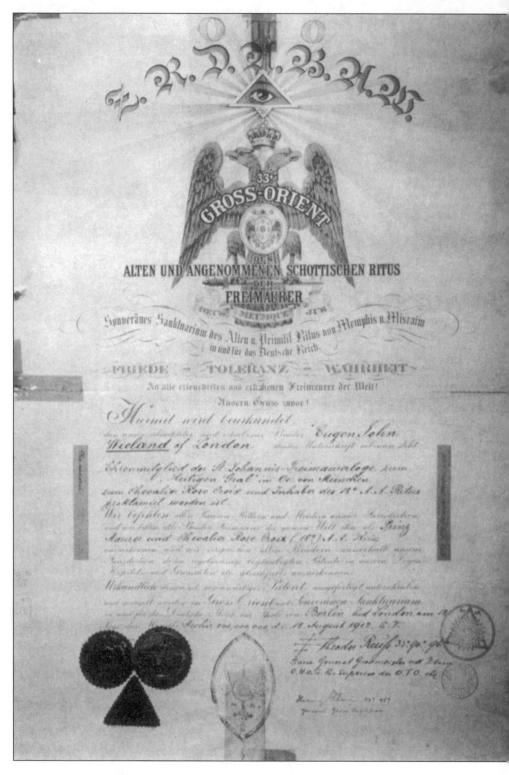

Certificate of membership of the Ordis Tempis Orientalis, issued by Theodor Reuss,
August 18, 1912 (Collection of Gerald Yorke; photograph by Michael Holford)

6

NAZISM AND
THE OCCULT TRADITION

During World War I, an Austrian artist named Adolf Hitler served in the First Company of the Bavarian Reserve Infantry Regiment and took part in the Battle of Ypres. He was one of six hundred survivors from the regiment's total enlistment of thirty-five hundred and was awarded the Iron Cross. This decoration was given to Hitler for capturing a French officer and fifteen men single-handedly and armed only with a Luger pistol. In 1916, Hitler was wounded in the leg, but he recovered and became a messenger, carrying documents between regimental headquarters and the front line.

His fellow soldiers regarded Hitler as a rather peculiar character because of his habit of spending the long periods between engagements in silent meditation. After one of these contemplative sessions, Hitler surprised his companions by leaping to his feet and shouting that Germany would soon lose the war. To the astonishment of his fellow soldiers, he claimed that the German people faced invisible enemies who were a greater danger to the war effort than the Allied troops.

Kaiser Wilhelm had already received a similar message even before the outbreak of the war. The kaiser was fascinated with spiritualism and was present at a séance when a medium predicted that the German royal house would fall in a war to end all wars. When the kaiser was forced into exile in Holland in 1918, he spent his time studying in his occult library. He blamed World War I on a conspiracy among Czar Nicholas II, King George V of England, and secret societies.

It is impossible to know the source of Hitler's prophecies about German defeat, but he was convinced that the war would end with an Allied victory. In the last month of the war, Hitler was caught in a British mustard gas attack. Temporarily blinded, he was sent from the front line to recover his health in a small town near Berlin. When he had fully recovered, Hitler was posted to a prisoner-of-war camp on the Austrian border, where he carried out guard duties. In 1919, the camp was closed and Hitler returned to Munich, where he became attached to the German military intelligence department. His task was to act as an undercover agent and to spy on the Communist revolutionaries who had engineered a coup in Munich, which had briefly given them power. Hitler helped unmask their leaders, who were shot by firing squad. Initially as an undercover agent, he also attended meetings of the German Workers Party, which opposed the Communists, but he was converted to the party's policies and rose to become its leader.

The German Workers Party had been founded in 1919 to promote racial superiority, German nationalism, and anti-Semitism. It was a socialist political party founded and funded by the Thule Gesselschaft or Thule Society, which was one of the most important secret societies in Germany, mixing extreme right-wing politics with occultism and Teutonic paganism. The society had originated with Baron Rudolf von Sebottendorf, a self-styled Saxon aristocrat who was in fact the son of a railway worker. He worked variously as a stoker and electrician on steamships visiting New York, Naples, Australia, Egypt, and Constantinople (now Istanbul). While visiting Egypt, von Sebottendorf became interested in the occult arts, and while in Turkey, he contacted the Sufis and began to study astrology, alchemy, and Rosicrucianism. In 1901, von Sebottendorf was initiated into a Masonic lodge, which, like many in the Middle East, had connections to the French Grand Orient. The Turkish lodge also had links to the

Society of Union and Progress, founded to promote liberal politics during the repressive regime of the sultan.

In 1910, while living in Istanbul, von Sebottendorf decided to found his own secret society based on a combination of Sufi mysticism, Freemasonry, alchemy, and a right-wing political philosophy that was anti-Bolshevik and anti-Semitic. It was at this period that he began to claim aristocratic links, adopting the name of the von Sebottendorfs, an ancient Silesian family who had served with both the Prussian and Habsburg armies. He fought in the Balkan War of 1912 and, as a result of wounds he received, returned to Germany. In 1916, von Sebottendorf made contact with the German Order, and in the next two years, he played a prominent role recruiting new members. By the end of the war, von Sebottendorf had moved to Munich and the German Order had adopted the name Thule Society to prevent its activities from being disturbed by the Communists, who were opposed to the German Order's right-wing, pro-monarchist views.

In 1918, the Thule Society had over two hundred fifty members in Munich and nearly fifteen hundred members scattered across the Bavarian countryside. Its membership list included many local dignitaries—judges, lawyers, police chiefs, aristocrats, doctors, university lecturers, scientists, military officers, industrialists, and businessmen. Among its leading members were Franz Gurtner, the Bavarian minister of justice, who later held the same position in the Nazi regime; Pohner, the police commissioner of Munich; and Wilhelm Frick, the assistant police chief who became the minister of the interior in the Third Reich. Another leading member of the Thulists was an occultist named Deitrich Eckart, who held séances with two White Russian émigrés. Eckart was associated with a White Russian printing house that produced an anti-Communist newspaper specializing in stories alleging that the Jews had financed the Bolshevik revolution.

At the occult séances organized by Eckart, the medium was a peasant woman who allegedly manifested ectoplasm from her vagina. This ectoplasmic substance formed into human shapes representing long-dead spirits. While she was in trance, the medium spoke in foreign languages and predicted the rise of a messiah who would lead Germany to victory and world domination. Also at these séances, dead members of the Thule Society materialized, including Prince von Thum und Taxis, who had been murdered in early 1919 by the Communists. The prince had been a member of the Order of Bavarian Mystics, which claimed descent from the Illuminati.

The Thule Society took its name from the mythical hyperborean island that once existed in the north Atlantic between Scandinavia and Greenland. It was believed by occultists that this island had once been part of Atlantis and was the source of the occult wisdom of the northern mystery tradition. Politically, the Thulists were committed to the establishment of a pan-German state based on the Habsburg dynasty, which had abdicated in November 1918, when faced with a socialist revolution in Austria. With the Communist uprisings in 1919 in defeated Germany, the Thule Society went underground, organizing a terrorist network that supplied arms to the rightist counterrevolutionaries and distributing German nationalist and anti-Semitic literature that called upon the people to rise up against the Bolsheviks, who had seized power in several German cities.

As part of their popular movement against the Communists, the Thulists started the German Workers Party. The idea was to attract ordinary Germans away from left-wing socialism to a new kind of socialist politics based on nationalism and Aryan racial supremacy. The Communists were well aware of the Thule Society's political activities by this time. In the April 1919 coup, the Communist militia raided the society's headquarters in Munich, and several leading Thulists, including Prince von Thum und Taxis and several titled aristocrats, were taken hostage and later shot dead. When the hostages were shot, the Thulists organized a citizens' army against the Communists, and on May 1, troops loyal to the counterrevolution entered Munich and regained control of the city.

In the prewar years, Hitler had been exposed to the racist and occult theories of Guido von List and was conversant with both Nordic and German mythology. It is possible that through this interest, Hitler decided to adopt the swastika as the emblem for the German Workers Party. This symbol had already been used by several German nationalist groups, including the German Order and the Thule Society. In fact, it was a leading Thulist, Dr. Frederick Kohn, who provided Hitler with the final design for the Nazi flag that became the national emblem of the Third Reich.

Hitler was impressed by Guido von List's political philosophy, which involved the relegation of the Jews to a slave race that would work for its German masters in a future Aryan-dominated Europe. Where Hitler disagreed with von List and the Thulists was in the idea of a new pan-European dynasty centered on the Habsburgs and a revived Holy Roman Empire. Hitler frequently spoke out against the Habsburgs, whom he regarded as traitors who had betrayed the German-speaking peoples of Europe. In *Mein Kampf* Hitler wrote, "How could one become a faithful subject of the House of Habsburgs, whose past and present policy is a betrayal of German origin?"

Von Sebottendorf had resigned as head of the Thule Society by the time Hitler joined the German Workers Party, but his pro-monarchist views may have been responsible for his failure to revive Thulism during the Third Reich. In the 1920s, he had been inducted into the Imperial Constantine Order, which was virulently anti-Bolshevik, and he acted as a secret agent for this group when he returned to Munich from abroad in 1933. With the rise of National Socialism, von Sebottendorf believed Hitler would encourage the rise of the new Thule Society. In fact, von Sebottendorf was arrested by the Gestapo in 1934 and interned in a concentration camp. When he was released, von Sebottendorf returned to Istanbul, where he claimed he was working for the Sicherheitsdienst, the Nazi intelligence service. He committed suicide in 1945, when he heard the news of the German surrender.

Hitler was influenced in his attitudes toward the Jews by a publication called *The Protocols of the Elders of Zion*. This document was said to be an account of the World Congress of Jewry held in Basel, Switzerland, in 1897, during which a conspiracy was planned by the international Jewish movement and the Freemasons to achieve world domination. At the beginning of World War I, copies of this publication had been imported into Germany from Russia by the Thule Society, which had used it to suggest that the Russian Revolution in 1917 had been financed by the Jews.

The Protocols was also used by the German nationalists to prove that the defeat of the Second Reich in 1918 was caused by a global Jewish conspiracy. The report of the World Congress had allegedly been smuggled out of Switzerland by a Russian journalist, who had then placed the document in the safe keeping of the Rising Sun Masonic lodge in Frankfurt. Before handing over the document, however, he had made several copies that he then circulated in rightist circles in Moscow and St. Petersburg. In fact, The Protocols was a forgery created by dissident members of the czarist secret police. They planned to use the document to undermine the influence on Nicholas II of several leading Freemasons who were urging the monarch to adopt liberal policies. Although The Protocols was exposed as a fraud in 1921, its influence was widespread for many years after and it is still regarded by some conspiracy theorists as genuine. Even today, it is still being used by intelligence services and the secret police in several Arab countries as anti-Israeli propaganda. In Mein Kampf, Hitler, obviously influenced by his reading of The Protocols, denounced the Jews as agents of an international conspiracy devoted to global domination through the control of the world's financial centers and money markets.

Once he was established in the German Workers Party, Hitler decided to modify the Thulist philosophy to produce a political movement that would have mass appeal. He wanted to use the party to create a right-wing counterrevolution that would sweep away the Jews, the Communists, and the Social Democrats, whom he, along with many other Germans, believed had betrayed the country during the war. Like the kaiser before him, Hitler suspected the Freemasons of playing a part in the defeat of Germany. He interpreted the Masonic myths based on King Solomon's temple as evidence that the Freemasons belonged to the international Jewish plot for world domination.

In 1920 the German Workers Party changed its name to the National Socialist Party and Hitler prepared his grand plan to gain supreme political power in post-war Germany. Assisted by Deitrich Eckart, he transformed National Socialism into a mass political movement. Eckart knew that the party needed a charismatic leader and he saw in Hitler the messiah predicted by the old peasant woman in her séances. Eckart taught Hitler social manners and introduced him to wealthy Thulists and White Russian émigrés who provided the funds for the embryonic Nazi Party. These people were frightened that a Bolshevik revolution could still sweep through Germany and were eager to finance a new political party that promoted German nationalism. The early meetings of the German Workers Party had been advertised in the Thulist newspaper *Volkisher Beobachter,* which later became the official organ of the Nazi Party. Police protection for Hitler was also provided by the Bavarian police, whose members included many leading Thulists.

Hitler's early career was dominated by another occultist, Karl Hausofer, who had been the German military attaché in Tokyo before the war and was in contact with several Eastern secret societies. During the war, Hausofer was a general in the imperial army, and after the armistice he became a professor of geopolitics at Munich University, where Rudolf Hess, later deputy führer in the Third Reich, was his assistant. Hausofer's son, who was an astrologer and a student of the prophecies of the medieval French mystic Michel Notre Dame, or Nostradamus, later became involved in Hess's disastrous peace mission to Britain in 1941.

Hausofer traveled extensively in the Far East in pursuit of occult knowledge. He believed that the Aryan race had originated in central Asia and he was later to try to persuade Hitler to extend the Third Reich's political influence to Persia, India, and Tibet. While visiting Tibet in 1908, Hausofer met George Ivanovitch Gurdjieff, the extraordinary Russian occultist who is not only believed to have been influential in the foundation of the German Order but is also said to have had contact with the Soviet dictator Josef Stalin when the latter was a student and stayed as a lodger in the Gurdjieff household.

Gurdjieff was born on the Russian-Turkish border and at an early age was introduced into a secret society known as the Community of Truth Seekers, a group of powerful occultists who believed that there had been a single world religion in ancient times that had fragmented into the various religious beliefs and occult doctrines that exist today. The teachings of this once-universal religion now survive only in legends, folklore, music, and the secret teachings of esoteric fraternities. It was the task of the Truth Seekers to travel the remoter parts of Europe, the Middle East, and Asia, contacting the secret societies that still preserved the Ancient Wisdom and reestablishing the ancient world religion.

During his own travels in Asia, Gurdjieff masqueraded as a carpet salesman and fashion designer selling ladies' corsets. He was also acting as a spy for the Russian secret service against the British in India and Afghanistan. He stayed for ten years in Tibet as the tutor of the dalai lama and hatched a plan to convert Czar Nicholas II to Buddhism. While in the East, Gurdjieff was initiated into the Sarmoung Brotherhood, which had been founded in Babylon in 2500 BCE. Shortly before the outbreak of World War I, Gurdjieff returned to Russia to teach his own occult system based on his Eastern studies. With the rise of the Bolsheviks, however, he was forced to leave and he established in France a spiritual commune, which attracted writers and intellectuals from all over western Europe.

It was through his contact with Gurdjieff that Hausofer was first introduced to the legend of the subterranean city of Agarthi. According to occult doctrine, Agarthi was a mysterious underground kingdom situated in a remote part of the Far East. The city was constructed over sixty thousand years ago by occult adepts who fled the cataclysm that allegedly destroyed Atlantis. Agarthi supposedly had huge libraries of rare volumes containing ancient esoteric wisdom. It is said to have been the source of the material in *The Secret Doctrine* written by the founder of the Theosophical Society, Madame Blavatsky.

Considering the relationship between Hausofer and Hess, it seems possible that Gurdjieff's assertion that the human race was spiritually and morally asleep and had to be wakened from its dream state by the application of occult techniques may have reached Hitler. Occultists have pointed out that the use of the Nazi slogan "Germany Awake" could be traced back to Gurdjieff. The concept of the Aryan master race and the creation of supermen who would rule a Nazi-dominated world may also link to the legend of Agarthi and its immortal occult adepts. It was the German philosopher Nietzsche who gave us the superman concept, but it was occult doctrine that refined the idea in the minds of the early Nazis.

Another source for the master-race theory in the early days of the Nazi Party was the occultist Alfred Rosenberg who, while Hitler was in prison from 1922 to 1924, was the acting leader of the National Socialists. Rosenberg and Eckart had been instrumental in importing copies of *The Protocols of the Elders of Zion* into Germany and both men acted as gurus to Hitler. Rosenberg was convinced that the Aryan race had originated on the lost continent of Atlantis and that Atlantis was the source of all ancient occult beliefs. He claimed that the mythical island had been destroyed because the gods condemned Atlantean experiments, which mated animals with women to create a hybrid race that was half animal and half human to be used as slaves. When Atlantis was threatened with cosmic destruction, the priesthood received prior warning and some of its members fled to Asia, where they established themselves as rulers of the indigenous aboriginal inhabitants. Rosenberg believed the modern Hindu caste system was a pale imitation of the original racial subdivisions imposed by the Atlanteans on their conquered inferiors.

Rosenberg also believed that the fleeing Atlanteans had established colonies in the Middle East, including Persia, where they founded the Zoroastrian religion with its dualistic philosophy of the eternal struggle between light and darkness. This religious belief, as we have seen, gave birth to the Manichean heresy that was promoted in medieval Europe by the Cathars until they were exterminated by the Roman Church. In an altered form, this philosophy was revived in Germany between the wars by the occultist Rudolf Steiner, who was a member of the German Theosophical Society and who was later persecuted by the Nazis for his occult beliefs.

The short career of Alfred Rosenberg as leader of the Nazis marked the beginning of the movement's flirtation with neo-paganism. He asserted that Christianity could not provide the spiritual force needed in the Third Reich because its dogmas were opposed to the ancient beliefs of the Germanic race. When the Nazis came to power, Rosenberg said that the crucifix and the Bible would be removed from church altars and replaced with the symbol of the swastika. On each altar would be a copy of *Mein Kampf* and a sword symbolizing the unconquerable will of the German people. When Hitler was released from imprisonment, however, he rejected Rosenberg's idea of a new German religion. He realized that millions of his fellow countrymen and women found comfort in the Church and any attempt to outlaw Christianity would be political suicide for the new party. Yet after Hitler gained power in 1933, several attempts were made by occultists in the Nazi Party to revive neo-paganism as the spiritual framework for the political ideals of National Socialism.

Hitler initially seems to have supported the idea, but only in a sublimated form because he believed it would never get the support of the German masses. While he despised Freemasonry as a Jewish invention, he used it as the model for the inner circle of the Nazi Party. He said, "They [the Masons] have developed an esoteric doctrine, not formulated it, but imparted it through the medium of symbols and mysterious rites . . . our party must be of this order—an order, the hierarchical order of a secular priesthood." In 1934, Hitler moved this idea a step forward when he declared, "We shall form an order, the Brotherhood of the Templars, around the Holy Grail of the pure blood."

Heinrich Himmler was to become the creator of Hitler's dream of a new Templar Order with the formation of the Schutzstaffel, or SS, which had originally acted as the führer's personal bodyguard in the 1920s. Himmler transformed the SS into an elite unit of crack troops that was ruthlessly dedicated to the Nazi ideology. They were destined to become feared throughout occupied Europe and were responsible for controlling the network of special concentration camps set up in 1942 to deal with the Jewish "problem." Himmler was a disciple of the occult doctrines that were at the root of the racial policies of the Third Reich. He believed that the SS would be the vehicle through which the racial purity of Germany would be reestablished by scientific breeding programs designed to create the master race of supermen.

Himmler drew on many historical precedents when he reformed the SS into a secret society within the German military machine. These included the Jesuits, the Freemasons, the Knights Templars, the Teutonic Knights, the Order of the Garter, and the Fellowship of the Round Table. The headquarters of the SS was established in the castle of Wewelsburg, which had been modeled on the castle in the Arthurian myth of the Holy Grail. In the castle, members of the SS officer corps were initiated in neo-pagan rites and were given a special ring carved with a skull, runes, and the swastika.

A special investigation group staffed by top SS officers was also formed under Himmler's direction. This group was given the task of studying history from a Nazi viewpoint with special emphasis on the secret societies in medieval Europe, including the Templars and the Cathars, and occult symbolism. For some reason, Himmler was convinced that the British secret service had been infiltrated by the Rosicrucians. To him, this apparently explained its successes during World War I, for its agents had been trained in occult and psychic techniques. Himmler also established the H-Unit (Hexen Unit) and gave it the task of investigating the medieval witch trials. It has been claimed that he planned to extend the Final Solution to suspected witches.

It was the influence of Himmler and his SS troops that was to make the extermination of the various "sub-human" and "inferior races" in occupied Europe such a success from the Nazi viewpoint, although the energy and resources that were poured into the Final Solution considerably weakened the overall German war effort and assisted the

Allies in defeating the Nazi evil. Hitler's hatred of the Jews was long-standing, as we have seen, but his attitude toward the gypsies (Roma) is more difficult to trace without reference to the occult beliefs that predominated in the early years of the National Socialist movement and that affected the political decisions of the Third Reich.

In the 1920s, the Nazis displayed quite a lot of interest in gypsy (Roma) culture. They believed that this culture should be preserved because the gypsies were the descendents of the Indo-European race that had settled in Asia. Hitler's plan was to settle the gypsy population of Germany in one area. In 1937, the Gestapo rounded up isolated gypsy bands and settled them in residential camps outside the cities. In fact, this was the prelude to the mass extermination of the gypsy race, which had suddenly become condemned as a "carrier of disease" and "tainter of the pure Aryan race."

Why did Hitler persecute the gypsies? Possibly because their swarthy, dark physical characteristics were the opposite of the idealistic Nazi image of the Aryan race as blonde, blue-eyed supermen. If, as Nazi racial experts claimed, the gypsies were related to the Aryans, the whole master race theory was undermined. Another possible if more speculative reason for their extermination was the Nazi belief that the gypsy population possessed a storehouse of occult knowledge. Superstitious Nazi leaders believed that this knowledge could be used to threaten the Third Reich. For this bizarre reason, four hundred thousand gypsies died in the gas chambers. Hitler was terrified of anyone with occult power who might pose a threat to his rule. In 1937, the Nazis prohibited several leading occult groups, including the Theosophists, the followers of Rudolf Steiner, the OTO, the Hermetic Order of the Golden Dawn, and the Order of New Templars.

Hitler's fear of occult opposition was well founded. There were many practicing occultists who had become aware of Nazi involvement in the black arts and were prepared to fight them on the magical and psychic level. It was well known that extremist political groups of all types had used the occult movements in the period between the two wars. Writing in the 1930s from her own personal experience, in her book *Psychic Self-Defense* the occultist and Golden Dawn member Dion Fortune describes the way revolutionary groups exploited occult fraternities for political purposes. Fortune cites two cases known to her: In one incident an attempt was made by political extremists to use the headquarters of an occult society as a post box for the collecting of certain letters. This bypassed the normal channels that were being monitored by MI5 (the British secret intelligence service responsible for counterespionage and countersubversion). In the second case, Fortune herself was asked to give shelter to a political agitator who faced deportation. Although a sum of several thousand pounds was offered for this service, she refused the request.

An occult involvement in the General Strike in 1926 has also been claimed. According to the Roman Catholic exorcist Dom Robert Petitpierre, he and his colleague Father Gilbert Shaw were convinced that Russian occult adepts were projecting psychic forces at Britain in the 1920s to precipitate industrial unrest. They hoped this would lead to a socialist revolution and the overthrow of the monarchy and the government. Both men were attending a theological college in Essex situated near a prehistoric burial mound. This site was allegedly on a ley line extending from Russia to Mount Snowdon, in north Wales, and they claimed it was being used by the Russian occultists to focus psychic energy.

Several well-known occultists played a role in the psychic opposition to Hitler and the Nazis, including the controversial magician Aleister Crowley. His activities extended from acting as a spy in pre-war Berlin to playing a part in the 1941 peace mission by Rudolf Hess. Crowley, however, had displayed a distinct lack of patriotism during World War I, when he actively supported the kaiser. He was living in Switzerland when the war began and had offered his services to the British government, but they refused to have anything to do with him. In October 1914, Crowley sailed to New York, and in 1915, he became interested in German nationalism. A chance meeting on an omnibus with a mysterious Irishman named O'Brien led Crowley to denounce his British citizenship, tear up his passport, and call on the

Irish people to support Germany by rising up against their English oppressors.

While living in the United States, Crowley wrote pro-German propaganda for two right-wing publications, *The Fatherland* and *The Internationalist*. He later claimed that he carried out this work as an agent for MI6 (the British secret intelligence service) and had been secretly working for the Allied cause all the time. Yet the British secret service denied all knowledge of this arrangement and denounced him as a "small-time traitor" who acted from a desire for self-advertisement rather than treason. As a result of this condemnation, however, the police did raid his occult temple in London and seized numerous documents and magical regalia.

After the war, it was suggested that Crowley should be prosecuted, but he seems to have persuaded the authorities that he was trying to help the Allies by writing tongue-in-cheek articles that in fact ridiculed the Germans. Crowley offered his services as an agent to MI6 after informing it that the head of the OTO, which he had joined in 1912, was a German intelligence officer. In the 1920s and 1930s, Crowley worked on an informal basis for MI6, supplying it with information about the European Communist movement and the links among the German nationalist groups, occult fraternities, and the Nazis. It is possible that Crowley's employment by the British secret service was well-known to the Germans. While he was living in Berlin, the bisexual magician shared a home with an Englishman who was a German agent.

The head of the OTO whom Crowley suspected of spying was probably Karl Germer, who used the magical pseudonym Frater Saturnus. He had fought in World War I and had been awarded the Iron Cross for unspecified special services. His intelligence activities had brought him in touch with Theodor Reuss, the founder of the OTO, and Germer was initiated into the secret society. When Reuss died, Germer became the new head of the OTO. In the 1920s, Germer was working as the manager of a publishing house in Munich and was responsible for the translating and publishing of several of Crowley's occult books.

Both Germer and Crowley were associated with an occult secret society known as the Fraternitus Saturni, or the Brotherhood of Saturn, from whom Germer derived his magical name in the OTO. This order had been founded in seventeenth-century Denmark and Sweden and also had lodges in Poland. Its modern history began in 1921, when a neo-Rosicrucian named Gregory Gregorius founded the Pansophic lodge of the order in Berlin. This event was attended by the grand master of the German Rosicrucian Order, Aleister Crowley, in his role as British head of the OTO, and the grand masters of several other European and American secret societies in the Rosicrucian-Masonic tradition. In 1933, the Brotherhood was outlawed by the Nazis and several of its leaders were thrown into prison. It was reorganized after the end of the war, however, and became a prominent neo-Rosicrucian society in early 1950s Germany.

Despite his past work for the German intelligence service, Germer was arrested by the Gestapo in 1935 because of his connections to Freemasonry. He was tortured in prison before being dispatched to a concentration camp but was mysteriously released ten months later. Germer fled from Germany at the beginning of the war but was arrested by the Belgian police and then deported to France. After a period of imprisonment in an internment camp, Germer left France for the United States, where he died in 1962.

Crowley made up for his lack of patriotism in World War I when hostilities broke out in September 1939. Because Crowley had extensive contacts with European secret societies, his specialist knowledge was used by the Secret Intelligence Service (SIS) for "black propaganda" purposes. When Crowley met the writer Aldous Huxley in Berlin in 1938, he confided to him that Hitler was a practicing occultist. He also claimed that the German branch of the OTO had helped the Nazis gain power.

In May 1941 Crowley was involved in the Hess peace mission. Crowley had come into contact with MI5 some years earlier through his friendship with Dennis Wheatley, the popular thriller writer who authored novels about black magic and the occult. In 1943, Wheatley had offered his services to the ministry of information at the suggestion of his wife, who was in MI5. He was appointed as an officer on the future operations staff and worked until 1944 as one of Winston Churchill's special staff officers. In this position, Wheatley had access to the official minutes and reports of the defense committee, the war cabinet, the chiefs of staff, the home office, the foreign office, and the joint intelligence committee, which was responsible for the activities of MI5, the SIS, and the Special Operations Executive (SOE).

In the 1930s, Wheatley had become friendly with a high-ranking MI5 officer, Maxwell Knight. Both men had been cadets on HMS *Worcester* at different periods in their naval careers, shared an interest in the occult, and had written crime thrillers. In 1933, the year the Nazis came to power, Wheatley's stepson Bill Younger was recruited by Knight when he was at Oxford University. His job was to spy on fellow students who were involved in Communist activities or who had fascist sympathies. After he left university, Younger became a full-time MI5 agent, working in the countersubversion department. Younger was also interested in the occult and was a friend of Joan Grant, who wrote several "fictional" historical novels based on her past lives.

Dennis Wheatley had been introduced to Crowley by the journalist Tom Driberg, who later became a Labor MP. He had also been used by MI5 to infiltrate the British Communist Party. Wheatley used his introduction to Crowley to obtain material for his black magic novels such as *The Devil Rides Out,* published in 1936. On one of his visits to the Wheatleys in 1937, Maxwell Knight met Crowley and later described the occultist to friends as a well-dressed middle-aged eccentric with the manner of an Oxford don. Knight became very friendly with Crowley and he and Wheatley attended magical ceremonies organized by the magician. The purpose of these visits was to research material for Wheatley's occult novels.

Because of his link to Maxwell Knight, Crowley became entangled in the attempt by the British secret service to lure Rudolf Hess to Britain in the early summer of 1941. At the outbreak of war,

Commander Ian Fleming, later to become world famous as the creator of the fictional spy James Bond, was working for naval intelligence. He knew Knight and was aware of the MI5 officer's interest in the occult and his friendship with Crowley. He was also aware, perhaps through Crowley's intelligence reports for the SIS, that many of the leading Nazis were engaged in occultism.

Fleming suggested that a trap could be laid that would persuade Hess to fly to Britain. Hess's subsequent capture would provide a superb propaganda coup for the Allied war effort. Fleming used a Swiss astrologer to infiltrate the occult circles in Germany that were frequented by Hess. The Nazi leader was fed the information that an organization known as the Link, which had actively supported the Nazis during the 1930s in England, was still operating underground in wartime Britain and still retained an influential membership of pro-German activists who were secretly plotting to overthrow the Churchill government. Once this was accomplished and the traitors were in power they would be capable of negotiating peace terms with Hitler.

Hess was told that the duke of Hamilton was willing to talk to him personally as the representative of the Link. In January 1941, Hess was further told by an astrologer working for SIS that on May 10, the position of six planets in the zodiac sign of Taurus coincided with the full moon. This was regarded by Hess as a favorable omen, and he chose that date for his ill-fated mission to contact the Link. The duke of Hamilton was working for the Royal Air Force (RAF) in Scotland, and when Hess parachuted into the country and was arrested by the police, he asked to see the aristocrat.

Originally, Fleming had asked MI5 to induce Crowley to use his wide contacts in the German occult fraternities to trap Hess. Unfortunately, British Intelligence knew that Crowley's influence was limited because of his activities as an MI6 agent in pre-war Berlin, when he spied on both the Communists and the Nazis. In one of his infamous radio broadcasts, Lord Haw Haw (William Joyce) had claimed satirically that when the Nazis occupied London, Crowley would celebrate a Black Mass in Westminster Abbey. Crowley believed he had become a specific target for the Nazis in the Blitz and moved out of London to a house on Richmond Green in Surrey.

When Hess was captured, Ian Fleming suggested to his boss, Rear Admiral John Godfrey, the director of the Naval Intelligence Department (NID), that Crowley should be allowed to interview Hess about the role of the occult in Nazism. Maxwell Knight was also keen on this idea, but others in MI5, MI6, and the NID were less happy about the idea and it was dropped. In fact, the intelligence services seem to have seriously mishandled the whole Hess operation and any chance to embarrass the Nazis with his capture was quickly lost.

In Germany, Hitler's reaction to the affair was swift and violent. He knew nothing about the mission and his first reaction when he heard the news was that Hess had suffered a brainstorm. Hess was dismissed in the official Nazi newspaper as a sick man who had been led astray by his interest in the occult and astrology. Several hundred astrologers, occultists, and members of secret societies were rounded up by the Gestapo and questioned to establish whether they knew Hess or other leading members of the Nazi Party. In June 1941, the public practice of the occult arts, astrology, fortune-telling, and psychic powers was banned by the Nazis.

Previous to his savage reaction against esoteric activities in Germany, Hitler, it is alleged, sanctioned the use of occult groups to raise psychic power to block the radar of RAF aircraft flying over Germany. The idea was that the planes would miss their target, get lost, and fly into the searchlights of the German antiaircraft batteries. It has been rumored that a similar psychic operation had also been set up in Britain by British intelligence involving psychics who worked from a secret location in Wales. Their purpose was to deflect the Luftwaffe during their raids on English cities into ambushes set up by the RAF's fighter command.

MI6 became interested in the Nazi preoccupation with the occult early in the war. Several occultists were employed by the SIS to combat the Nazis on a psychic level. A Hungarian born astrologer named Louis de Wohl, a ranking major, was attached to the Psychological

Warfare Department. His job was to examine Hitler's birth chart and send regular reports to the war office detailing what Hitler's astrologers were advising the German leader to do in the war. It has been said that the SIS employed several other astrologers, who produced fake predictions that suggested that Germany would lose the war. Faked astrological publications were smuggled into occupied Europe by SIS agents, who circulated them widely. They also used the prophecies of the sixteenth-century seer Nostradamus, who predicted the rise and fall of a European dictator called Hister (Hitler).

One of the most successful psychics employed during the war by the British intelligence service was known simply by the code name Anne. She had offered the intelligence service her psychic services, which included the ability to project her mind to remote locations and report what was happening there. At her interview, she impressed the assembled intelligence officers by entering a trance state and projecting her mind to the next room. She described how a group of men were sitting reading the *Times* and circling certain advertisements with blue pencils. This information was checked out and found to be correct.

In the following weeks, Anne was rigorously tested by the secret service, which tried to prove that her powers were fake. She astounded the testers by repeating conversations among British troops stationed overseas. Eventually, the intelligence officers had to admit that her powers were genuine and they used her gifts on several occasions. Anne achieved her most astonishing coup when she successfully projected her mind to the Nazi high command's headquarters in Berlin. There she read certain top-secret documents and, when she had recovered from her trance, reported their contents back to her British intelligence colleagues.

The psychics working for the secret service were not the only occultists engaged in anti-Nazi activities. Before the war, there had been a revival of witchcraft and it was alleged that a Hungarian occultist had organized witch covens in the Cotswolds and used psychic powers to fight the Nazis. This person also had contacts with the

British intelligence service and had recruited occult circles in the West Midlands area to use telepathy to combat the Germans.

One of the leading personalities in the witchcraft revival was a retired customs officer, Gerald Gardner, who had returned from the Far East and settled in the New Forest in Hampshire. Gardner was interested in spiritualism and the occult, and as a result, he joined a Rosicrucian theater company operating in Christchurch before the war. This theater had been founded by disciples of Annie Besant, who were Co-Masons and had formed a group known as the Corona Fellowship of the Rosy Cross, which was an unofficial offshoot of the Temple of the Rose Cross founded by Besant in 1912. Gardner soon discovered that several of these neo-Rosicrucians were also members of a witch coven, and in 1939, he claimed he was initiated as a witch by their high priestess, an old lady named Dorothy Clutterbuck who lived in a large house in the New Forest.

In June 1940, when England faced invasion from the Nazis, Gardner claims that the high priestess of his coven called a huge gathering of witches in the New Forest, where the great circle was erected. This was a magical ritual performed only in cases of extreme emergency. Previously, it had been raised only twice: in 1588 to combat the Spanish Armada, which was defeated by both Drake and his ships and the help of a great storm, and in the 1800s when it looked as if Napoleon would cross the Channel. The ritual in the forest involved raising a cone of psychic power and directing it toward the French coast with the command "You cannot cross the sea, you cannot cross the sea, you cannot come." According to Gardner, this ritual involved the use of the life force of the gathered covens and as a result several elderly witches died. The ritual was repeated four times, and then the elders said, "We must stop; we must not kill too many of our people."

At the opposite end of the occult spectrum, the Theosophical occultist Dion Fortune was also working against the Nazis on the psychic level, although her organization was linked to theirs by their shared Rosicrucian affiliations. She used racial and national archetypes in magical practices to protect Britain from invasion. From the autumn of 1939 to 1942, Fortune produced a series of newsletters that replaced the official journal of her magical group, the Fraternity of the Inner Light, which could not be produced because of the wartime paper shortage. These newsletters provided the membership of the Inner Light scattered all over the country with a series of meditation exercises that were practiced each Sunday.

Each Sunday morning the inner circle of initiates of the fraternity met at the group's London headquarters in Bayswater. All the other members nationwide linked with those in London to form a network of trained minds. In her first newsletter, sent out in October 1939, Fortune explained that the idea was to contact the spiritual influences that ruled the British race, using the symbol of a cross surmounted by a rose and surrounded by golden rays of light. This particular symbol had been common to the medieval Rosicrucians and to modern occult groups such as the Hermetic Order of the Golden Dawn, which Dion Fortune had joined just after World War I. By 1940, the Inner Light was involved in magical rituals to invoke the guardian angels of the British Isles, who were visualized as robed and armed patrolling the shores of the country to prevent the German invasion.

There has been considerable speculation concerning the occult beliefs associated with National Socialism and the role played by secret societies in its rise to power. This has led to exaggerated and sensational stories that have confused the real facts of the matter. This confusion was helped by the Allied attitude toward the true nature of the Nazi political doctrine after the war. Churchill allegedly suppressed the facts about the Nazis' involvement in occultism; he ordered that under no circumstances should the general public be informed of the extent of the occult activities engaged in by the Third Reich. At the Nuremburg trials of the major Nazi war criminals, including Rudolf Hess, the truth about their esoteric activities and practices was hidden from the world. It was believed that if this information had been revealed in open court, many of the war criminals on trial would have been declared insane and would have escaped the death penalty demanded by Allied prosecutors.

7

SECRETS
IN THE VATICAN

In the alternative history of secret societies, the position taken by the Vatican and whoever occupied the papal throne at any point in that history has always been a matter of great importance. The relationship between the pope and the grand masters of secret societies was an explosive one. It could be nothing else. The Roman Church regarded the members of secret societies as spiritual anarchists and the agents of a satanic conspiracy against organized religion. On the other hand, the Freemasons and Rosicrucians accused the Church of suppressing the true teachings of Jesus of Nazareth. Other secret societies, such as the Illuminati and the Carbonari, were fervently anticlerical. They plotted the overthrow of the Catholic Church because it opposed the old pagan religions and the Manichean heresy, from which these groups drew their spiritual inspiration, and supported the wealthy landowning class that was oppressing the masses.

At first, papal support for some of the secret societies was freely given. Chivalric orders such as the Knights Templar, which were nominally Christian, were granted special papal favors. Even the Priory of Sion, which we are led to believe promoted the heresy that Jesus survived the crucifixion, was allegedly granted a charter by Pope Alexander III in the twelfth century (the same pontiff who had given the Templars special dispensations). In addition, the medieval Church patronized the masonic guilds whose craftsmen had built the Gothic cathedrals, even though their legendary origins predated Christian belief and were firmly rooted in the pagan mysteries.

It was only when the Vatican perceived secret societies to be a political and ideological threat to the Church that the climate of tolerance began to change. The creation of a church within the Church by the Templars and rumors of their heretical and pagan practices had forced the Vatican to support King Philip of France's personal crusade to wipe out the order in the early fourteenth century. The Church had previously acted against the Cathars and other heretics to retain its spiritual monopoly in the face of a growing alternative religion.

In taking this kind of action, the Vatican was following a historical tradition, for the early Church had moved to neutralize dissent within its ranks by a series of councils that established the officially recognized tenets and doctrines of Christianity. These councils, principally the infamous Council of Nicaea convened by the Roman emperor Constantine in the fourth century CE, rejected pagan beliefs such as reincarnation that had been held by some of the early Christians and presented Jesus as God incarnate rather than as a human spiritual teacher. Anyone who disagreed with these decisions was branded a *heretic*, meaning "one who chooses," and they could expect little tolerance from the new breed of Christian leaders who were in political control of the new Church.

One of the first victims of the intolerance of the early Christian Church was Celtic Christianity, which was dissolved by the Council of Whitby in 664 CE. Celtic Christianity had developed its own unique character during the Roman occupation of Britain and was heavily influenced by druidism. According to legend, the first Christian church in this country was built by the uncle and foster father of Jesus, Joseph of Arimathea, at Glastonbury in Somerset on the present site of the medieval abbey. Joseph was a wealthy merchant who visited the tin mines of Cornwall for trading purposes. He took his young nephew on one of these business trips, the legend says, and the nephew was initiated into a druidic college. Glastonbury had been a spiritual center since prehistoric times, and the version of Christianity introduced by Joseph and his disciples intermingled with the native paganism. A separate branch of the Celtic Church was established in Wales during the fifth century CE by Irish monks who blended Eastern traditions with the old pagan beliefs of Ireland.

In addition to druidism, the Celtic Church was influenced by Coptic Christianity. This unorthodox version of the new faith was founded by Clement of Alexandria through blending the teachings of Jesus with gnosticism, Judaism, and Neoplatonism. Clement founded his Coptic Church on the Gospel of Mark, written by the evangelist in Alexandria following the death of Jesus. This gospel claimed to preserve the inner teachings given by Jesus to his closest disciples, whom he initiated into the Christian mysteries. It is interesting to note that Ormus, the legendary first-century founder of the secret society that allegedly became the historical Priory of Sion, lived in Alexandria and was converted to Christianity by Mark.

Our contemporary knowledge of the Gospel of Mark dates to 1958, when an American professor of theology, Dr. Morton Smith, discovered references to it in a letter by Clement preserved in a desert monastery. According to Dr. Smith, Jesus passed his inner teachings to the disciples during an initiation rite resembling those of the pagan mysteries. Dr. Smith interprets the ritual communion meal practiced by early Christians as a pagan rite descended from the mysteries of Isis and Osiris. The medieval secret societies accepted this esoteric interpretation of Christianity in contrast to the censored version offered by the Church.

Before it became an established power structure protected by the might of imperial Rome, early Christianity operated underground much like the pagan mystery cults and suffered persecution for its beliefs. The Roman hatred of Christians was based on the belief that their teachings were politically subversive and threatened the status quo. By the third century CE, when the Roman Empire had entered a crisis period, Christians infiltrated all levels of Roman society and held important positions despite the fact that they were regarded as dissidents whose alien ideas posed a danger to the social fabric of the Empire. This persecution of Christians coincided with major conflicts within the Church itself concerning the imperial power of the Roman emperors. In the first decade of the fourth century, a situation arose in which several rival emperors fought to occupy the Roman throne. From this internecine struggle emerged one candidate who was to play a decisive role in both the history of the Roman Empire and Christianity during his long reign from 306 to 337 CE: Constantine the Great.

Constantine had been reared on the pagan religious beliefs of the Sol Invicta cult, which taught that the emperor was the incarnation of the sun god. This cult was the first attempt in Roman culture to impose a monotheistic structure on the polytheistic pantheon of gods and goddesses worshipped by the ordinary people. It was similar in many ways to the Aton religion of ancient Egypt created by the heretical pharaoh Akhenaton. Initially, Constantine was a devout pagan, and it is recorded that while fighting in Gaul (France), he saw a vision of the solar god Apollo, who was worshipped in Rome as the supreme incarnation of the divine sun. While marching on Rome to establish his right to be emperor, however, Constantine saw another vision: this time, a blazing cross in the sky and above it in letters of flame the motto *In hoc signo vinci,* or "In this sign I conquer." When he won his battle the next day, the opportunist Constantine decided the Christian god was a powerful deity who was worthy of his worship.

From that moment, though he did not fully accept Christianity until a dramatic deathbed conversion, Constantine became more tolerant of the new religion. The Christian community soon realized they had a friend occupying the Roman throne and turned this fact to their advantage. Christian leaders identified the new emperor as "the beloved of God" who "guides and steers, in imitation of the Lord, all the affairs of the world." With these words, the early Church had clearly marked out the Roman emperor as the representative of God on earth. It even embraced the symbolism of the pagan solar cult by describing Constantine as "the light of the sun [who] illuminates those farthest from him with his rays."

Constantine in turn increased the political power of the embryonic Church by appointing Christians to key positions in his court;

by prohibiting the private practice of magical rituals; and by declaring Sunday, the Christian holy day, a public holiday. During his reign, however, paganism still flourished and sacrificial rites were practiced as an important aspect of state ritual. Despite this, it was understood that while Constantine tolerated this paganism, he secretly favored Christianity. Any doubts in this direction were finally swept away when, in 324 CE, the emperor officially declared that Christianity would become the state religion of the Roman Empire.

The sympathetic approach to Christian beliefs pioneered by Constantine was continued by his sons who followed him to the throne but suffered a brief reversal during the short reign of his nephew, Julian, from 355 to 363 CE. Julian was a mystical intellectual and as a young man, he had been initiated into the pagan mysteries of the Greek goddess Hecate. While he pretended to be a devout Christian, Emperor Julian worked to reverse the advances made by the Christian religion during the previous forty years. He provided a high degree of freedom for all religious beliefs, including Christianity, but was biased toward paganism. Yet his death in the war against the Persians brought a sudden end to the neo-pagan revival in the Empire. Rumors quickly spread that Julian had not been killed by the Persians, but instead had been assassinated by a Christian in his own army who objected to the emperor's pagan beliefs.

With the death of Julian, the Christian religion quickly reestablished itself in Rome, and under Emperor Theodosius (378–395 CE), the worship of the old pagan gods was finally prohibited. This event coincided with attacks on Rome by barbarian tribes, which marked the end of the city's imperial glory. In 452 the dwarfish Attila the Hun appeared at the gates of Rome, but the barbarian was repulsed by the bishop of the city, who declared that the temporal power of the Roman emperor had been passed down to him.

In the bloody aftermath of the barbarian invasions and the beginning of the so-called Dark Ages, the Roman Church began to establish its political power. In the fifth century, the Church recognized the royal family of the Franks, the Merovingians, or "long haired kings," by baptizing Clovis the first Catholic monarch in Europe. The Church had decided that a strong leader was required to forge European unity against foreign invasion and insure the survival of Christianity in the face of pagan opposition. In 751, when the Merovingian throne was usurped by a court chancellor, the Vatican swiftly recognized the new regime. The last Merovingian king, Childeric III, was deposed and imprisoned. His flowing hair, which was of spiritual significance to the family, was ritually shorn by the reigning pope as a symbol of the dynasty's broken power. The Merovingian bloodline survived, however, by marrying into the family of the dukes of Habsburg and Lorriane.

By the late eighth century, the relationship between the Frankish kings and the bishop of Rome had grown stronger. In 795, Pope Leo III recognized the Frankish monarch Charles the Great of Charlemagne as the patrician of Rome. When Charlemagne saved the pope from the disgrace of an adultery charge, the grateful pontiff crowned him the new Roman emperor. The Holy Roman Empire ruled by the Frankish king was the first attempt by the medieval Church to expand its power base from the spiritual realm into the world of international politics. The Vatican's aim was to form a united Europe based on Christian values and chivalry through which it could exert absolute spiritual and temporal power.

With the death of Charlemagne, this dream of European unity quickly faded. His grandson was crowned Holy Roman Emperor in 915, but when he died nine years later, the imperial throne lay empty for two decades. In 936, Otto, the son of Henry the Fowler, was elected king by the German aristocracy. He declared his intention to fight the enemies of Christ and drive the pagans out of his land. The Vatican saw in this German warlord the potential for a new Roman emperor.

In 951, Otto was crowned the king of Lombardy and became the ruler of northern Italy. Following his defeat of the pagan Magyars in 955, Otto took the title of Protector of Europe. In Rome, Pope John XII, a notorious womanizer who turned the Vatican into a brothel during his papacy, appealed to Otto for help to fight his enemies. As a result, he rewarded the German king by crowning him the Holy

Roman Emperor in 962. For the next century the Italian popes and the German emperors ruled Europe, with the latter considered by the Church to represent the temporal power of God on earth.

The election of Pope Gregory VII in 1073 brought this cozy alliance under stress. The new pope asserted his belief that the Vatican was the master of the Roman emperors and the chosen vicar of Christ on earth, representing God. He claimed that the crowning of the Holy Roman Emperor by the pontiff demonstrated in public that the political power of the Empire derived from God through his chosen emissary in the Vatican. Emperor Henry IV challenged this view and was promptly excommunicated by the pope for treason. Faced with local revolts that threatened to topple him from the throne, Henry was forced to retract this view and submit his authority to the pope.

This ideological battle between the popes and the Roman emperors they had created raged for several hundred years. The point where we can discern the beginning of the secret societies' influence in this power struggle was in the reign of Frederick II, crowned as Holy Roman Emperor in 1215. Frederick was a man possessed of a great spiritual vision and he followed in the footsteps of his grandfather, Frederick Barbarossa, who had defiantly declared, "We hold our kingdom and our Empire not as a fief of the pope but by election of the princes from God alone." Frederick II became king of Sicily, and in 1228, he left on a Crusade to the Holy Land that resulted in him being crowned the king of Jerusalem. Frederick was rumored to have been involved in occult practices, including astrology and alchemy. He kept a harem at his court in Sicily, spoke Arabic, and had allegedly been inducted into the Muslim faith. This may explain why Pope Gregory IX denounced Frederick as a heretic and the personification of the Antichrist.

Frederick's political ambitions in the Middle East had brought him into open conflict with the Templars after he negotiated the return of Jerusalem from Muslim hands to Christian armies. In the treaty, Frederick agreed that the Muslims should retain the site of the temple of Solomon, which was then occupied by a mosque. This concession angered the Templars and they regarded it as an insult and betrayal because of the spiritual significance of the temple to the order. In their view, it was essential that while the order survived, Solomon's temple should be in the possession of the Christian Crusaders. Frederick was well aware of their anger and it is said that he fled Jerusalem, fearing that the Templars or their allies, the Assassins, were plotting to kill him.

Frederick's opposition to the Templar Order was determined by the fact that he shared their political aspirations. The Holy Roman Emperor had founded his own chivalric order, the Teutonic Knights, as a rival to the Templars. From 1230 to 1239, several battles were fought between the two orders for supremacy in the Holy Land. It is possible that Frederick, as an occultist, was opposed to the Templars because he did not share their spiritual beliefs and thought they had strayed from the true path. Frederick knew any attempt to overthrow the order by force was doomed to failure because of their support in the Vatican. Yet his opposition to the order in the Holy Land seriously weakened their political power, and the loss of the temple in Jerusalem sapped their morale. These circumstances contributed to the eventual downfall of the Templars.

With the death of Frederick in 1250, the Holy Roman Empire collapsed. For twenty years Europe was devastated by war until, in 1273, the concept of the old empire was revived with the crowning in Austria of a new Holy Roman Emperor, Count Rudolf von Habichtsburg, or Habsburg, meaning the "castle of hawks." For the next three hundred years, under the patronage of the Vatican, the Habsburgs extended their empire throughout Europe, based on their temporal power and the spiritual power of the Roman Catholic Church.

Yet the successful alliance between the Habsburgs and the Vatican was seriously weakened by the actions of one man, a crusading reformer who used the symbol of the rose and the cross on his personal seal: the German monk Martin Luther, who, in 1517, disgusted by the corrupt practices of the Church, nailed a document to the door of his local church condemning the selling of papal indulgences. Pope Leo X immediately issued a bull against Luther, who promptly burned it in public, leading to his excommunication in 1521. The Reformation, allegedly supported by the Rosicrucians and other secret societies opposed to the Roman Church, swept through Europe. It became a popular movement supported by the ruling classes and stopped the Vatican's relentless progress through European society.

This period of the Reformation represents a key time in history during which the relationship between the Church and secret societies was changed. In the twelfth and thirteenth centuries, the Church had used the powers of the Inquisition to crush the heretical Cathars and the Albigensi, who had challenged its rule in southern France. In the early fourteenth century, it had destroyed the Templars, and by the end of that century it had begun persecuting suspected witches. With the Reformation, the Church was faced with an enemy within whom it could not destroy without bringing down its own edifice. With the Reformation, the whole concept of organized religion in Europe was revolutionized overnight. If the Reformation had been helped by secret societies, then it was a masterstroke of genius on their part.

In 1529, the German princes who supported Luther and his reforming policies protested to Emperor Charles V about the restrictions imposed on the new Christian movement. It was from this outcry that the word Protestant came into being, and a campaign to reform the Roman Church from within was transformed into an alternative religion that challenged the spiritual authority of the pope and the material power of his Holy Roman Empire. Support from the grand masters of the secret societies was offered to the religious reformers because they recognized the Reformation as a means to weaken the influence of the Catholic Church in European political affairs.

The Reformation effectively emasculated the power of the Church. It laid the foundation of the Puritan movement, whose members fled religious persecution in Europe to found a new nation in the Americas based on spiritual principles drawn from Rosicrucian sources. It also provided an atmosphere of open-mindedness and allowed the seeds of the Renaissance to flower based on the best ideas of the pagan classical world. Indirectly, the Reformation gave the impetus for the scientific revolution of the seventeenth century, which centered on well-known Rosicrucians such as Sir Francis Bacon and Sir Isaac Newton, and led after the trauma of the English Civil War to the founding of the Royal Society. In Europe, although the Habsburgs were to rule as Holy Roman Emperors for another three hundred years until Francis II relinquished the crown in 1806, the Reformation destroyed any hope of a united Continent controlled by the Roman Church. Above everything else, the religious reforms of the sixteenth century marked the beginning of the period when the Roman Church became determined to exterminate secret societies because they had weakened its power base.

The seventeenth-century rise of the Rosicrucian Order, which preached political equality, religious freedom, and liberty, and the eighteenth-century revival of the Masonry, which now used the symbolism of medieval craft masonry as spiritual metaphors, posed a further threat to the Church, whose authority over ordinary people was based on its claim to exercise power through apostolic succession from Jesus through St. Peter. The medieval Church had created a climate of fear by promoting the existence of a satanic conspiracy involving anyone who dared to resist Christian doctrine. In contrast, secret societies provided an alternative version of spirituality to their followers. Not only did these societies claim the Church had deliberately subverted the teachings of Jesus, but they taught their followers that there were other sources of spiritual knowledge that were just as valid as Christian belief but predated it by thousands of years.

When the Masonic lodges began to spread throughout Europe, the Church reacted by conducting a smear camp against them similar to the one used against heretics and witches. Anti-Masonic tracts were distributed alleging that unnatural sexual practices including sodomy and flagellation took place in the new Masonic lodges. In 1738, the first papal bull to combat Freemasonry was issued by Pope Clement XII; it threatened any Catholic who became a Mason with excommunication—at that time an extremely serious punishment.

As a result of this bull, some limited police action was taken against Masons in France and elsewhere.

In the 1780s, claims that secret societies such as the Illuminati were using Freemasonry as a cover for radicalism and revolution gave the Church fresh charges to level against it. Many European governments comtemplated action to curb the political excesses of the Masons and they received support from the Vatican in their efforts. Yet the Reformation and the Age of Reason, with its humanistic and rationalist philosophies, had further undermined the Roman Church's authority. The bulls issued by the popes condemning secret societies had an effect only in Catholic countries and, because many of the occult fraternities had influential friends in high places, the extent of the clerical action was very limited.

The climax of the Church's crusade to destroy the influence of Freemasonry came in the nineteenth century. In 1864, Pope Pius X condemned both socialism and the secret societies in his *Syllabus of Errors,* which he published following an investigation of revolutionary activities in Italy. The Carbonari, which had recruited its membership from army officers, policemen, and landowners, had been active in the first three decades of the century and, in 1848, revolution had spread like wildfire across many European countries, including Italy. Twelve months after the publication of *Syllabus of Errors,* the pope again condemned secret societies and specifically attacked Freemasonry as anti-Christian, satanic, and pagan in origin. In 1884, Pope Leo XIII issued a proclamation identifying Masonry as one of the secret societies working to establish Satan's kingdom on earth. He also condemned Freemasonry because he claimed it was attempting to "revive the manners and customs of the pagans."

The nineteenth-century concept of Masonry as a satanic plot was finally dispelled following the exposure of the sensational and bizarre confessions of the high priestess of an occult group called the New Reformed Lodge of the Palladium. These confessions were an elaborate hoax perpetuated by a French journalist, Leo Taxil, who, in 1885 and 1886, published a series of pamphlets allegedly revealing Masonry to be a revival of the Cathar heresy. Taxil presented to a gullible public the high priestess of a secret Masonic order—Diana Vaughan, who, he said, descended from the seventeenth-century alchemist Thomas Vaughan. The lodges of her order admitted both men and women on equal terms and practiced satanism. Vaughan claimed she was associated with the Society of Rosicrucians in Anglia, founded by William Wynn Westcott of the Hermetic Order of the Golden Dawn. Westcott, she claimed, was secretly the leader of the English Luciferians. Taxil informed his readers that Diana Vaughan had given up "the satanic cult of Freemasonry" and had become a convert to the Roman Church.

Diana Vaughan's memoirs, ghostwritten by Taxil, became an overnight bestseller in France. The cover of his anti-Masonic tract *Les Mysteres de la Franc Macconerie* depicts a group of Freemasons worshipping the Baphomet, the idol of the Templars, inside a Masonic temple. In the foreground stands the cloaked figure of an assassin clutching a knife and a female figure with an Arabic scimitar holding up a decapitated head. These lurid books were eagerly accepted by the Vatican and used as evidence of the evils of Freemasonry. Taxil's anti-Masonic campaign was so successful that a conference was organized and was attended by thousands of people eager to hear further revelations. The pope sent a telegram blessing the event and it was read out loud to cheers from the crowd. At the conference, delegates called on Taxil to present his star witness, but the wily journalist told the assembly she had been forced into hiding after threats to her life from Masonic assassins.

The anti-Masonic crusade continued unabated until 1897, when Taxil finally confessed at a press conference that Diana Vaughan had been a figment of his imagination. He claimed to have written the books to expose the ludicrous excesses of the Roman Catholic Church's attacks on Freemasons. This statement, plus the use of Templar symbolism and connections to the Golden Dawn, suggests the anti-Masonic crusade was a "dirty tricks" operation of the secret societies to discredit future attacks on them by the Church. It certainly had that effect, although Taxil was set upon by his outraged journalistic colleagues, who were angry at being duped by his lies, and he had to be rescued by the police.

It has often been claimed that the ultimate objective of the secret societies was to infiltrate the Vatican and place their own man on the papal throne. After all, the Illuminist conspiracy had been exposed in 1785, when a member of the order who was a priest died in an accident. He was killed by lightning while on a secret mission and his body was taken to a nearby convent. A nun preparing the body for burial found a cache of documents sewn into the lining of his cassock that outlined plans for the destruction of the Catholic Church from the inside. The authorities promptly outlawed the order, and its leader, Adam Weishaupt, was banished from Bavaria. Although he died in obscurity some years later, in the period immediately following his banishment, Weishaupt laid the foundation for the completion of his grand plan, which many believe is still in operation today.

Certainly, one of the main objectives of the Carbonari was to infiltrate the Church at all levels and eventually have one of its own members elected as pope. Some modern critics of the Roman Church, especially those with right-wing political views who support ultratraditionalist doctrines such as the Latin Mass, see in the liberalization of the Church in recent years proof that its hierarchy has been penetrated at the highest level by agents of secret societies who are working for its eventual downfall.

In his book *The Broken Cross,* Piers Compton, an ex-editor of the Catholic newspaper the *Universe,* traces the alleged infiltration of the Roman Church by the Illuminati. He cites as evidence the use of the Illuminatist symbol of the eye in the triangle by leading Catholics. It has been used by the Jesuits, has appeared as the seal of the Philadelphia Eucharistic Congress in 1976, and has been featured on a special issue of Vatican stamps in 1978. Compton further claims that Pope John XXIII, who died in June 1963, used the symbol on his personal cross.

According to Compton, Pope John (formerly Bishop Angelo Roncalli) was an initiate of a secret society. Roncalli was consecrated as a bishop in 1935 and entered the Vatican Diplomatic Service as the apostolic visitor of the Holy See in Sofia, Turkey. It was while he was in Turkey that Roncalli allegedly became a member of a secret society whose emblem was the rose and the cross. During the papacy of John, from 1958 to 1963, there were instigated the first major reforms in the Catholic Church's theology since the Middle Ages. In the eyes of traditionalists, these reforms were a program of radical change dictated by the grand masters of secret societies to their papal puppet.

In his book, Compton claims that several hundred leading Catholic clerics are members of secret societies. He quotes a 1976 Italian journal article listing over seventy-five Vatican officials who were associated with these groups—including the private secretary of Pope Paul VI, the director general of Vatican Radio, the archbishop of Florence, the prelate of Milan, the assistant editor of the Vatican newspaper, several Italian bishops, and the abbot of the Order of St. Benedict. It is presumed that the secret society involved is Freemasonry, although at least one name on the list is said to have family connections to the Rosicrucian Order.

In his exposé of secret societies and their alleged influence on the Vatican, Compton singles out the nineteenth-century Cardinal Mariano Rompalla (1843–1913) as one of their key agents inside the Church. This Sicilian liberal had radical political views and rose to the position of secretary of state in the papacy of Leo XIII. When the pope died in 1903, Rompalla emerged as the leading candidate to follow him. He failed in his bid only because the cardinal of Krakow, acting on behalf of Emperor Josef von Habsburg, exercised a veto. As the rulers of the Holy Roman Empire until 1806, the Habsburgs had retained the right to veto any papal candidate they regarded as unfit to hold office.

Considering the Austrian emperor's dislike of secret societies and their meddling in European politics, his action is significant. Following his defeat, the cardinal seems to have had very little influence in Vatican affairs. It is said that after his death, documents were found among his papers linking him to both the OTO and Aleister Crowley. Unfortunately, the incumbent pope was so horrified by the documents' contents that he ordered them burned, so we will never know what they contained.

With the death of the reforming Pope John in 1963, the Catholic

Church entered a turbulent period in its history that saw the Vatican shaken by financial scandal caused by its doubtful relationship to a secret Masonic lodge, the Mafia, and right-wing extremists. The new pope, Giovanni Montini, the former archbishop of Milan, was regarded by his critics as a socialist. It was claimed that he attempted to make a pact with the Italian Communist Party after World War II. In fact, the new pope's political views were more complex than this flirtation with left-wing politics might suggest. Montini certainly had very strong anti-Nazi views, and he exercised these from 1940 to 1945 as a section head in the Vatican intelligence service in occupied Europe.

Archbishop Montini's father was a leading Social Democrat and his family connections allowed his son, as Vatican secretary of state, to meet with leading Italian Communists in 1944 to discuss power sharing with the Socialists and Democrats in a postwar Italy. According to a Central Intelligence Agency (CIA) report of the meeting, Montini was hopeful that communications could be established after the war between the Vatican and the Soviet Union, despite the anti-Communist views of Pope Pius XI.

Montini's political affiliations seem to have changed dramatically after the war. By the early 1950s, he had become directly involved with the CIA through its front organization, the American Committee for a United Europe (ACUE), and he allegedly worked for the agency spying on fellow priests with left-wing opinions. The ACUE was founded in 1949 and its first chairman was William "Wild Bill" Donovan, a wartime hero of the Office of Strategic Services (OSS), which was a forerunner of the CIA. The secretary of the ACUE was a director of the Council on Foreign Relations (CFR) and a coordinator of the later Trilateral Commission, both groups that are regarded by conspiracy theorists as front organizations for the modern activities of the Illuminati in international power politics.

The aim of the ACUE was, as its name suggests, to provide American assistance to the plan for the political unification of Europe in the postwar period. This idea had the support of many leading politicians, including Winston Churchill, who frequently endorsed the proposal for a "united states of Europe" after the war. The ACUE was a product of Cold War mentality and it promoted a policy of anti-Communism. It was secretly funded by the American government and had links to Prince Bernhard of the Netherlands and a former director of the British Special Operations Executive (SOE). This elite secret unit had been set up by Churchill and it parachuted undercover agents into occupied Europe to perform acts of subversion and sabotage.

When Cardinal Montini was elected as Pope Paul VI in 1963, his critics noted that the Vatican's previous hard line on Freemasonry notably relaxed. In 1917, coinciding with World War I and the Bolshevik Revolution, the Vatican had forbidden Catholics to become Freemasons. Any Catholic who was found to be a Mason or a member of "any other secret society, which plotted against the state" could be excommunicated. With the papacy of Paul, this harsh stricture was relaxed and Catholics could join a Masonic lodge, provided membership did not involve anticlerical activities. This relaxation led to the celebration of a special Mass in 1975 by a Brazilian archbishop to mark the fortieth anniversary of a local Masonic lodge.

In 1978, Pope Paul became aware of rumors of an imminent Communist takeover in Italy. It was reported that the Vatican transferred five billion dollars of its financial holdings from Italy to the United States because the pope had lost confidence in the European democratic system. Paul allegedly believed that Europe was on the verge of a left-wing revolution. Rumors circulated in the Vatican that the pope was even willing to break with tradition and retire. His chosen successor, a non-Italian European, could then be elected and could make a deal with the Eastern Bloc to preserve the Church in a future Communist-dominated Europe.

The pope's fear of a left-wing takeover was shared by secret societies and especially by members of the Masonic lodge in Italy. Its public exposure highlighted the clandestine financial and political intrigues within the Vatican and possibly led to the murder of the next occupant of the papal throne. Propaganda Two, or P2, as it became more popularly known, was an elitist Masonic lodge founded in 1960 by a wealthy businessman, Licio Gelli, who had fought with the fascist Italian Black Shirts in the Spanish Civil War in the 1930s and had fraternized with the Nazis during the 1939–1945 conflict. Despite his right-wing views, Gelli had also established links to Communist partisans during the hostilities, so he escaped prosecution as a war criminal. Gelli had connections to various fascist groups in Latin America, the CIA, and the Mafia. He regarded his membership in Freemasonry as an important aspect of his political work. In 1976, he told friends, "Freemasonry hates Communism because it is contrary to the idea of the dignity of personal individualism, is the destroyer of fundamental rights, which are the divine inheritance of all men, and is the enemy of the Masonic principle to have faith in God."

The anti-Communist crusade motivating Gelli and the other members of the P2 lodge allowed it to become a front for the CIA's subversive activities in Italy during the 1970s. Several leading members of P2 received financial support from the agency to fight Italian Communism, and they channeled funds to other anti-Communist and anti-Soviet groups overseas. The political philosophy of P2 was centered on the creation of an alternative government that would take power if Italy was ever faced with a Communist uprising or even a victory by the Communists in a democratic election. The plan was for P2 to create a "white coup" by counterrevolutionaries, with the outside assistance of the CIA and American troops if required, and to establish a right-wing, pro–United States regime.

In common with political secret societies of the past such as the Illuminati and the Thule Society, the P2 lodge drew its members, estimated at twenty-five hundred, from the highest levels of the social, political, and military establishment. They included three cabinet ministers; the heads of the Italian secret service; the chiefs of staff of the army, navy, and defense ministry; the commanders of the paramilitary and customs police; eighteen members of Parliament; twenty-one judges; leading businessmen; journalists; and political commentators. P2 also had overseas branches in Cuba, South America, and the United

States and was described by an official Italian government report as "a secret sect that combined politics with business with the intention of destroying the constitution of the country."

According to an article by Jonathan Marshall in the parapolitical journal *Lobster,* P2 also had connections to neo-Templar groups in France. As grand master of P2, Gelli had made contact with Jacques Massie, a Marseilles police inspector who was a member of an extreme right-wing group called Service d'Action Critique (SAC). Massie and five members of his family were gunned down when he allegedly betrayed the secrets of the group to his police colleagues. Other members of SAC included prominent political figures, former mercenaries who had fought with the OAS terrorists in Algeria, and underworld elements. Massie was involved in smuggling arms from Turkey to both the left-wing Red Brigade and neo-Nazi terrorists in Italy to fund the political activities of SAC. Conspiracy theorists say this support for opposing political viewpoints is one of the hallmarks of the Illuminati, which uses both sides for its own ends.

While he was in Marseilles visiting Massie, the grand master of P2 had meetings with representatives of a neo-Templar order who sympathized with the aims of SAC. Gelli allegedly discussed his plans for the future of Italy with his new friends. In France, the modern Templar orders included top government officials, bankers, army and police officers, and members of the French secret service (SDCE), the equivalent of the British MI6. The orders were divided up into several different branches, some of whom were associated with Masonic and political groups in France, which financed anti-Communism activities.

One of these neo-Templar groups was exposed in the 1960s and was discovered to have wealthy members with Vatican connections. This group was pro-Catholic, pro-monarchist, and anti-Communist, and one of its leaders, Constantin Melnik, was associated with the French secret service, Radio Free Europe (a CIA front organization), and the Rand Corporation (a right-wing think tank financed by the Pentagon). Melnik was of French birth but his parents were White

Russians and he claimed his grandfather had been the personal physician of Czar Nicholas II.

A further, if unlikely, link among the Vatican, the Romanovs, and secret societies was also provided in the 1960s when the deputy head of the Polish secret service defected to the United States. Mikael Goliniewski provided the CIA with a flood of sensational revelations concerning the alleged penetration of Western society by Soviet moles. The agency became suspicious, however, when the Polish defector changed his name to Alexi Nicholaevitch Romanov and announced publicly that he was the secret son of Nicholas II.

Goliniewski was supported in this claim by a right-wing chivalric order called the Knights of Malta, who traced their pedigree back to the Crusaders who fought in the Holy Land. According to occult tradition, one of the grand masters of the Knights of Malta, Manuel de Fonseca, was an initiate of the Templar tradition in the eighteenth century and had introduced Count Cagliostro to Templar thought and practice. The modern order boasted it had sympathizers inside the Vatican, the Russian Orthodox Church, and the White Russian émigré groups in the West who were seeking to reestablish the monarchy in their homeland. This Russian connection derived from 1778, when Napoleon invaded Malta and the knights were offered sanctuary by Czar Peter I, who is credited with forming a clandestine group of army officers and Russian Orthodox priests known as the Secret Circle, which was fanatically dedicated to the preservation and protection of mother Russia. The Secret Circle, which had links to the Knights of Malta, allegedly survived the Bolshevik Revolution and infiltrated its agents into the Western intelligence services with the aim of destroying Communism and restoring a White Russian regime in Moscow.

The modern Knights of Malta supported the ultratraditionalist, right-wing faction among the cardinals in the Vatican who opposed the reforms of Pope John and those who supported him. It campaigned for the return of the old Latin Mass and regarded the liberals in the Church as enemies of the true faith. In recent years, rumors have circulated linking the Knights of Malta to both extreme right-wing political groups and the CIA.

Goliniewski had an odd connection to the British Royal family. Lord Louis Mountbatten, uncle of Prince Charles, was a leading critic of the Polish defector's claim that he was a descendant of the Romanovs. Mountbatten was related to the Russian royal family through Queen Victoria, and he was also a strong opponent of the Knights of Malta and a critic of their association with the CIA. Mountbatten's name had been raised when Winston Churchill and President Roosevelt, who was allegedly a member of an Illuminist-inspired secret society, discussed the revival of the old Habsburg empire in the postwar period as part of their grand plan for a united Europe. Churchill believed the revival of a European supermonarchy would act as an antidote to Communist expansion plans in postwar Germany, France, Italy, and Austria. Mountbatten was proposed as a suitable candidate for emperor, as was Dr. Otto von Habsburg, who was a leading exponent of a pan-European federation. In the 1970s, when there were rumors circulating in Britain of a right-wing coup against the Labor government of Harold Wilson, it was said that Lord Mountbatten was approached by the plotters to be the head of a new military government, but he refused.

The exposure of the illegal activities of the P2 lodge not only revealed a web of right-wing conspirators engaged in subversive acts but it also exposed a financial scandal involving high officials in the Vatican. This scandal came to light with the collapse of the Banco Ambrosiano, whose managing director was Roberto Calvi, a staunch Catholic but also a leading personality in the P2 lodge. In 1971, Calvi had been introduced to the director of the Vatican Bank, Bishop Marcinkus, by another P2 member who was a financial advisor to Pope Paul. When the bishop became a director of Banco Ambrosiano, it was claimed that its subsidiaries were actively engaged in laundering illegal funds for the Mafia. Links were quickly established between the Banco Ambrosiano and the Vatican Bank, entangling the Catholic Church in a financial operation that connected it to Freemasonry, right-wing extremists, and organized crime.

Calvi's task in P2 was to use his extensive contacts among international bankers to set up an overseas structure that could act as an alternative to the Italian banking system in the event of a Communist government coming to power. Although a devout Catholic, Calvi ruthlessly used his membership in P2 to further his own financial ends. When he apparently committed suicide by hanging himself under Blackfriars Bridge in London, it was rumored that he had been murdered to prevent him from revealing the inside secrets of the links among the Vatican, the Mafia, and international Freemasonry. This theory was reinforced by the fact that his briefcase, allegedly containing documents implicating the Vatican with Banco Ambrosiano and the P2 lodge, vanished after his death.

The P2 scandal came to light after the death of Pope Paul VI in the summer of 1978. Albino Luciani, who had been the patriarch of Venice, was elected by the College of Cardinals and took the name John Paul I. He held socialist views and seemed determined to bring a new style of papacy to the office of vicar of Christ. John Paul was quickly dubbed the smiling pope by the media because of his relaxed manner, sense of humor, and informality. He was not just a good public relations officer for the Church but was also a sophisticated liberal who advocated artificial birth control and wanted to relax the Catholic hard line on divorce, abortion, and homosexuality.

It would also appear that the new pontiff planned to investigate the Church's recent financial affairs, sell off many of its financial holdings to provide money for the poor, and reform the Vatican's banking system, which had been dominated by the influence of the P2 lodge. John Paul I further shocked many traditionalists by openly referring to God as both the father and the mother in a sermon to the crowds in St. Peter's Square. Liberal-minded theologians had been discussing for many years the androgynous nature of God, but such a controversial view had always been regarded by Vatican hard liners as a heresy. Within a few days of the new pope's election, gossip was circulating in the corridors of the Vatican that he was a heretic, a practicing homosexual, and a crypto-Communist.

Predictably, John Paul I faced severe opposition from conservative elements in the Church to his campaign to cleanse the corruption that had been allowed to fester during the previous papacy. Shortly after he was elected, the pontiff was presented with a list of prominent Masons in the Catholic hierarchy. He also became aware of the activities of the P2 lodge and how it had supported and nurtured the ultratraditionalist elements in the Vatican to create divisions in the Church. The new pope had powerful enemies, and when he died suddenly in September 1978, there were many people inside the Vatican and in the shadowy world where criminals, political extremists, and renegade members of secret societies plot and conspire who were secretly relieved. Since his death, rumors have spread that John Paul I was poisoned by assassins who feared his reforming policies and investigations into the links between the Church and the P2 lodge.

After the death of the smiling pope, a Polish cardinal was elected as the next pontiff and took the name John Paul II in reverence to his short-lived predecessor. At first, the media portrayed the Polish pope as a liberal in the same mold as his namesake, but it soon became clear that he was a traditionalist in matters of Catholic doctrine. In a series of keynote sermons, John Paul II reinforced the Church's traditional teachings on birth control, homosexuality, and family life. As a possible response to the public uproar over the P2 revelations, the pope also reinforced the Church's historical opposition to Freemasonry. In 1981, the Congregation for the Propagation of the Doctrine of the Faith, which is the modern equivalent of the medieval Inquisition, issued a declaration condemning Freemasonry and confirming that any Catholic who belonged to its lodges would be excommunicated.

Yet the new pope did very little to deal with criticisms of the Vatican's dealings with the Banco Ambrosiano. In fact, in 1987 the pope defended his long-time friend Archbishop Marcinkus when special prosecutors investigating Calvi's mysterious suicide accused him of fraud. The prosecutors decided that the archbishop should face legal charges, but the pope responded by granting Marcinkus sanctuary inside the

Vatican, where, because the Holy See was an independent state and outside Italian legal jurisdiction, the arrest warrant was not valid. This act by the pope can be interpreted as an attempt to limit the damage to the Church by the Banco Ambrosiano affair and an example of loyal friendship, rather than a conspiracy involving secret societies.

The financial investments made by Pope Paul VI in American banks in the 1970s, when he feared a Communist coup in Italy, were relocated, according to Vatican insiders, following the assassination attempt on John Paul II by a Turkish gunman in 1981. A disinformation cover story was spread in the media by Western intelligence services alleging that the shooting had been an attempt by the KGB, who used the Bulgarian secret service, to silence the pope's support for solidarity in his native Poland. Insiders pointed out, however, that the would-be assassin had no obvious links to the Eastern Bloc and in fact was a member of the Grey Wolves, a right-wing Turkish terrorist group funded by the CIA and Italian neo-fascists.

It has been alleged that the Vatican was warned in advance of a possible plot to kill the pope. The source for this information was a high-ranking official in the Soviet embassy in Rome. Because of this tip-off and information collected by the Vatican intelligence service, the pope was convinced the murder attempt was not a Soviet conspiracy but instead the work of Western business interests. On the day he was shot, John Paul II planned to launch an attack condemning the immorality of Western capitalism and demanding a return to spiritual and moral values in European and American society.

Despite his traditional views on moral issues, there were still some extreme voices within the Vatican who speculated that Pope John Paul II might be under the influence of secret societies. Since the days of Pope John XXIII, a radical movement had existed within the Church that sought closer links among Catholicism and other Christian churches, with the ultimate aim of reversing the divisions of the Reformation that weakened Christianity. A special report was leaked in 2007 that suggested that the Anglican and Roman Churches should unite under the leadership of the pope. This event would certainly not be welcomed by secret societies, but in the pope's desire to support this idea, the ultratraditionalists had seen evidence of an anti-Catholic conspiracy because generally the Anglican Church is today more liberal in its policies on such subjects as abortion, married clergy, and women priests.

At the celebrations in honor of St. Francis of Assissi in 1986, which stressed the unity of all the world's religions, the pope participated in a multireligious prayer for world peace. Traditionalists were horrified to see the pontiff happily sharing a platform with a Tibetan lama, a Hindu swami, a Native American medicine man, a Jewish rabbi, and a Maori high priest. It was noted that the unity of all the world religions and the recognition that they all derived from the same ancient source was the central philosophy of the secret societies.

8

THE OCCULT
AND MODERN POLITICS

The involvement of the P2 lodge with neo-fascism and the Vatican is only one example, albeit a negative one, of the way in which occultism and secret societies have influenced modern politics. Exactly how great this influence has manifested since the end of World War I, except for their role in the early history of National Socialism in Germany, is a matter of debate. Frequently, writers on the subject have fallen into the trap of projecting onto the subject their own ideological views, both left and right, and their personal prejudice. This has created sensational scenarios of the sinister motives of those groups and individuals who allegedly operate in modern times as agents of the Illuminati and other occult-related secret societies.

Typical of these politically motivated conspiracy theorists was Nesta Webster, author of a series of bestselling books in the 1920s that allegedly exposed the secret Jewish plan for world domination. She claimed that the Jews, working through secret societies and the international banking system, were the éminences grises behind the revolutionary movements of the eighteenth and nineteenth centuries. The fact that the Templars revered Solomon's temple and were international bankers, the allegation that the House of Rothschild financed the Illuminati, and the use of Judaic symbolism in Freemasonry apparently added fuel to Webster's speculative theories of a historical Jewish conspiracy. Webster believed she was the reincarnation of a countess who had been executed in the French Revolution and was convinced it was her duty in this lifetime to expose the secret societies that had plotted the 1789 uprising.

In the 1920s, when anti-Semitism was rife, Webster's theories were widely accepted by the British establishment, including such well-known politicians as Sir Winston Churchill, who quoted extensively from her works in his attacks on the Bolsheviks in Russia. Webster came to be regarded by the British government as an unofficial expert on secret societies and revolutionary movements and she gave lectures on the subject to the armed forces and the secret service. Webster revealed her true political colors in 1923. Her books had reviled Marxism as the modern cover for the "Jewish menace," and in that year she went a step further by joining the British Fascist Party, which imitated Mussolini's new political movement in Italy. This organization later developed into the British Union of Fascists, led by Sir Oswald Mosley, which received considerable media attention and public support in the 1930s.

Although Webster's researches were heavily prejudiced by her anti-Semitic views and hatred of Communism, the basic theme of her books was the alleged manipulation of historical events by politically motivated conspirators who used secret societies and the occult tradition as their cover. This theme has since been taken up by other modern researchers, who claim to be able to recognize the influence of the occult puppet masters in modern politics. To establish how deeply secret societies have penetrated international politics, it is necessary to understand how the history of the twentieth century has been molded by a hidden power group. This group is not necessarily aligned to either the left or right wing of the conventional political movements that have taken a public role in shaping world events in the years since the end of World War I. It operates within both capitalism and communism and has as its ultimate goal a politico-spiritual vision transcending both these materialistic systems used to control the masses.

The four years from 1914 to 1918 represent one of the most

significant periods in modern history. They saw the destruction of three of the great imperial powers that had dominated European politics in the previous century: In this short period of time the Habsburg, Romanov, and Hohenstauffen dynasties were destroyed. World War I also saw the weakening of the foundations of the British empire, and both America and Russia emerged from the war as potential superpowers of the future. The war also saw the climax of a long history of German nationalism, which through its messiah Adolf Hitler, spawned a new political force that twenty years later would be responsible for another major European conflict. From that terrible holocaust was born the nuclear age and the suicidal confrontation between the opposing power structures of West and East that held the world hostage with the threat of imminent global destruction for nearly fifty years.

If we are to accept the role played by secret societies in World War I, the Russian Revolution, and the rise of National Socialism—as did the leaders of the defeated nations in 1918—it has to be realized that these influences, both positive and negative, did not wane with the defeat of Germany in 1945. They continued into the postwar period and are still with us today. In general, as far as it can be detected by those who are not directly in contact with its working, this influence could be categorized as basically benign in nature. Yet the unpalatable fact must also be faced that in many instances the pursuit and exercise of power in the political arena has a corrupting effect, especially when it encounters the inherent weaknesses of human nature.

The exposure of the P2 lodge in Italy was a rare example of the workings of a renegade secret society becoming public knowledge through the misdeeds of its leadership. Usually, because of their very nature, secret societies work behind the scenes and their activities seldom become known to the outside world. Any interpretation of their activities must therefore be confined to an analysis of the outward signs of their influence within the overall pattern of international politics. These signs are occasionally revealed in major historical events or sociopolitical movements whose impact on mass consciousness is so great that the hidden hands behind them are briefly revealed to general view, albeit in a shadowy and indistinct form.

One classic example is the one-world government movement, which, in the decade following World War I, seemed to have become the focus for the efforts of the leaders of respectable secret societies who played no role in the events leading up to the 1914–1918 conflict. Their goal seemed to have been the elimination of the risk of any future outbreaks of war on a global scale. One of the political figures who played an influential role in this new movement was President Woodrow Wilson of the United States, who was allegedly a secret member of the Rosicrucian Order. Wilson was a statesman with an unusually idealistic view of world politics. This sometimes led his more realistic critics to denounce him as a naive romantic. His foreign policy reversed past trends by respecting the rights of small nations and promoting nonintervention in the domestic disputes of other countries.

This foreign policy was responsible for Wilson's reluctance to allow the United States to be drawn into the war between Germany and Britain in 1914. He adopted a neutral stance and in fact engaged in protracted negotiations with the German kaiser to attain a peace settlement. Yet when details were revealed of a proposed military alliance among Mexico, Japan, and Germany, which would have involved Mexican troops invading Texas, Wilson was reluctantly forced to act. In April 1917 the U.S. Congress approved the president's declaration of war on the Axis powers and American troops were committed to the European conflict. It has been suggested that this alliance was in fact false and an excuse used by warmongers to commit America to the European war.

While the war was waged, influential power groups had already been urging the developed nations to create a neutral organization dedicated to international cooperation. Wilson was a prominent advocate of this idea, which he saw as a unique historical opportunity to prevent future armed conflict between nations and to secure a lasting world peace. This concept was also supported by secret societies. Following the entry of the Americans into the war, popular uprisings in the Austro-Hungarian empire and public protests in Germany forced the Axis powers to seek a negotiated settlement, and in 1918 a peace conference was convened in Paris to discuss terms.

President Wilson had already sent his special advisor, Colonel E. M. House, to begin talks with several of the Allied governments with the objective of creating an international organization for world peace. Wilson himself traveled to the Paris peace conference, where the foundations of the new League of Nations were laid. A covenant was drawn up by the founding members who agreed on a joint policy of collective security. The nations who participated in the formation of the League of Nations pledged to act jointly against any aggressor. They also promised to solve international disputes by arbitration, pursue graduated disarmament, and establish an international court of justice.

In the 1920s, the League of Nations set up its headquarters in Geneva, a city regarded by secret societies as one of the world's major sacred power centers, and it began to pursue the arduous task of promoting world peace and security. Unfortunately, the failure of the U.S. Congress to ratify the covenant of American membership weakened the position of the League. In the 1930s, the organization's impotence in preventing the Sino-Japanese War, the invasion of Abyssinia (now Ethiopia) by Italy, and the annexation of Poland by Hitler contributed to its eventual demise with the outbreak of hostilities in 1939.

Despite the failure of the United States to become a full member of the League of Nations, President Wilson did not abandon his dream of world government, which he pursued on different lines. In 1919, Colonel House traveled back to Paris, this time to have discussions with members of a British quasi-political group called the Round Table, which also had branches in North America. In a meeting held at the Majestic Hotel in May 1919, the idea was proposed for an alternative international organization to the League of Nations. This new group would act as the coordinating agency for the establishment of a future world government dominated by Britain and the United States.

The Round Table had been conceived by the nineteenth-century diamond and gold magnate Cecil Rhodes, who gave his name to Rhodesia (now Zimbabwe). Rhodes was a fanatical exponent of the one-world government concept, and the idea behind the Round Table was to promote British imperialism worldwide. Conspiracy theorists have identified Rhodes's group as a classic example of a semipublic secret society with internationalist ambitions. It had been founded because Rhodes fervently believed that British values should be extended throughout the world to an imperial global power capable of rendering war impossible. He was allegedly a disciple of Professor John Ruskin, the radical Oxford don who taught philosophy and art in the 1870s and has been claimed as a follower of Adam Weishaupt and his Illuminist doctrines. In his will, Cecil Rhodes left instructions to the international banker and financier Lord Rothschild that requested Rothschild expand the work of the Round Table, which was modeled on the organizational structure of the Jesuits and the Freemasons.

From its inception, the Round Table had been influential in shaping British government policy, especially as it related to foreign affairs. It is believed to have played an important role in the events leading up to World War I. With the successful outcome of the 1918 peace conference, the Round Table was anxious to extend its political influence on an international scale. An American branch of the group had already been founded, and when Colonel House approached it with his president's grand plan for a world government, the organization was more than eager to become involved in his idealistic venture.

The new international grouping that came out of the Paris meeting was on a smaller scale than the League of Nations, reflecting its more modest ambitions, but it shared the same aspirations. In Britain, the organization was called the Institute for International Affairs (IIA), while in New York it operated as the Council for Foreign Relations (CFR). The finances for the group came from wealthy international bankers, and the organization quickly recruited prominent American and British political figures known to support its aims. Initially, its critics regarded the CFR as an elitist, right-wing power group, which was even accused of helping to finance Hitler's rise to power, although no evidence has ever been found to support this claim. Following World War II, however, the CFR was labeled a promoter of international socialism through the United Nations. Conspiracy theorists claim it was the CFR who supported Henry Wallace's plan to have the Illuminist symbol of the eye in the triangle on the one-dollar note. The CFR's apparent contradictory political ideals are said to be typical of modern Illuminati front groups, which allegedly use both right and left political ideologies to further a cause that transcends conventional politics.

In the eyes of its opponents, the CFR is currently dedicated to destroying the sovereignty of the United States, reversing the democratic process, which instigated the American Revolution in 1776, and promoting internationalism and the foundation of a world superstate that embraces both capitalism and communism in a new political order. The evidence for this seems to be largely based on the neutral stance the CFR adopted in American politics. It recruited its membership from both the Democratic and Republican parties, and leading members of the CFR have included Adlai Stevenson, Robert and Edward Kennedy, Hubert Humphrey, John Foster Dulles, Robert McNamara, Henry Kissinger, and Nelson Rockefeller. Several men who were CFR members early in their political careers later became presidents of the United States, such as Dwight Eisenhower, John Kennedy, Richard Nixon, and Jimmy Carter.

After World War II, the CFR turned its attention to supporting the United Nations Organization, founded in 1945. The idea for this international organization developed in U.S. state development policy documents drawn up at the beginning of the war. A study group called the Committee on Post-War Problems (CPWP) was set up with the brief to formulate plans for a new international and social organization to replace the old League of Nations. This policy unit was allegedly staffed by undercover CFR agents working within the State Department and manipulating the American government's foreign policy.

President Franklin Roosevelt, who is said to have had secret society connections, first used the term United Nations in the January 1942 Declaration of United Nations, which was issued by twenty-six nations that had pledged to fight the Axis powers of Germany, Italy, and Japan.

It was not until the end of the war, however, that plans to form the United Nations were seriously considered. A conference on international organizations met in San Francisco from April to June 1945, and deliberated on proposals that had been previously worked out by China, the USSR, the United Kingdom, and the United States during a series of high-level meetings from August to October 1944.

The United Nations officially came into existence in October 1945, with the purpose of securing international peace in the postwar period. As with its predecessor, the League of Nations, the United Nations immediately found this a difficult task, even with the use of an international peace-keeping force drawn from the armies of its member states. Its first challenge was involvement in the Korean War, which threatened to turn into World War III after the military intervention of China. Since the 1960s the United Nations has become more concerned with economic and social issues, including education, science, environmental protection, health, the refugee problem, disaster relief, drug abuse, racism, and human rights. Although the United Nations has had some success in these areas, it seems unlikely that the organization will provide the basis for a future world government.

Conspiracy theorists have always regarded the United Nations with suspicion because of the alleged involvement of the CFR in its creation. Further suspicion was cast on the organization by the activities of a shadowy group called the United World Federalists (UWF), founded in 1947 by two CFR members. The UWF promoted setting up a world governmental structure under the auspices of the United Nations and involving powerful countries from both the East and West. Right-wingers who opposed the alleged Soviet influence on the United Nations saw in this plan an Illuminist conspiracy to create a one-world state based on Marxism. Left-wingers, on the other hand, interpreted it as an attempt by right-wing governments to achieve global domination for their ideology.

The activities of the CFR have been linked to two other political think tanks that emerged in the postwar period and whose secret origins and unorthodox political views have labeled them as covers for secret societies: the Bilderberg Group and the Trilateral Commission, which have been suspected of being covert power groups engaged in the secret manipulation of international affairs. Because these groups go to extraordinary lengths to avoid publicity, hold their meetings in private, and guard their important members by taking extreme security measures, the speculation concerning their real motives has become more and more sensationalized over the years.

The Bilderberg Group was founded in May 1954. Its first meeting took place in the Bilderberg Hotel in Osterbeck in Holland, hence the name it adopted. The chairman at the first meeting was Prince Bernhard of the Netherlands, who remained in this position until he was forced to resign in 1976 over the financial scandal involving the Lockheed Aircraft Corporation. Bernhard was replaced by the ex-British prime minister Sir Alec Douglas-Home. There is no official membership list for the group, but at its meetings held once or twice a year, eighty to a hundred people drawn from the political, financial, and media spheres are invited to attend, although few reveal afterward the discussions that take place behind closed doors.

What prompted the foundation of the Bilderberg Group? In his book *The Global Manipulators,* Robert Eringer links them to the CIA and international Freemasonry. According to Eringer, the first Bilderberg conference was organized by the mysterious Dr. Joseph Retinger, who had been involved in secret activities for nearly half a century and was reputed to be the top agent for international Freemasonry. Retinger knew everybody who was anybody in European politics, although it was rumored that he had been banned from 10 Downing Street when he accused the wife of the then prime minister, Lord Asquith, of being a practicing lesbian.

During World War I, Retinger was in Mexico working for President Wilson when be uncovered a conspiracy by Texas oilmen to spark a war between the Mexicans and the United States. Despite his Masonic connections, in the 1920s he was involved in special missions for the Vatican, and in 1924 he established a secret organization dedicated to European unity. Despite the rise of Nazism, he continued his crusade for a united Europe, and when war broke out, he joined the Polish Free Forces in London. He parachuted into occupied Poland with the British SOE to assist the Resistance during the abortive Warsaw uprising.

In 1946, at a lecture given to the Institute for International Affairs (the British branch of the CFR) in London, Retinger expanded on his personal vision of a united Europe as a bulwark against postwar Soviet expansionist policies. His morbid fear of Communism led him to join the American Committee for a United Europe (ACUE), which was channeling funds to anti-Communist groups in Europe and had as its top agent in the Vatican the future Pope Paul VI. In his function as a member of ACUE, Retinger approached Prince Bernhard of the Netherlands and suggested that he use his royal influence to help assemble a group of influential Europeans who shared the two men's anti-Communist views and belief in a united Europe. This new group would act as a select think tank, coordinating policies designed to combat the alleged Red menace to Western society. In 1952, Retinger made contact with the CIA and asked the agency to provide financial and moral support for the venture. Two years later, the first meeting of the group was held in Holland with delegates attending from Europe and the United States.

Conspiracy theorists who see the Bilderberg Group as an Illuminist front cite the fact that its steering committee consists of the odd number 39, which is 13 + 13 + 13. In occultism, the number 13 has many mystical meanings and sinister associations. They also point out that Prince Bernhard's wife, Queen Juliana, had been involved in occult practices, including spiritualism and healing. Her daughter, Crown Princess Beatrix, attended a Bilderberg conference in 1965. This meeting was also attended by Prince Phillip and Lord Mountbatten and was held at the Villa d'Este on Lake Como in Italy. Como was of course the ancient headquarters of the Order of the Comacine—the forerunners of the medieval Freemasons.

The Bilderberg Group was originally founded as an anti-Communist organization with a predominantly right-wing membership. In 1976, however, fifteen representatives from the Soviet Union attended one of its conferences in the Arizona desert. This move was interpreted by many observers as a shift in focus by the group from a united Europe opposing the Eastern Bloc to the idealistic concept of a world government as promoted by internationalists within secret societies. This change of emphasis coincided with the new policy of détente with the Soviet Union supported by CFR member Jimmy Carter when he became president.

Another mysterious power group associated with the CFR and the Bilderberg Group is the Trilateral Commission, which dabbles in international politics and supports the world government movement. The Trilateralists were the brainchild of certain American politicians who, in the early 1970s, became concerned that the traditional links between the United States and Europe were weakening. Their plan was to create a new community of nations centered on North America but that included western Europe and Japan, which they identified as a future superpower. The plan for this community was to begin with a policy group composed of industrialists and politicians from each geopolitical sphere. While on paper the Trilateralists are confined to cooperation among the United States, Japan, and Europe, the high number of CFR members who also belong to it suggests that its inner doctrine is based on the establishment of a world government.

The director of the Trilateral Commission in the 1970s was Zbigniew Brzezinski, a special advisor on national security in the Carter administration and a member of the CFR. He was quoted as saying, "The world is not likely to unite behind a common ideology or a supergovernment. The only practical hope is that it will now respond to a common concern for its own survival. The active promotion of such trilateral cooperation must now become the central priority of U.S. policy."

Both the Bilderberg Group and the Trilateralists act as shadow governments, promoting internationalist policies of European unity and world government. They act as a form of political Freemasonry, offering world leaders and national insiders the chance to meet in secret to exchange information and discuss undisclosed social changes that are then put into practice in their respective countries. Individual members of these groups deliberately play down the real significance of these meetings, but world leaders and top politicians take out valuable time from their work schedules to attend them. Of course, it is mere speculation to recognize in the workings of these covert power groups any resemblance to the invisible college of the sixteenth-century Rosicrucians writ large on the modern stage of international politics.

Originally, Utopian and libertarian concepts were promoted by the medieval Freemasons and the Rosicrucians. The occult adepts who operated at the highest levels in these secret societies were genuinely concerned with the progress of humanity on both the material and spiritual levels. They supported the political concept of an equalized society in which everyone had the right to worship God in whatever form he or she believed and to follow the politics of his or her choice, providing they were based on democracy and freedom of thought and action. At a time when millions were enslaved in the medieval feudal system, secret societies taught that all men and women were free individuals.

Secret societies advocated the reform of those social conditions that imprisoned the soul, universal education for the masses, and civil liberty. They believed the advantages of the new scientific research and the gifts of artistic creation were not the hidden treasure of a few, but instead should be available to everyone. Secret societies also believed that if knowledge were made more widespread, a natural social progress would lead to the evolution of the individual from the common herd, and this was their long-term objective. The foundation of specialist organizations such as the Royal Society, social reform movements, and alternative religious groups were only staging posts for the grand plan of uniting religion, science, and the arts into a universal philosophy for the mass enlightenment of the human race.

A very important aspect of the work of these secret societies has always been the ultimate unification of world religions. This aim was based on the restoration of the pre-Christian mystery tradition, which had been persecuted by the early Church and forced to go underground in medieval Europe, and the recognition that all religions had originated in a universal spirituality variously referred to as the Perennial Philosophy, the Primordial Tradition, and the Ancient Wisdom. The mystical beliefs of the secret societies were, and indeed are, based on the Hermetic maxim "As above, so below," which teaches that the natural world is a material reflection of the spiritual. This motto forms the esoteric basis for ancient Egyptian mysteries, gnosticism, esoteric Christianity, the kabbalah, the Hermetic tradition, alchemy, and secret societies such as the Templars, Freemasons, and Rosicrucians. The occult doctrines of geomancy, alchemy, astrology, and sexual magic taught by these secret societies were used to aid the progression of the individual member from material darkness to the spiritual light of understanding and gnosis (knowledge).

We have traced how the political philosophy of secret societies developed in the twentieth century, but how did these esoteric teachings express themselves in the mass consciousness? Secret societies such as the Rosicrucians have very seldom exposed their inner activities to the public gaze, preferring to work within established occult organizations that, because of their elitist structure, have concealed their real work from the profane. In rare instances these esoteric teachings have been presented by an initiate to the public in a way that has made the teachings accessible to the average person. A classic example of this was the foundation of the Theosophical Society in 1875 by Madame Helena Blavatsky. The formation of this group seems to have been a deliberate act to establish the occult tradition in materialistic European society and to unite the spiritual beliefs of East and West.

Another initiate of secret societies who was instrumental in the public spread of esoteric teachings in the early part of the twentieth century was Rudolf Steiner (1861–1925), who had been a member of the German Theosophical Society and had connections to various Masonic and Rosicrucian groups and other secret societies. He spent some years as the secretary of the German Theosophical Society and had extensive contacts with Annie Besant, the left-wing activist who replaced Madame Blavatsky as the leader of the organization. In 1909, however, Steiner separated from the Theosophical Society, declaring that he was opposed to the policy that had become popular in Theosophical circles with regard to the emergence of a new messiah. Steiner's later work was Christ-centered, and he strongly believed that Christ incarnated only once, as described in the Christian scriptures, and would not return. Because of the new direction the Theosophical Society was taking, Steiner resigned to form a new occult group called the Anthroposophical Society.

He began to tour Europe to lecture on his theories about the spiritual value of art and alternative education. His ideas seem to have been deeply rooted in Rosicrucian tradition, though he gave them a modern gloss. Like the medieval Freemasons, Steiner believed that the new spiritual impulse flowing through the world had to be expressed through the medium of radical architecture. This led him to design an ultra-modern building in Basle in Switzerland to house the headquarters of his new society. His unconventional ideas on educating children based on self-expression and artistic skills were crystallized in the founding of special Steiner schools, which still flourish today.

At the end of World War I, Rudolf Steiner was briefly involved in politics when, being sympathetic to the world government concept, he advocated a solution to the problems of central Europe based on the ideas of liberty, fraternity, equality, and freedom, which seemed to have been drawn from Masonic and Rosicrucian teachings. He also promoted a vision of human development and evolution that drew its inspiration from a neo-Manichean doctrine of the eternal struggle between the powers of darkness and the forces of light. These teachings, however, were largely eclipsed by his ideas in the fields of organic farming, alternative medicine, the spirituality of art, and the education of young children, where he brought together the latest scientific research with ancient occult techniques to offer a unique solution to many social problems.

It is significant that many of Steiner's ideas have now been accepted and adopted by followers of the modern New Age movement, which arose in the early 1970s but had its spiritual roots in the counterculture of the 1960s. Today, it has become fashionable to regard the 1960s as a wasted period of permissive self-indulgence that was responsible for spawning our present social problems of drug abuse, political extremism, and sexual immorality. Such a view is a simplistic one, however, and it ignores the fact that the period represents one of the most important influxes of spiritual energy ever experienced by Western society. On one level, it was a time of change and social upheaval when young people threw aside the moral shackles imposed by convention and elected to follow a radically different lifestyle from that of their parents. This new way of living embraced self-sufficiency, vegetarian diets, psychedelic drugs, astrology, radical politics, pacifism, free love, rock music, bizarre clothes, and a spiritual devotion to exotic forms of religion based on Eastern mysticism and Western paganism.

Because of the fragmented nature of the counterculture, it is difficult to identify clearly the esoteric sources at work behind the scenes or to pinpoint any actual involvement by the inheritors of the Rosicrucian and Masonic traditions. Yet the sixties movement brought into public consciousness many of the symbols and beliefs of the occult tradition, and these have now become generally accepted as a natural part of daily life. The concepts, philosophies, and ideals that arose from this important historical period were deeply influenced by more traditional esoteric beliefs, and these were later taken on board by the New Age movement of the 1970s and 1980s.

Central to the beliefs of the new spirituality is the imminent dawning of the Aquarian Age. According to esoteric tradition, every two thousand years the world enters a new zodiacal age. The Piscean Age began with the birth of Jesus and was dominated by Christianity as the most influential of the world religions. The beginning of a new zodiacal age provides a unique chance to accept the eternal truths of the Ancient Wisdom in a new form. The changeover period between the Piscean and the Aquarian Ages is an important one because it is the first time in recorded history that our species has had the ability to commit global genocide and to destroy the planet by either a nuclear holocaust or an ecological disaster.

This changeover period, as we can see from the daily events recorded in the mass media, is a time of confusion, apprehension, and extremism on a planetary scale. Dark forces are manifesting in the world, symbolized by international terrorism, famine, ultramaterialism, dictatorship, and religious fanaticism. Such manifestations are to be expected because, according to occult belief, the new waves of spiritual energy that flow through the planet at these changeover periods meet with resistance from the old energies that are the psychic leftovers from the dying age.

The impulse of the Aquarian Age, which motivated the 1960s generation, encompassed an idealistic, if romantic, vision of a Utopian society based on love and peace. War would be eliminated by common consent and all countries would unite in a nonpolitical planetary brotherhood of nations. In this idealistic society of the future, every individual would have the right to worship whatever God (or gods) he or she chooses and there would be complete freedom and equality between the genders. It was a dream that would have been instantly recognizable by sixteenth-century Rosicrucians such as Sir Francis Bacon and the grand masters of the Masonic lodges who influenced the American and French Revolutions.

In the counterculture, the hybrid forms of mysticism that arose as a side effect of the search for individual freedom and that developed into the New Age movement drew from historical sources identified with secret societies. The late 1960s and early 1970s saw a tremendous revival of interest in occultism, spiritualism, paganism, astrology, and magical practices. This was an obvious reaction to the failure of orthodox religion to provide spiritual sustenance for the new educated class. Like gnosticism, the New Age movement attempted—and still attempts—to synthesize Eastern and Western forms of religion and offers the individual seeker the ability to communicate with God without the interference of a priestly middleman.

The New Age movement and the occult revival, while claiming to present a new style of spirituality, still relies on the traditional philosophies of past occultists such as Blavatsky, Besant, Steiner, Alice

Bailey, and Aleister Crowley to provide its theological framework. Rare texts of medieval magic have been unearthed and reprinted in cheap editions and interest in ley lines, stone circles, Celtic mythology, and ancient Egyptian religion flourishes in neo-pagan revivals supported by the formation of numerous magical groups and witch covens.

One of the most important aspects of the New Age movement is its holistic approach to spirituality. It embraces such varied subjects as ecology and green politics, alternative medicine, hi-tech science, Eastern religion, quantum physics, and feminism in an attempt to look at society in a unified way. In common with the Rosicrucian-Masonic tradition, the New Agers have realized that if society is to be transformed, then a common ground must be found among religion, science, art, spiritual concepts, and principles applied to these disciplines. The "one planet" ideal of the New Age groups shares many similarities with the secret societies' aspirations toward one world government. In fact, many of the Theosophically derived occult fraternities and New Age groups are strong advocates of the ideal of global governance.

The New Age concern for gender equality and the importance of the feminine principle is another aspect of Aquarian spirituality and it also links it with the aims of secret societies. In the last two thousand years, our planetary culture has been dominated and stifled, in both the religious and political sense, by the forces of patriarchy. They have formed a primary restriction on the progressive work carried out by those who follow the tenets of the Ancient Wisdom. We have seen in our historical investigation of secret societies that one of the common beliefs shared by the pagan mystery cults, the gnostics, the Cathars, the troubadours, the Templars, the Freemasons, and the Rosicrucians was a reverence for the feminine principle. This has always been a key focus for adherents to the secret tradition and is the key to understanding the occult symbols they used to reveal their spiritual truths to initiates and to the outside world.

The Aquarian Age, whose spiritual movement is at present undisciplined and immature, is, according to the inner teachings of secret societies, destined to provide a new balancing of the male and female energies. This will in turn create a better relationship between humanity and Mother Earth and will usher in a period of increased spiritual awareness. The various spiritual ideals expressed in New Age teachings are gradually filtering through to society and creating subtle changes in the way ordinary people look at their planet and fellow human beings. On a mundane level, the opening of health stores; the trend toward alternative medicine and organic foods; the practice of meditation by tired businessmen; widespread support for ecological action groups such as Greenpeace and Friends of the Earth; the interest in Eastern religions, Christian mysticism, and Western paganism; and the widespread practice of occult techniques such as astrology are all examples of the social and spiritual changes that can be expected to accelerate as we enter the Aquarian Age around the year 2025.

While the New Age movement has updated the occult tradition and presented it in a way that has mass appeal, it often produces a simplistic and superficial version of the Ancient Wisdom. By contrast, traditional Rosicrucianism (as the inherited tradition of the pre-Christian mysteries) has been widely represented in modern times by several semisecret groups that claim descent from the original fraternity of the Middle Ages. These groups include the Rosicrucian Fellowship, the Fraternity of the Rosy Cross (FRC), the Ancient and Mystical Order of the Rosy Cross (AMORC) and, most recently, the Lectorium Rosicrucianum.

These neo-Rosicrucian fraternities all claim genuine connections to the medieval Order of the Rosy Cross and are linked by either common membership or affiliation. The Rosicrucian Fellowship was founded by a German-American of Danish extraction, Max Heindel (1865–1919), who had been a leading member of the German Theosophical Society. While living in Europe, Heindel claimed he was initiated in a secret Rosicrucian temple in Bohemia (now the Czech Republic) and given instructions to form a new branch of the order in the United States. Because he was a practicing astrologer, Heindel introduced elements of astrological symbolism into his neo-Rosicrucian tradition.

The Fraternity of the Rosy Cross (FRC) claims descent from

P. B. Randolph, who was involved in sex magic and had been connected with the OTO. The FRC itself has been linked to groups that in turn derived their inspiration from Continental occult fraternities that mixed Rosicrucian and Masonic beliefs, including the Kabbalistic Order of the Rosy Cross, founded in France in 1889. The AMORC has a high public profile and places regular advertisements in popular newspapers and magazines and offers a correspondence course to its new members. It has over fifty thousand members in the United States, and from its worldwide headquarters in San José, California, it operates lodges in Britain, France, Australia, Germany, Switzerland, and South Africa. Its teachings involve the occult use of color and light, alchemy, the perfection of the physical body, the development of will, the nature of matter, and the mysteries of time and space. In common with the traditions of medieval Rosicrucianism, AMORC advocates a synthesis of science and religion.

In contrast to these groups, the Dutch-based Lectorium Rosicrucianum sidesteps the medieval Rosicrucians and claims to trace its ideology directly to the pre-Christian pagan mystery schools. Formed in Holland in the 1920s, it holds public meetings in European capital cities to introduce its neo-gnostic teachings to interested parties. It would appear to draw some of its beliefs from the Cathar heresy and is a unique phenomenon among modern neo-Rosicrucian fraternities.

Even less orthodox survivals of the Rosicrucian tradition exist today that have emerged from the occult revival of recent years and the influence of several different groups that claim to preserve the traditional workings of the Hermetic Order of the Golden Dawn and other nineteenth-century magical and occult societies. In addition, there exist several rival organizations in Europe and the United States, which claim to be the genuine OTO, and there are new occult groups following Crowley's teachings, including the Nu-Isis Lodge, the Knights of the Solar Cross, and the Order of Maat. Although there is little evidence to suggest that any of these branches or imitators of the OTO are involved in political activities, Crowley's personal brand of anarcho-liberterianism summed up by the Assassins' famous slogan "Nothing is forbidden; everything is permitted" has been described by his critics as magical fascism. Since the 1960s, Crowley has attracted a new generation of would-be magicians and occultists.

The Templar tradition is also represented in many different forms today by chivalric orders and Masonic fraternities that claim descent from the original knights, but they can usually be traced back only to the eighteenth-century revival of Templarism. There were new revivals of Templarism in France during the nineteenth century linked to Freemasonry. One branch of this Templar tradition exerted its influence during the days of the wartime Vichy government, when Masonry was forbidden, in keeping with Nazi policy on secret societies. In this period, the neo-Templars became involved with *synarchism,* a new political movement that combined bureaucratic socialism, pacifism, and the technological control of society. It seems to have received support from foreign intelligence agencies, including the British MI6, as an anti-Vichy and anti-Nazi movement. In common with the original Templars and most wartime Allies politicians, it was committed to a united Europe after the war. As we have seen in the 1960s and 1970s, however, Templarism in France was associated with extreme right-wing politics and it forged international links to politically motivated Masonic groups such as the P2 lodge in Italy.

The most recent of the modern neo-Templar groups in France is the oddly named L'Ordre Internationale Chevalvesque Tradition Solaire (OICTS), or International Order of Chivalry, Solar Tradition. It was founded by a Templar Order in 1984 and was charged with the task of reviving genuine Templarism in the modern world in preparation for the coming Aquarian Age. The impetus for this resurgence of Templar activity came in 1952, when representatives of the order met secretly at an old country house in Switzerland that had once been owned by the Knights of Malta.

According to its manifesto published in 1987, the OICTS encourages the ancient civilizing ideals of chivalry, campaigns for spiritual unity, fosters the fraternity of all races, integrates spirituality into everyday life, and works to improve the quality of life through the adoption of spiritual principles. The new order established itself in North America because it believed the continent would have an important role to play in the Aquarian Age. Its theology is based on esoteric Christianity, the Grail mysteries, and a respect for the feminine principle. For this reason, women are admitted to the order on equal terms with men, which is a direct departure from the medieval Templar tradition.

In the modern occult groups that claim to follow the traditions of the medieval secret societies—and these include the neo-Templars, various esoteric Masonic lodges, and such shadowy organizations as the Priory of Sion—several common themes come together: Politically, they include a unified Europe based on spiritual principles. At present the European Union (EU), with its overweight bureaucracy and food surpluses, seems a transitory shadow of the great plan envisioned for Europe in the twenty-first century by those who are working on an esoteric level behind the scenes of international politics.

9

THE NEW WORLD ORDER

In the last twenty years there have been many dramatic changes in the world—so many that the term *historic* as used to describe them is the most overused word in the media's vocabulary. There has been the collapse of the Soviet Union, the fall of the Berlin Wall, the unification of Germany, the dismantling of the Warsaw Pact, the end of the Cold War, the rise of democracy in Eastern Europe and Russia, and peace in Northern Ireland. In 2004, membership in the European Union (EU) was extended to ten new countries, including several former Communist nations—a momentous event that few would have dared to predict in the 1980s, when the Cold War was at its most icy.

Such economic measures as the introduction of the euro as the single European currency and attempts to agree on an EU constitution have revived optimistic talk of a new pan-European Federation or United States of Europe. On the negative side, we have experienced civil war and ethnic cleansing in the former Yugoslavia, genocide in Rwanda and Sudan, mass starvation and the AIDS epidemic in Africa, the Gulf War, 9/11, the so-called war on terror, Anglo-American interventions in Iraq and Afghanistan, the ongoing struggle between Israel and the Palestinians in the Middle East, and the possible development of nuclear weapons by Iran and North Korea.

Despite major changes in the world order, the events of the late twentieth century continue to haunt international politics at the beginning of the new century. During World War II, Pope Pius XII, the so-called Nazi pope, was accused of failing to speak out against the evils of Nazism and the Holocaust. Critics alleged this was because the Roman Church had always been anti-Semitic. In 1997, American documents were released showing that the Vatican had obtained quantities of gold from Holocaust victims from the pro-Nazi puppet regime in Yugoslavia during the war. This was worth in excess of two hundred forty million dollars and allegedly was used to finance the so-called ratlines organized by Catholic priests to smuggle Nazi war criminals out of Europe in 1945.

More Nazi links were revealed when Cardinal Joseph Ratzinger was elected Pope Benedict XVI. It was revealed that as a young man in Germany, he had been a member of the Hitler Youth and was thus dubbed the Panzer* Pope by the media. As a young Nazi, he had manned an antiaircraft battery that fired at Allied bombers, and after deserting at the end of the war, he was briefly interned by the Americans. Benedict followed in the papal slippers of his reactionary predecessor as he quickly reaffirmed the Church's orthodox policies on homosexuality, abortion, married priests, and birth control. The new pope also condemned the growth of "New Age religions" and the younger generation's fascination with witchcraft and the occult. In 2003, when he was Cardinal Ratzinger, he was the head of the Holy Office for the Propagation of Faith (formerly the Inquisition) and publicly attacked Wicca and neo-paganism, the Chinese practice of feng shui, spiritual healing, and the use of crystals. Astrology and yoga, however, received the Vatican's approval because it was claimed that their practice was unlikely to lead to eternal damnation. As for neo-paganism, the Holy Office for the Propagation of Faith said that it corrupted young people by teaching them to hug trees and love Mother Nature. While a love and respect for nature was acceptable and recommended, ascribing Divinity to the earth was wrong. Ratzinger said that practicing Catholics had to choose between the

---

*A "Panzer" is a German war tank used in World War II.

Church and New Age beliefs because they could not follow both.

In 2006, Pope Benedict caused worldwide controversy when he spoke out against the new threat of Islam. He quoted from a medieval text that described Islam as a warrior religion that achieved its aims through warfare and violence. Following widespread protests and demonstrations in many Muslim countries, the pope was forced to qualify his statement and assure his critics that he meant no disrespect to Islam. The Vatican later set up a meeting between the pope and Muslim leaders as a public relations operation to promote religious tolerance. Meanwhile, the pope faced opposition within his own ranks in the United States and Central America from progressive priests who demanded that the Church become more involved in social issues in the developing world and reform its traditional views on abortion and birth control in the face of world overpopulation. At the same time, the Church faced mounting lawsuits from members who claimed that as children they had been sexually abused by priests.

In the last twenty years, more public revelations have surfaced concerning the ongoing activities of the P2 lodge and its links to the Vatican. In 1993, the Italian secret service investigated the murder of two Sicilian judges killed in a bomb attack. They were looking into claims that renegade intelligence officers were involved because of the two men's anti-Mafia stance. Apparently, at the time of their deaths the judges were engaged in a full-scale investigation of possible links between the criminal organization and secret Masonic lodges in Sicily. P2 was also said to be still operating on the Italian mainland. Allegedly, it was laundering funds on behalf of organized crime using Swiss banks. In 1990, the Vatican officially protested a new film being made that depicted the papacy in a conspiracy with the Mafia, Freemasons, international bankers, and arms dealers. The film claimed that laundered money from criminal sources had been used by the Church in the 1980s to finance anti-Communist and pro-democracy activities in Eastern Europe.

In November 1992, the London *Times* reported that the Italian police were launching a new investigation into a high-level conspiracy among politicians, criminals, and Masons. Top political figures, judges, civil servants, and journalists were believed by the police to be implicated in an antistate plot. A separate investigation into gunrunning and drug smuggling had surprisingly thrown up evidence connecting the gangs involved to Freemasonry. A computer was seized that contained records of the membership of well-known Mafiosi in Masonic lodges. Again there were rumors of links among organized crime, politicians, and the Vatican.

As late as 2002, the British antifascist magazine *Searchlight* claimed that P2 still existed and that the Italian prime minister at the time, Silvio Bellusconi, had been one of its members. There is no evidence, though, that he was ever involved in any criminal activity. In 2006, however, Bellusconi was indicted on charges of corruption. The magazine speculated that P2 was still actively involved in plans for a new wave of terrorism designed to destablize the Italian government and bring about a right-wing coup. P2 had also allegedly been involved in the assassination of the Swedish premier, Olav Palme, in 1986. Rogue elements in the CIA, whom some conspiracy theorists believe are the secret puppeteers behind P2, were also involved in the politician's murder because of his public criticism of U.S. foreign policy.

The P2 lodge has been linked in the past to the U.S.-sponsored Operation Stay Behind, which recruited fanatical anti-Communists in several European countries during the Cold War and trained them to form nationalistic resistance movements if these countries were invaded by Soviet forces. Critics of the operation claim that these clandestine militias had a secret and subversive agenda and were also trained to overthrow the existing legitimate government if it showed signs of pro-Soviet tendencies or Communist ideals. In Italy, the stay behinds were known by the code word *gladio,* from the short sword used by Roman gladiators. Gladio operatives have been accused of assassinating Italian prime minister Aldo Moro in 1978 and also allegedly of using extreme left-wing terrorist groups to create a climate of fear that they hoped would lead to a right-wing coup. In 1974 the Italian minister of defense, Andre Guilo Andreotti, who later became prime minister, announced that Operation Gladio had been closed down. In November 1990, however, General Paolo Inzerilli of the Italian security service told the European parliament that his government had only just disbanded the gladio units.

In 1997, it was revealed that a new investigation by the city of London police had concluded that the Vatican's banker, Roberto Calvi, had not taken his own life but had been murdered. His body was exhumed in 1998, and in 2002 forensic experts announced there was evidence of foul play in his death. They said they had found marks on his neck suggesting he was strangled before being hanged from London's Blackfriars Bridge. More evidence was produced claiming the banker was killed by Mafia hit men from Naples because he knew too much about the illegal connections among the Vatican, organized crime, and Italian Freemasonry. This was confirmed by Calvi's son, who said his father had owed money to the Mafia and had been killed because of that debt and his insider knowledge of its dealings with the Catholic Church and the P2 lodge.

In 2005, several people, including a well-known Mafia chief, were arrested and charged with Calvi's murder. The police now believe that the banker was lured by his killers to a boat moored on the River Thames and was garroted from behind with a rope. His body was then suspended from the bridge using the rope as a noose. The death was thus faked as a suicide with ritualistic Masonic elements to throw the police off the scent. Allegedly, the boat had been hired by a known Italian drug dealer, who was found murdered in his London flat three months after Calvi's "suicide."

Another famous secret society involved in parapolitics and the occult was also in the news in the 1980s and 1990s. In 1982, Henry Lincoln, Michael Baigent, and Richard Leigh published the U.S. version of their mega-bestseller *Holy Blood, Holy Grail,* in which they put forward the idea that there had been a historical conspiracy by secret societies such as the Templars and the Priory of Sion to conceal the fact that Jesus did not die on the cross. Instead, the book suggests, he and his wife, Mary Magdalene, fled to France, and there she gave birth to his child. It was alleged that this child became the ancestor of the French royal Merovingian family and established a sacred bloodline referred to as the *sangrael,* or "royal blood." In the last few years, this theory has been boosted by the worldwide success of Dan Brown's novel *The Da Vinci Code* and the subsequent Hollywood movie starring Tom Hanks. It also led to a sensational court case in 2006, when Baigent and Leigh claimed that Brown had plagiarized their work in his fictional account.

Much of the research in *Holy Blood, Holy Grail* was based on documents provided to the authors by a self-styled French aristocrat named Pierre Plantard St. Clair, who claimed to be the current grand master of the Priory of Sion. Plantard claimed that the secret society had been founded in the Middle Ages and was the éminence grise behind the Knights Templar. Recently, it has been revealed that the documents provided to Lincoln, Baigent, and Leigh were fakes and it has been claimed that the Priory was a surrealist hoax concocted by Plantard and some friends in the 1950s. Plantard has also been exposed as a confidence trickster, fantasist, and fraudster who falsely claimed to be descended from the Merovingians and the French royal family. The founding of the Priory was allegedly part of Plantard's grandiose dream of restoring the monarchy to France.

These revelations might have been the end of the story of the Priory of Sion, but two British researchers, Lynn Picknett and Clive Prince, who incidentally featured as extras sitting on a London bus in the film of *The Da Vinci Code,* investigated the society and its origins more closely. They claimed that instead of being just an elaborate practical joke, the Priory had been founded as a right-wing, Catholic traditionalist, pro-monarchist, politico-occult secret society and its true origins went back to Vichy, France, in World War II. Its ethos, they claimed, could basically be described as anti-Communist, anti-Semitic, and anti-Masonic.

According to Picknett and Prince, Pierre Plantard's bizarre beliefs, fantastic historical claims, and faked documents have obscured the Priory's real political connections and significance in the modern history of France. They claim that Plantard was linked to the pro-Nazi Vichy government and that, more recently, the Priory was connected to right-wing extremists, the criminal underworld, neo-Templar orders, and both the French and British intelligence services. Allegedly, the secret society supported a military conspiracy in 1958 that restored General Charles de Gaulle to power. The two authors' final revelation is that the Priory of Sion is no less than a cover for a secret political and occult movement working behind the scenes to establish a united Europe based on a Franco-German alliance.

The sacred bloodline of Jesus is supposed to have passed to the ancient Merovingian dynasty of French kings, which was featured in one of the most dramatic and controversial events of the last twenty years. On August 31, 1997, Diana, princess of Wales, and her boyfriend, Dodi Al Fayed, were killed in a car crash in a Paris underpass. Within a few days of this tragic event, conspiracy theories were already circulating that blamed her death on MI6, Mossad, international arms dealers, or the British royal family. These conspiracy theories continued unabated despite the findings of a December 2006 official government report by Lord Stevens, the former commissioner of London's metropolitan police, which stated that the princess had been killed in a simple motor accident and that there had been no interference from outside forces.

Some of the more sensational of the conspiracy theories around this event contained elements of the occult. The most fantastic claimed that Princess Diana's death was a ritual murder or a human sacrifice that had allegedly been carried out on the orders of an international cabal of highly placed occultists whose leaders were the royal House of Windsor. Those who believe this extraordinary theory say that the tunnel where the accident occurred is close to the Pont Alma, an area of Paris historically associated with the Knights Templar and the Merovingians. Before they converted to Christianity, the latter were pagan worshippers of the princess's mythological namesake, the Roman moon goddess Diana. According to a Merovingian legend, anyone who dies near the Pont Alma is a very special person and will go straight to heaven.

For many years, rumors have circulated that the Windsors are involved in occult activities. They have been linked to a network of European aristocratic and royal families that conspiracy theorists call the Black Nobility—families whose bloodlines are said to go back thousands of years to Babylonian and Sumerian times. President George W. Bush has been linked to this ancient occult bloodline because he, like George Washington, is related to the British royals. In fact, George W. Bush is a distant cousin of Queen Elizabeth II. It has even been claimed that Princess Diana was supposed to marry a prominent American after her divorce from Charles Windsor, which would have sealed a connection between the occult bloodlines of the New World and the Old World. When she refused, it is said the secret power elite ordered her death.

Among the apocryphal stories linking the Windsors to the occult is the tale that the late Princess Margaret, the queen's sister, was the high priestess of a royal coven that met in the White Tower at Windsor Castle. Prince Charles was also said to have subscribed to an American neo-pagan magazine called *Green Egg* and Princess Diana was allegedly an avid reader of a well-known British witchcraft magazine called *The Cauldron*. Unfortunately, no evidence has been presented to support these claims.

Just before the arranged marriage of Princess Diana and Prince Charles, an anarchist magazine in London said that the princess had been initiated into witchcraft in a ceremony held on the queen's Balmoral estate in Scotland. Allegedly, the ritual involved the sacrifice of a stag and was her introduction to the hidden side of the royal family that the public has never seen. Allegedly, it was feared that her unstable mental condition after the breakup of her marriage might cause her to reveal the secrets of the Black Nobility to the media. Whatever the truth, or otherwise, in these fantastic and bizarre claims, it is a matter of public record that Diana's brother, Earl Spencer, made a very unusual speech in the House of Lords in 1994 that mentioned Satanism: He said he had evidence that a satanic cult was secretly holding ceremonies on his family estate that involved animal sacrifice.

Why he should mention this, and why Satanists should have been attracted to a place where, three years later, Princess Diana was buried is wide open to speculation.

An alleged connection between an occult secret society and European royalty was revealed in 1994, when members of the Order of the Solar Temple, a ceremonial magical group claiming descent from the Knights Templar, committed ritual suicide. The order's leaders, Joseph di Mambro and Luc Journet, had persuaded the gullible members that after they died, they would ascend to the star Sirius and become advanced spiritual beings. Deluded parents murdered several of the children who were too young to take their own lives.

It has been claimed that one of the high priestesses of the Solar Temple was Princess Grace of Monaco, formerly the Hollywood movie star Grace Kelly. Luc Journet was supposed to have met her husband, Prince Rainer, and through him he recruited the princess, who allegedly had an interest in the occult. Princess Grace was said to have donated millions of dollars to the order's founders. When she was killed in a car crash, conspiracy theorists said the princess had either been murdered because she had refused to give the cultists any more money or had committed suicide because she believed she would ascend to a higher spiritual plane. Unfortunately for these theories, there is no real evidence that Princess Grace was connected to the Solar Temple apart from the dubious testimony of a convicted con man who used to be a driver for one of the order's leaders. It is true, however, that in the 1980s, Luc Journet was busy recruiting wealthy new members among the high society in the south of France. It would appear he was more interested in money than their souls, because the group was largely a scam to relieve the gullible of their fortunes. As with other phony secret societies of this type, the Order of the Solar Temple attempted to give itself some credibility by association with the Knights Templar.

The phenomenal success of Dan Brown's thriller *The Da Vinci Code* has focused more attention on the original Knights Templar, and specifically on Rosslyn Chapel in Scotland. Nonfiction books about

Rosslyn and the Sinclair, or St. Clair, family have become a cottage industry since the novel was published. There has been wild speculation that the chapel is the secret hiding place of the Holy Grail, the treasure the Templars allegedly excavated from Solomon's temple, or even the burial place of the heads of Jesus and John the Baptist. Today, Rosslyn is associated with a modern Scottish Order of Templars, which claims to be its guardian. Another group claiming descent from the original knights has emerged from the shadows in Hertfordshire, England. They wrote to the pope and demanded a pardon for the medieval order in the spirit of reconciliation and religious tolerance. The papal reply, if there was any, is not known.

In a separate development, documents were found in the Vatican library suggesting that the Templars may have been involved in some of the heretical practices that led to their suppression. It was revealed that at the time, the Vatican instigated its own clandestine investigation into the charges made against the order in 1308. The Inquisition questioned many of the leading members, who freely confessed without torture that they had denied Christ, spat on a crucifix, and kissed their initiator on intimate parts of his body. The reason the knights gave for these practices was that it was a test of their faith: They were told that this is what they would be forced to do if they were captured and tortured by the Saracens. Whether or not this was a cover story to conceal real occult practices, it does indicate that, for whatever reason, the Templars did indulge in the blasphemous rites the Church accused them of practicing.

In November 2000, after a contested election that many observers believed was won by the former vice-president Al Gore, George W. Bush became president of the United States. It was soon revealed that when he was a student at Yale University, Bush had been a leading member of a secret society known as the Skull and Bones. This student fraternity, also known as Chapter 332 and the Order of Death, was founded in 1832. Allegedly, it had connections with the esoteric Scottish Rite Masonry and the Egyptian Rite Freemasonry founded by the Illuminati agent Comte Cagliosto.

New members are initiated into this death-obsessed society at its impressive headquarters on the Yale campus known as the Tomb. Although secrecy surrounds its rituals, they are said to feature coffins; a skull; confessions of sexual activity; mock human sacrifices; some homoerotic horseplay; and members dressed up as Death, in skeletal masks and black hooded robes, the devil, and the Hangman. The skull used by the society was said to have been robbed from the grave of a Native American leader by George W. Bush's grandfather, Prescott Bush, in 1918. When Native American elders demanded its return, however, the story of this robbing was exposed as a Skull and Bones legend.

During the nineteenth century, the Skull and Bones recruited its members from elite American families that had been engaged in commerce and politics since before the Revolution. Its foundation allegedly derived from the activities of the British East India Company in the previous century. During the American War of Independence, the company was heavily involved in the opium trade and allegedly came under the influence of the Illuminati-linked House of Rothschild. The company sponsored wealthy merchants in New England, and it was the scions of these families who founded and ran the Skull and Bones in its early years. Today, it exists to promote traditional Anglo-Saxon values and to groom suitable young men for future careers in law, banking, the intelligence community, and the government.

Critics of this secret society have also claimed links among the Skull and Bones, the CIA, and the drug trade, which were presented to the public in 2007 in *The Good Shepherd,* Robert De Niro's film about the origins of the agency. Leading figures in the CIA, including its former director George H. Bush, were Yale students and belonged to the Skull and Bones. In fact, the agency has always used the university as a recruiting ground for new agents, as did its wartime predecessor, the Office of Strategic Services (OSS). American intelligence also has a long history of alleged involvement in the drug trade, from the nineteenth-century opium wars to the modern Iran-Contra scandal. Shortly after the Skull and Bones was founded, the university authorities regarded its activities as sinister and it was condemned for its alleged "criminal influence."

The Bush dynasty was involved in the Skull and Bones almost from its inception. Prescott Bush, as we have seen, was a leading member and became a legendary figure in its history. Originally, it has been claimed, the Skull and Bones was the American chapter of a college fraternity in Germany that promoted nationalism. It has been alleged that Prescott Bush was one of the many American businessmen who helped finance industry in Nazi Germany before the war. Conspiracy theorists even claim that the skull and crossbones motif of the secret society derives from the infamous death head logo of the Waffen SS, despite the fact that the Skull and Bones was founded a hundred years before the Nazis came to power.

The society, however, does have an almost mystical attitude toward militarism that echoes the old Prussian army code and the later National Socialist philosophy. George H. Bush's mentor in the fraternity was Henry Stimson, who had some interesting ideas about the role of warfare in modern society: Stimson maintained that frequent wars were a healthy thing because they had a cleansing effect on a nation and enabled its people to rally behind a patriotic and uniting cause. For that reason, when Skull and Bones members left the university in the past, they were actively encouraged to pursue careers in the armed forces. We can wonder how this militaristic philosophy of the Order of Death may have influenced America's postwar foreign policy, especially after 9/11.

George W. Bush and his father, along with many other former presidents and prominent politicians, belong to another secret cult-like group with death-related symbolism that many claim has a sinister influence in modern political affairs. In fact, this group has been described as an offshoot of the Skull and Bones and is where these younger members "graduate" to after they leave Yale and take up important positions in public life. Some bored San Francisco journalists, writers, and artists who led a bohemian lifestyle founded the so-called Bohemian Group in 1872. Its early members included such literary luminaries as Mark Twain and Jack London.

Shortly after its foundation, the Group was taken over by a cabal of wealthy businessmen, who bought a twenty-seven hundred acre redwood forest near Santa Rosa in northern California as a leisure retreat. Now, every summer several thousand politicians, business leaders, showbiz personalities, and media moguls gather at Bohemian Grove for a two-week campout. During their stay, the members are split up into different camps with exotic-sounding names and have access to a wide range of luxury facilities, including a hotel, log cabins, a clubhouse, bars, and game rooms. At the Grove, the all-male membership can drop their inhibitions, relax, and party in complete privacy.

It all sounds very idyllic, but conspiracy theorists believe that the Bohemian Group is another front organization for the Illuminati and an intellectual think tank where plans for world domination are discussed and implemented by the secret power elite. As evidence they cite the fact that over the years, those attending the midsummer gatherings of the rich and famous have included nearly every Republican president since 1923 and many Democratic ones as well. In addition, there are heads of global financial organizations such as the World Bank; Supreme Court judges; senior military officers; defense contractors; and selected foreign leaders, including former British prime ministers. Cultural exemplars such as Hollywood movie stars and film producers have also been in attendance, along with royalty such as Prince Phillip. His involvement is significant because the British royal family is not supposed to get involved in politics, yet the prince had also attended meetings of the Bilderberg Group.

Talks and meetings at the retreat include topics of interest to the guests. In the 1990s, these included such significant subjects as the first Gulf War, the development of so-called smart weapons, defense problems in the coming century, and the new world order. It has been alleged that the Manhattan Project to build the first atomic bomb was conceived at Bohemian Grove. Other military projects that came out of these gatherings allegedly included the construction of the B2 stealth bomber and Ronald Reagan's grandiose "star wars" plan for an antimissile defense shield. If this is true, the Bohemian Group is far more than just an excuse for tired businessmen and politicians to have some private R & R.

During the gatherings at Bohemian Grove, the participants allegedly indulge in such bizarre practices as mass open-air urinating, cross-dressing in female clothes, amateur cabaret revues, nude swimming, homosexual activities, and sex with prostitutes. The major event is a quasi-pagan ceremony called the Cremation of Dull Care. It features a torchlight procession at an artificial lake at the center of the grounds and the mock sacrifice of a human effigy representing the "dull care" the guests have left behind in the outside world. This ritual takes place in front of a fifty-foot-high stone image of an owl, which is alleged by conspiracy theorists to be the representation of an ancient Caananite god called Moloch, who is worshipped by the Illuminati. The ceremony is presided over by hooded and black-robed figures led by a high priest dressed in black and red with a silver cloak. The effigy of the human body is ferried across the lake on a boat and the master of ceremonies makes references to ancient Babylon and the sacrifice of Gallic prisoners-of-war by the Celtic druids. The effigy is then burned Wicker Man–style to the sound of loud cheering and cries of "burn him, burn him!" from the assembled crowd.

The participants in this strange ritual say it is just a pantomime and harmless fun. Critics say that in pagan times, Moloch was a bloodthirsty deity who demanded child sacrifices as burned offerings and this ritual is a modern revival of that barbaric practice. In the 1980s, a local newspaper, the *Santa Rosa Sun,* reported that it had uncovered evidence that Bohemian Grove was a cover for a modern Moloch-worshipping cult that practiced human sacrifice. It was claimed that on special occasions, a real human victim replaced the effigy. There were also unconfirmed reports of children going missing in the area and rumors of murders in the woods that had been covered up by local and national law enforcement agencies. Investigators attempting to penetrate the Grove have been chased off by military vehicles and black 4x4s with tinted windows, which some think belong to the U.S. Secret Service. The other elements of the security force guarding the area include local sheriff's deputies and the personal bodyguards of the rich and famous who attend the gathering.

Whether or not the Bohemian Group is a cover for a satanic cult practicing human sacrifice, which seems very unlikely, the fact is that its secretive meetings and weird rituals have been attended by such heavyweight political players as Vice-President Dick Cheney, ex-Secretary of Defense Donald Rumsfeld, and ex-Secretary of State Colin Powell. Their presence, along with the current commander-in-chief of the U.S. Armed Forces and former presidents, only adds to the sensational speculation about what really goes on at the Grove. It may be just an excuse for famous people to let their hair down once a year and indulge in some juvenile fun and games, but it does underline the fact that secret societies and their rituals fascinate many powerful politicians and leaders of society.

In January 1991, President George H. Bush told the Congress that the impending first Gulf War to liberate Kuwait from Saddam Hussein was part of a "big idea—a new world order where diverse nations are drawn together in a common cause to achieve the universal aspirations of mankind." This concept of a new world order was seen by the paranoid as a coded reference to one world government and the role America would play in establishing it in the new century. Six years later, a magazine editor named William Kristol founded a think tank called the Project for a New American Century (PNAC), which put forward an agenda for this new world order that many observers believe was accepted by the American administration.

William Kristol was a leading member of the neo-conservative (neocon) movement founded in the Cold War by a group of prominent anti-Communist intellectuals, including his father, Irving Kristol. Several well-known politicians who supported the neocon philosophy joined the PNAC in its early days, including Paul Wolfowitz, Dick Cheney, Jeb Bush, and Donald Rumsfeld. When George W. Bush became the new president, Wolfowitz, Cheney, and Rumsfeld became important members of his administration. Jeb Bush, brother of George W., had been elected governor of Florida and was involved in the controversial recount in the disputed 2000 presidential election.

In 2000, the PNAC issued a report recommending that "in the interests of world peace" the United States should establish military bases around the world to protect its interests and deal with any possible threat to the homeland from an enemy. With the collapse of the Soviet Union and the end of the Cold War, the new enemy was soon identified by the neocons in Washington and the Pentagon as radical Islamists. The report also recommended that the United States develop biological weapons of mass destruction (banned under the Geneva Convention) for use in future wars.

Critics of the PNAC saw it as an attempt to establish an American empire stretching from the Middle East to Asia in the twenty-first century. With Russia no longer regarded as a superpower and major player in international politics, America could achieve global military supremacy. This, the conspiracy theorists claimed, would lead to George H. Bush's new world order and pave the way for a U.S.-dominated world government secretly controlled by the Illuminati. Unfortunately, the PNAC and the Bush dynasty seem not to have foreseen 9/11, the rise of Islamic terrorism, and the failure of the occupation of Iraq. At the beginning of the twenty-first century, these events appear to have stalled the grand plan, if only temporarily.

When the three planes crashed into the World Trade Center and the Pentagon on the morning of September 11, 2001, the conspiracy buffs saw it as evidence of an anti-Illuminati plot. Masonic symbolism was seen in the twin towers of the WTC, which allegedly represented the pillars of Boaz and Joachim outside Solomon's temple or the fallen Tower of Babel. The original idea for the building is credited to David Rockefeller, one of the members of the alleged Illuminati-controlled banking family. He was serving as the chairman of the Chase Manhattan Bank in the 1950s when he suggested that a complex dedicated to international trade should be built at the east end of New York's financial district. With the help of his brother Nelson, then the governor of New York State, David Rockefeller initiated the project and plans were made public in 1961. Work began five years later. By destroying this symbolic edifice, those who were responsible were making a very public statement about the shadowy forces working behind the scenes of international politics and commerce to control the world.

After 9/11, President Bush spoke of a "war on terror" and a "crusade" against Islamic extremism. Conspiracy theories alleged that, despite his public persona as a born-again Christian, Bush was a puppet of the Illuminati, who opposed all religions. A war between the Christian West and Islam, it was argued, would further their plans for world domination because they were advocates of the policy of "divide and conquer." Allegedly, Bush was given the go-ahead to invade Iraq at a Bilderberg meeting. On the eve of the Anglo-American invasion in 2003, political commentators said that history was at a turning point and we were witnesses to an epic "clash of civilizations" in the Middle East. American and British tanks were preparing to roll into the ancient region of Mesopotamia, which had been the cradle of the first civilizations and the legendary sites of the Garden of Eden, Babylon, Ninevah, Ur, and the Tower of Babel. This fact was not lost on some of the military commanders who led the assault. Addressing British troops on the eve of the invasion, Lieutenant Colonel Tim Collins summed up the area's historical importance in biblical times when he told them, "Iraq is steeped in history. It is the site of the Garden of Eden, the Great Flood, and the birthplace of Abraham. Tread lightly."

In fact, after the invasion and the subsequent breakdown of law and order when the Iraqi army was disbanded, widespread looting took place. Many priceless artifacts were stolen from the Baghdad Museum and important archaeological sites were robbed and destroyed. Some conspiracy theorists claim this desecration of ancient places was deliberate; the Illuminati were trying to cover up evidence of the Anglo-American occult bloodline and its alleged origins in the area thousands of years ago.

The biblical significance of Iraq was doubtless not lost on President George Bush. As a born-again Christian, he believed he was a man of destiny placed in the White House by God to liberate the

Bible lands from tyranny and establish democracy there, whether the citizens of the lands wanted it or not. He was even reported to claim that the invasion was a divine mission and that he had been told by God to wage war on Iraq. The neocon hawks and the Christian Right also supported the invasion in an unholy alliance based on the biblical prophecy of the Second Coming and the Rapture, when it is said that God's chosen will be taken up to heaven and the wicked who are left are to be ruled by the Antichrist. Many Christian fundamentalists saw the Illuminati or the society's hidden leader as this evil figure and the world government, established under the auspices of the United Nations, as his tool for controlling what was left of the human race. As a result of this view, liberals condemned as a plan to create a theocratic dictatorship the political moves by the Christian Right to change the policy of the separation of church and state, guaranteed under the U.S. Constitution as drawn up by the Masonic Founding Fathers.

After 9/11, the role of the United Nations in world affairs was seriously weakened and was not helped by allegations of high-level corruption in the organization. Before September 2001, conspiracy theories had depicted the United Nations as an Illuminati front dedicated to the goal of one world government. Information leaking from a recent Bilderberg Group meeting now suggested that the North Atlantic Treaty Organization (NATO), set up in 1949 to secure a lasting peace in Europe and counter the military threat from the USSR, would take that role in future. NATO was seen as the vanguard global security force to replace United Nations peacekeepers in hotspots and to fight the war against Islamic terrorism. In fact, NATO had already taken on the role of an international police force in the Balkans in the 1990s and has more recently assumed this role in Afghanistan.

It is alleged that the Bilderbergers visualized NATO as the armed force of a proposed supernational government led by America with support from Britain and possibly newly liberated Eastern European states such as Poland and the Czech Republic. In early 2007, rumors circulated that the United States wanted to base in these countries its new antimissile system, dubbed "son of star wars." Lack of support for the Iraq invasion by America's traditional allies in "old Europe," such as France, has shifted the balance of power across the Atlantic. The United Kingdom has also moved away from the European Union since 2003 and has opted for a closer relationship with the United States, which may have given it a future role in the establishment of a new world order. This was reflected in Prime Minister Tony Blair's comment in November 2006, when he visited British troops fighting the Taliban in Afghanistan: He said that what they were doing was very important for the future, for they were "fighting for world security in the twenty-first century" (The London *Times*, November 2006).

The momentous events of the first few years of the new century indicate that the administration of President George W. Bush sees America as the leader of a new world order that is dedicated to spreading Western democracy across the world. Yet the apparent failure of this policy in Iraq and the ongoing military campaign in Afghanistan appear to be stumbling blocks in the process. This has been underlined by the lack of support from the United States's former European allies and the rejection of American cultural values by the political green movement, which arose out of the counterculture of the sixties and is opposed to the globalization that is seen as another U.S.-Illuminati plot. Economic experts also predict that within fifty years, the United States may be replaced by either China or India as a world superpower. If that happens, the international balance of power will move from the West to Asia. This seems unlikely to occur, however, without a possibly violent power struggle between the old guard and the new kids on the block.

The story of the occult conspiracy and the role that secret societies have played in it in the last two decades has been a conflict between opposing forces that seek ultimate power for different reasons. It also reveals a sinister agenda on the part of those who have hijacked the concept of one world government and corrupted it for their own selfish purposes. The historical conspiracy that has been outlined here is in reality a historical review of attempts by the initiates of secret societies and members of clandestine political groups to progress the evolutionary development of the human race in both the social and spiritual spheres. Unfortunately, as recent international events have made clear, this goal has been frustrated and perverted by lesser souls. Their only concerns are with the vainglories of the material world; the acquisition of personal power at any cost to others; the suppression of knowledge; and, with the advances in surveillance technology, the control of the masses. We can see this today in the increasing threats to personal freedom and expression in Western countries and in the rise of religious fundamentalism and the use of terrorism as a tool for political change.

Through the centuries, many renegade elements within the international power elite have attempted to sue secret societies and the occult movement as a cover for their (often) criminal activities and aims. Sadly, some of these renegades have worn the masks of initiates. In addition, the legitimate and sincere attempts by esoteric fraternities to eradicate ignorance and advance social progress have been misunderstood by the masses they have been trying to help. These attempts have also been deliberately misinterpreted by the fraternities' religious and political enemies who want to see their glorious mission fail.

In this look at the influences shaping world events behind the scenes, we have not ignored these negative aspects of its secret history, for they provide an invaluable if saddening insight into those evil minds that secretly plot the downfall of civilization and encourage anarchy and chaos. There is hope for the future, however, and evidence that even in our doom-laden, crisis-ridden times there are genuine initiates of the esoteric tradition working on a positive level to improve our society. It is unfortunate that their existence is not recognized— and is even denied—by those who have no knowledge or understanding of their activities and little or no awareness of the spiritual reality that exists beyond the physical world.

CHRONOLOGY

The following is not intended to be an exhaustive chronology of the influence of the occult tradition and secret societies on world history. It does, however, highlight key events that can be traced to these sometimes-ancient sources. Because of the nature of the subject, some of the events, especially those in prehistory, may be of a speculative nature.

40,000 BCE

The earliest mystery schools, as allegedly depicted in the Lascaux cave paintings, are established.

30,000 BCE

According to some occult traditions, Asia and Australasia are colonized by the inhabitants of the lost continent of Lemuria, or Mu. Goddess worship and matriarchal cultures are established worldwide.

10,000 BCE

Evidence suggests possible first contact between extraterrestrials and Stone Age tribes in Tibet.

9000–8000 BCE

The lost continent of Atlantis is destroyed because, according to occult tradition, its scientists start conducting genetic experiments that create half-human, half-animal hybrids they use as slaves. Some of the priesthood of the continent allegedly flee before the island is destroyed and establish colonies in the British Isles, western Europe, North Africa, and

South America. The northern mystery tradition arises, centered on the island of Thule and the Aryan culture. The runic alphabet is invented.

5000 BCE

The first primitive cities are established in the Middle East by the descendants of Cain. Agriculture begins with the domestication of animals such as sheep and goats. There is possible contact between extraterrestrials and early Sumerian culture is represented by the fish-headed god Oannes.

5000–4000 BCE

The Two Lands are formed in predynastic Egypt and are ruled by outsiders (Isis and Osiris). The Egyptian pantheon of gods, including Horus, Thoth, Set, Ra, Ptah, and Hathor, is established. Pharaohs are regarded as divine representatives of the gods.

4000–2000 BCE

Burial mounds and chambered tombs are built in western Europe and the Mediterranean. The Sphinx and the Great Pyramids of Giza and Cheops are built in Egypt. The ziggurat (Tower of Babel) is built in Ur. The Sarmoung Brotherhood is founded in Babylon. Stonehenge and other megalithic stone circles are erected in the British Isles.

2000–1000 BCE

Thothmes III reigns in Egypt (ca. 1480). The Rosicrucian Order is founded. Akhenaton reigns in Egypt (ca. 1370); he establishes the mystical Brotherhood of Aton, which is dedicated to the worship of the sun as a symbol of the Supreme Creator. Akhenaton's son Tutankhamun reigns; he reestablishes the old pantheon of Egyptian gods and goddesses. The Hebrew-Egyptian prince and initiate Moses leads the Children of Israel out of slavery in Egypt to the promised land of Canaan during the reign of Rameses II.

1000–500 BCE

The Dionysian Artificers are founded. Solomon's temple is built (ca. 950). The Greek city-states are established and the Olympic pantheon of gods replace earlier nature worship. The first temples are erected in Mexico, Peru, and southwest North America. Celtic culture is established in western Europe. Goddess worship declines and worship of patriarchal sky gods personified by priest-kings rises. Rome is founded (750).

500 BCE–1 CE

Druidic colleges are founded in the British Isles and are exported to Gaul (France). Odin is recognized as a major god of the northern mysteries and is credited with inventing the runes. Buddha, Lao-tzu, Confucius, Pythagoras, Plato, and Zoroaster preach their new religions and spiritual philosophies. Maya culture develops in South America. The Eleusinian mystery cults are established. The Essene sect rises in Palestine and Judaea. Jesus of Nazareth is born.

1–400

Jesus allegedly travels to India, Tibet, and Britain to be initiated into the esoteric traditions of East and West. He is crucified for his radical political and religious ideas (ca. 33). Jesus allegedly survives crucifixion and flees to southern France with Mary Magdalene, where their child is born. The Nazarenes break from Judaism to found the Christian Church (ca. 80). Joseph of Arimathea establishes the Christian Church in Britain at Glastonbury (ca. 37). Britain is invaded by Roman legions and the druids are suppressed (40–60). Paul travels to Asia Minor and Greece to preach his own version of Christianity (50). The Jews, led by the Zealots, revolt against Roman rule (66). The Essenes are suppressed and the Dead Sea Scrolls are hidden in caves. The Temple in Jerusalem is destroyed by the Romans (70). The Christian scriptures are written. Ormus is converted to esoteric Christianity by Mark. Mithraism and the mysteries of Isis compete with Christianity in the Roman Empire. Mani, a Persian high priest of Zoroastrianism, is crucified (276). Emperor Constantine declares Christianity the official religion of the Roman Empire. The Council of Nicaea defines heresy, condemns paganism, and lays the theological foundation for the Catholic, or Universal, Church (325). Constantine's successor, Julian the Apostate (361–363), briefly reestablishes the old pagan religion. Emperor Theodosius outlaws the worship of the pagan gods in Rome and closes the pagan temples (378). The barbarians, led by Attila the Hun, invade Rome, Greece, and Europe (395–480). The Roman legions withdraw from Britain (395). The Comacine Order is founded by ex-members of the Roman College of Architects.

500–1000

Muhammad (d. 632) founds Islam. Celtic Church practices are outlawed by the Council of Whitby (664). The first Sufi secret societies are founded (ca. 700). The Emerald Tablet of Hermes Trismegistus is translated in writing for the first time. Emperor Charlemagne allegedly founds the first Rosicrucian lodge in Toulouse (898). The Cathars, Druzes, and Yezedi are founded (900). Heretical Catholic monks found the first Rosicrucian college (1000).

1000–1400

The Order of the Assassins is founded by Hasan-i-Sabbah (1034–1124) and the Order of St. John is founded (1050). The First Crusade begins in the Holy Land (1095). The city of Jerusalem is captured by Godfrey de Bouillon, the alleged founder of the Priory of Sion (1099). Assassins infiltrate the Thuggee cult in India. The Order of the Poor Knights of the Temple of Solomon is founded in Jerusalem (1118). A charter is allegedly granted to the Priory of Sion by Pope Alexander II (1178). A crusade is launched against the Cathars (1208). The Inquisition is created to fight heresy (1215). The Cathars are massacred at Montségur in southern France (1241). The troubadours practice their cult of courtly love. Occult schools that teach the kabbalah and alchemy are established in Spain by the Moors. Count Rudolf von Habsburg is crowned as Holy Roman Emperor (1273). Members of the Knights Templar are arrested by King Philip of France on charges of devil worship, heresy, and sexual perversion (1307). The Templar Order is disbanded by papal decree (1313). The last official grand master of the Templars, Jacques de Molay, is burned at the stake and the order goes underground (1314).

1400–1600

Christian Rosenkreuz allegedly lives (1379–1482). The Order of the Garter is founded by Edward III (1348). The *Corpus Hermeticum* is first published by the Medici family in Italy (1460). *Malleus Malifiracum* is first published, as is the papal bull of Pope Innocent, both of which began the medieval witch-hunting hysteria (1484 and 1486). Martin Luther begins the Reformation (1521). Cornelius Henry Agrippa refers to the Templars as gnostics and worshippers of the phallic god Priapus (1530). Dr. John Dee lives (1527–1608). The British secret service is founded by Sir Francis Walsingham. Johann Valenti Andrea is born (1586). Sir Francis Bacon lives (1561–1626). The Spanish Armada is defeated by the British, allegedly with magical help from the New Forest witches (1588).

1600–1700

The Virginia Company is founded by James I (1606). The Romanovs become czars of Russia (1613). The Rosicrucian manifesto is published (1614). Elias Ashmole lives (1617–1692). The *Mayflower* voyages to New England and Sir Francis Bacon's novel *The New Atlantis* is published (1620). The pagan community of Merrymount is established in Massachusetts by Thomas Morton. The English Civil War begins (1642). The first English Masonic guild accepts nonstonemasons at its meetings (1646?). King Charles I of England is convicted of treason and beheaded (1649). General Oliver Cromwell allegedly makes a pact with the devil to retain power. Freemasonry is introduced to the American colonies by Dutch settlers (1658). The Order of Pietists is founded in Pennsylvania (1694).

1700–1800

The comte de Saint-Germain is born (1710). The Masonic Grand Lodge of England and the Druid Order are founded (1717). The first Masonic lodge is founded in France (1721). Benjamin Franklin is initiated as a Mason (1731). Chevalier Alexander Ramsey informs the French Masons that they are heirs to the Templar tradition (1736). The Roman Church condemns Masonry (1738). Count Cagliostro is born. Comte de Saint-Germain is involved in the Jacobite plot to restore the Stuart dynasty to the English throne (1743). The Society of Flagellants and Skoptsi are founded in Russia (1750). George Washington is initiated as a Mason (1752). Sir Francis Dashwood founds the Hell Fire Club. Franklin visits England to discuss the future of the American colonies with Dashwood (1758). The Rite of the Strict Observance, based on the Templar tradition, is founded by Baron von Hund. Frederick of Prussia founds the Order of the Architects of Africa and uses the title Illuminati to describe his neo-Masonic lodges (1768). Benjamini Franklin is elected grand master of the Nine Sisters lodge in Paris (1770). The Grand Orient is founded in France (1771). The Boston Tea Party occurs (1773). General George Washington is appointed commander-in-chief of the new American army (1775). The Order of Perfectibilists or Illuminati is founded. The American Revolution formally begins (1776). Czar Peter I founds the Secret Circle (1778). The comte de Saint-Germain allegedly dies (1784). The Grand Masonic Congress allegedly plots the French Revolution. Cagliostro is involved in the Diamond Necklace Affair. The Illuminati are banned in Bavaria and go underground (1785). The French Revolution formally begins (1789). There is an Illuminist conspiracy to overthrow the Habsburgs (1794).

1800–1900

Count Grabinka founds a secret society in St. Petersburg based on Martinism and Rosicrucianism (1803). Occultist Fabre d'Olivet leads a French republican plot to assassinate Napoleon Bonaparte by placing a bomb under his coach. Emperor Napoleon takes control of French Masonry (1805). The revived Templar Order in France celebrates the martyrdom of Jacque de Molay with a public requiem (1808). The Order of the Sublime Perfects is founded (1809). Eliphas Levi (1810–1875) reveals the secret symbolism of the Templar idol, the Baphomet. Czar Alexander I and Emperor Francis von Habsburg unite to defeat the Italian revolution incited by secret societies. John Quincy Adams, initiate of the Dragon Society, is elected U.S. president (1820). Czar Alexander outlaws Masonry in Russia (1822). The Decembrist secret society attempts a coup when Alexander dies (1825). The Anti-Masonic Party is founded in the United States to combat secret societies in American politics (1828). Wagner joins the Vaterlandsverein, a secret society dedicated to the formation of a pan-European federation of nations. The Masonic convention at Strasbourg plots a second French Revolution (1848). Napoleon III condemns the Grand Orient for dabbling in radical politics (1850). Paschal Randolph founds the Hermetic Brotherhood of the Light (1858). Abraham Lincoln is assassinated (1865). The Ku Klux Klan is founded (1866). The Society of Rosicrucians in Anglia (SRIA) is founded (1867). The Theosophical Society is founded by Madame Blavatsky allegedly on instructions of the Hidden Masters of the Great White Brotherhood. Aleister Crowley is born (1875). The mysterious suicide (murder?) of Archduke Rudolf von Habsburg occurs at a hunting lodge at Mayerling (1889). The Hermetic Order of the Golden Dawn is founded (1888). Empress Elizabeth von Habsburg is assassinated by anarchists (1898).

1900–1985

The Ordo Templi Orientis is founded (1900). The International Order of Co-Freemasonry is founded (1902). *The Protocols of the Wise Men of Zion in Russia* is published (1905). The Ancient and Mystical Order of the Rosy Cross is founded (1909). The Black Hand Society is founded (1911). Aleister Crowley is accepted as head of the British branch of the OTO. The Order of the Temple of the Rosy Cross is founded (1912). Archduke Franz Ferdinand and Archduchess Sophia von Habsburg are assassinated. The attempted murder of Rasputin occurs. World War I begins (1914). Kaiser Wilhelm abdicates. The Habsburg dynasty is overthrown. The Bolshevik Revolution occurs in Russia and the Russian royal family is murdered (1917–1918). The German Workers Party is founded by the Thule Society (1919). Hitler joins the German Workers Party and changes its name to the National Socialist Party (1920). Crowley is employed by MI6. Cardinal Roncalli, later Pope John XXIII, allegedly joins the Rosicrucian Order. Hitler becomes first chancellor of the Third Reich (1933). President Franklin D. Roosevelt places on the dollar bill the Illuminist symbol of the eye in a triangle (1935). The Nazi invasion of England is allegedly prevented by New Forest witches and other occultists (1940). Rudolf Hess is lured to Britain on a peace mission by fake astrological data (1941). The Templar Order is revived in France (1952). The Bilderberg Group meets for the first time (1954). The P2 lodge is founded (1960). Pope Paul VI dies and Pope John Paul I is elected and allegedly murdered. Pope John Paul II is elected (1978). The P2 conspiracy is exposed. An attempt to assassinate John Paul II occurs (1981). L'Ordre Internationale Chevelresque Tradition Solaire is founded on instructions of the revived Order of the Templars in France (1984).

1986–1999

The Berlin Wall falls (1989). The Soviet Union and the Warsaw Bloc collapse (1991). East and West Germany are unified (1990). The Vatican protests the film depicting the papacy in a criminal conspiracy with the Mafia, Freemasons, arms dealers, and international bankers (1990). President George H. Bush suggests the concept of a new world order in a speech on the first Gulf War (1991). The Italian police investigate top-level connections among politicians, organized crime, Vatican officials, and Freemasons. The Project for the New American Century (PNAC) is launched by neo-conservatives to promote the new world order in the twenty-first century as an American-led enterprise. Diana, princess of Wales, is killed in a car crash in Paris; conspiracy theories link her death to alleged occult activities by the British royal family and prominent American families (1997).

2000–2007

George W. Bush, a former member of the Skull and Bones fraternity and a member of Bohemian Grove and the Bilderberg Group, is elected president of the United States in a controversial election. The PNAC issues an influential report outlining a plan for American military global domination in the new century (2000). Hijacked planes flown by Arab terrorists crash into the World Trade Center in New York and the Pentagon in Washington, DC. President Bush launches a "war on terror" and a "crusade" against extreme Islam. The draconian and controversial Patriot Act is passed by the U.S. Congress and the Department of Homeland Security is established in wake of 9/11. Military tribunals are suggested to try terrorists held by the United States and the United States sets up detention camps in which prisoners are held without trial and access to lawyers (2001). The war in Afghanistan begins (2001). The P2 lodge is reported to have ongoing activities in Italy and is accused of plotting acts of terrorism designed to destabilize the government and launch a right-wing coup. A new police inquiry into the "suicide" of Vatican banker Roberto Calvi claims he was murdered by Mafia hit men (2002). The Anglo-American invasion of Iraq begins (2003). Cardinal Joseph Ratzinger, a German ex-member of Hitler's Youth and former head of the Holy Office for the Propagation of the Faith (formerly the Inquisition) is elected Pope Benedict XV. The membership in the European Union (EU) is extended to new countries, including former Communist republics of the Eastern Bloc. The creation of a single European currency (the euro) and discussions of a new European constitution revive talk of a United States of Europe (2004). Several people are arrested in connection with the murder of Roberto Calvi (2005). The claim is made that the Priory of Sion was originally created in Vichy, France, during World War II as an occult secret society promoting the return of the French monarchy and a united Europe. The British prime minister Tony Blair addresses troops in Afghanistan and tells them they are fighting for "world security" in the twenty-first century (2006). President Bush and Vice-President Dick Cheney are reported to be planning either a limited bombing raid or a full-scale invasion of Iran because of that country's plans to develop nuclear weapons. Conspiracy theorists see this as stage two in the American bid to occupy the area that was once ancient Mesopotamia and the establishment of a U.S.-dominated world government controlled by the Illuminati. Christian right-wing fundamentalists interpret it as another step toward Armageddon, the Second Coming, and the Rapture (early 2007).

BIBLIOGRAPHY

In any book that deals with controversial subjects and an alternative version of history, the issue of references will always be a contentious one. Some of the material in this book is based upon my own interpretation of historical events in the light of more than forty years of research into occultism, parapolitics, and secret societies. Other information was provided by insider sources who do not wish to be identified. The following list of biographical references is provided for those readers who wish to follow up my primary sources for most of the available esoteric material in the book.

CHAPTER ONE: THE ANCIENT MYSTERIES

Dionysian Artificers

da Costa, Hippolyto Joseph. *The Dionysian Artificers*. Los Angeles: Philosophical Research Society, 1996.

Hall, Manly P. *Masonic Orders of Fraternity*. Los Angeles: Philosophical Research Society, 1996.

Steers, Albert. *Cyclopedia of Fraternities*. London: Hamilton Publishing Co., 1899.

Freemasonry

Hall, Manly P. *Freemasonry of the Ancient Egyptians*. Los Angeles: Philosophical Research Society, 2000.

Heckleton, Charles. *The Secret Societies of All Ages and Countries*. London: George Redway, 1897.

Knight, Stephen. *The Brotherhood: The Secret World of the Freemasons*. New York: Stein and Day, 1984.

Ward, J. S. M. *Freemasonry and the Ancient Gods.* Whitefish, Mont.: Kessinger, 1997.

———. *Who Was Hiram Abiff?* Whitefish, Mont.: Kessinger, 1942.

Goddess Worship

Black, Barbara. *The Book of Lilith.* York Beach, Maine: Nicholas Hay, 1986.

Hall, Manly P. *The Secret Teachings of All Ages.* New York: Tarcher, 2003.

Patai, Raphael. *The Hebrew Goddess.* Detroit: Wayne State University Press, 1990.

Rosicrucian Order

Lewis, H. Spencer. *Rosicrucian Questions and Answers.* Whitefish, Mont.: Kessinger, 2004.

Temple Symbolism

Horne, Alexander. *King Solomon's Temple in the Masonic Tradition.* New York: HarperCollins, 1989.

Wood, David. *Genesis: The First Book of Revelation.* Tunbridge Wells, Kent, England: Baton Wicks Press, 1986.

Other Topics

Harrison, Michael. *The Roots of Witchcraft.* Fort Lee, N.J.: Lyle Stuart, 1975.

Pagels, Elaine. *The Gnostic Gospels.* New York: Random House, 1979.

Pennick, Nigel. *Sacred Geometry.* San Francisco: Harper and Row, 1982.

Spence, Lewis. *Myths and Legends: Ancient Egypt.* New York: Benjamin Blom, 1971.

CHAPTER TWO: THE CURSE OF THE TEMPLARS

Cathars

Keightley, T. *Secret Societies of the Middle Ages.* London: C. Cox and Co., 1848.

Death of Jesus

Baigent, Michael, Richard Leigh, and Henry Lincoln. *Holy Blood, Holy Grail.* New York: Delacorte, 2005.

———. *The Messianic Legacy.* New York: Henry Holt, 1986.

Islam and Christianity

Billings, Michael. *The Cross and the Crescent.* London: BBC Publications, 1987.

Islamic Sects

Burman, Edward. *The Assassins.* San Bernardino, Calif.: Borgo Press, 1989.

Daraul, Arkon. *Secret Societies: A History.* New York: MJF Books, 1998.

Knights Templar

Burman, Edward. *The Templars: Knights of God.* Rochester, Vt.: Destiny Books, 1986.

Howarth, Stephen. *The Knights Templar.* New York: Athaneum, 1982.

Levi, Eliphas. *Transcendental Magic.* London: Rider, 1958.

Mystery Cults

Begg, Ean. *The Cult of the Black Virgin.* London: Arkana, 1996.

Godwin, Jocelyn. *Mystery Religions in the Ancient World.* New York: HarperCollins, 1982.

Priory of Sion

Baigent, Michael, Richard Leigh, and Henry Lincoln. *Holy Blood, Holy Grail.* New York: Delacorte, 2005.

Sufism

Bennett, J. G. *The Masters of Wisdom.* Santa Fe, N.M.: Bennett Books, 1995.

Shah, Idries. *The Way of the Sufi.* New York: Dutton, 1969.

Other Topics

Boyce, Mary. *Zoroastrians: Their Religious Beliefs and Practices.* London: Routledge and Kegan Paul, 1979.

Jonas, Hans. *The Gnostic Religion.* Boston: Beacon Press, 2001.

Walker, Benjamin. *Gnosticism: Its History and Influence.* San Bernardino, Calif.: Borgo Press, 1986.

CHAPTER THREE: THE ROSICRUCIAN CONNECTION

Johann Valentin Andrea

Hall, Manly P. *Orders of Universal Reformation.* Los Angeles: Philosophical Research Society, 1949.

Elias Ashmole

McIntosh, Christopher. *The Rosicrucians: The History, Mythology, and Rituals of an Esoteric Order.* York Beach, Maine: Weiser, 1997.

Comte Cagliostro

Wilgus, Neal. *The Illuminoids.* Albuquerque: Sun, 1978.

John Dee

Deacon, Richard. *History of British Secret Service.* Chicago: Academy Chicago, 1980.

French, Peter. *John Dee: The World of an Elizabethan Magus.* New York: Dorset Press, 1989.

Smith, Charlotte Fell. *John Dee.* Whitefish, Mont.: Kessinger, 2004.

Comte de Mirabeau

Birch, Una. *Secret Societies and the French Revolution.* London: John Lane, 1911.

Jacques de Molay

Partner, Peter. *The Murdered Magicians: The Templars and Their Myth.* Oxford: Oxford University Press, 1982.

Comte de Saint-Germain

Hall, Manly P. *The Secret Teachings of All Ages.* New York: Tarcher, 2003.

Hermeticism

Scott, Walter. *Hermetica: The Ancient Greek and Latin Writings.* Boston: Shambhala Publications, 1985.

Knights Templar
Partner, Peter. *The Murdered Magicians: The Templars and Their Myth*. Oxford: Oxford University Press, 1982.

Masonic Lodge Neuf Sœurs
Birch, Una. *Secret Societies and the French Revolution*. London: John Lane, 1911.

Masonry
Frost, Thomas. *The Secret Societies of the European Revolution, 1776–1876*. Chestnut Hill, Mass.: Adamant Media Corp., 2001.

Andrew Ramsey
McIntosh, Christopher. *The Rosicrucians: The History, Mythology, and Rituals of an Esoteric Order*. York Beach, Maine: Weiser, 1997.

Rosicrucianism
Lewis, H. Spencer. *Rosicrucian Questions and Answers*. Whitefish, Mont.: Kessinger, 2004.

McIntosh, Christopher. *The Rosicrucians: The History, Mythology, and Rituals of an Esoteric Order*. York Beach, Maine: Weiser, 1997.

Royal Society
Hall, Manly P. *Orders of Universal Reformation*. Los Angeles: Philosophical Research Society, 1949.

Templar Revival in Germany
Partner, Peter. *The Murdered Magicians: The Templars and Their Myth*. Oxford: Oxford University Press, 1982.

Adam Weishaupt
Roberts, J. *Mythology of the Secret Societies*. New York: Macmillan, 1972.

CHAPTER FOUR: THE AMERICAN DREAM

American Flag
Hall, Manly P. *The Secret Teachings of All Ages*. New York: Tarcher, 2003.

Sir Francis Bacon
Dawkins, Peter. *The Great Vision*. Stratford-upon-Avon, England: Francis Bacon Research Trust, 1982.

Hall, Manly P. *America's Assignment with Destiny*. Los Angeles: Philosophical Research Society, 1994.

John Wilkes Booth
Wilgus, Neal. *The Illuminoids*. Albuquerque: Sun, 1978.

Christopher Columbus
Hall, Manly P. *America's Assignment with Destiny*. Los Angeles: Philosophical Research Society, 1994.

Sir Francis Dashwood

Colquhoun, Ithell. *The Sword of Wisdom.* New York: Putnam, 1975.

Towers, Eric. *Dashwood: The Man and the Myth.* Wellingborough, England: Crucible, 1986.

Benjamin Franklin

Towers, Eric. *Dashwood: The Man and the Myth.* Wellingborough, England: Crucible, 1986.

Hall, Manly P. *America's Assignment with Destiny.* Los Angeles: Philosophical Research Society, 1994.

Great Seal

Capt, E. Raymond. *Our Great Seal: The Symbols of Our Heritage and Our Destiny.* Thousand Oaks, Calif.: Artisan Sales, 1979.

Great White Brotherhood

Tomas, Andrew. *Shambhala: Oasis of Light.* London: Sphere, 1977.

Hermetic Brotherhood of the Light

McIntosh, Christopher. *The Rosicrucians: The History, Mythology, and Rituals of an Esoteric Order.* York Beach, Maine: Weiser, 1997.

The Holy Grail and The Aquarian Age

Tomas, Andrew. *Shambhala: Oasis of Light.* London: Sphere, 1977.

Johannes Kilpius and the Pietists

Hall, Manly P. *America's Assignment with Destiny.* Los Angeles: Philosophical Research Society, 1994.

Masonry

Hall, Manly P. *America's Assignment with Destiny.* Los Angeles: Philosophical Research Society, 1994.

Ordo Templi Orientis

McIntosh, Christopher. *The Rosicrucians: The History, Mythology, and Rituals of an Esoteric Order.* York Beach, Maine: Weiser, 1997.

Other Topics

Mannix, Daniel P. *The Hell Fire Club.* New York: Ballantine, 1959.

CHAPTER FIVE: GERMAN NATIONALISM AND THE BOLSHEVIK REVOLUTION

Disraeli

Roberts, J. *Mythology of the Secret Societies.* New York: Macmillan, 1972.

Dr. Gerard Encausse

de Jonge, Alex. *The Life and Times of Grigori Rasputin.* New York: Coward, McCann, and Geoghegan, 1982.

Habsburgs

Marek, George. *The Eagles Die: Franz Joseph, Elisabeth, and Their Austria.* New York: Harper and Row, 1974.

Bulwer Lytton

Jennings, Hargrave. *The Rosicrucians: Their Rites and Mysteries.* London: Hesperides Press, 2006.

McIntosh, Christopher. *The Rosicrucians: The History, Mythology, and Rituals of an Esoteric Order.* York Beach, Maine: Weiser, 1997.

Order of New Templars

Goodrick-Clarke, Nicholas. *The Occult Roots of Nazism.* New York: New York University Press, 1993.

Ordo Templi Orientis

King, Francis. *Sexuality, Magic, and Perversion.* Los Angeles: Feral House, 2002.

Racial Supremacy

Goodrick-Clarke, Nicholas. *The Occult Roots of Nazism.* New York: New York University Press, 1993.

Sarajevo

Brook-Shepherd, George. *Victims at Sarajevo.* London: Harville Press, 1984.

Vivian, Herbert. *Secret Societies.* London: Thornton Butterworth, 1927.

Secret Societies

Troyat, Henri. *Alexander of Russia: Napoleon's Conqueror.* New York: Grove Press, 2003.

Socialist League

King, Francis. *Sexuality, Magic, and Perversion.* Los Angeles: Feral House, 2002.

Other Topics

Bruce, Lincoln. *The Romanovs: Autocrats of All the Russians.* New York: Anchor, 1983.

CHAPTER SIX: NAZISM AND THE OCCULT TRADITION

Aleister Crowley

Deacon, Richard. *History of British Secret Service.* Chicago: Academy Chicago, 1980.

Gurdjieff

Bancroft, Ann. *Modern Mystics and Sages.* Chicago: Academy Chicago, 1981.

Kaiser Wilhelm

Aronson, Theo. *The Kaisers.* London: Cassell, 1971.

Psychic Warfare

Gardner, Gerald. *Witchcraft Today.* n.l.: Citadel, 2004.

Glass, Justine. *Witchcraft: The Sixth Sense, and Us.* London: Neville Spearman, 1965.

Hutton, J. Bernard. *Women in Espionage.* New York: Macmillan, 1971.

McCormick, Donald. *Murder by Witchcraft.* London: John Long, 1968.

Wulff, Wilhelm. *Zodiac and Swastika.* New York: Coward, McCann, and Geoghegon, 1973.

Society of Union and Progress

Goodrick-Clarke, Nicholas. *The Occult Roots of Nazism.* New York: New York University Press, 1993.

Other Topics

Fortune, Dion. *Psychic Self-Defense.* York Beach, Maine: Weiser, 2001.

King, Francis. *Satan and Swastika.* New York: Mayflower, 1976.

Masters, Anthony. *The Man Who Was M: The Life of Maxwell Knight.* New York: B. Blackwell, 1984.

Petitpierre, Robert. *Exorcising Devils.* London: Robert Hale, 1976.

Pool, James. *Who Financed Hitler?* New York: Pocket, 2006.

Wheatly, Dennis. *Gunmen, Gallants, and Ghosts.* London: Arrow Books, 1975.

CHAPTER SEVEN: SECRETS IN THE VATICAN

Frederick II

Burman, Edward. *The Templars: Knights of God.* Rochester, Vt.: Destiny Books, 1986.

Gospel of Mark

Smith, Morton. *The Secret Gospel: The Discovery and Interpretation of the Secret Gospel according to Mark.* Middleton, Calif.: Dawn Horse Press, 2005.

Illuminist Conspiracy

Webster, Nesta. *Secret Societies and Subversive Movements.* Whitefish, Mont.: Kessinger, 2003.

Priory of Sion

Baigent, Michael, Richard Leigh, and Henry Lincoln. *Holy Blood, Holy Grail.* New York: Delacorte Publishing Co., 2005.

Propaganda Two

Marshall, Jonathan. "Brief Notes on the Political Importance of Secret Societies." In *Lobster* 5 and 6 (1984).

Yallop, David. *In God's Name: An Investigation into the Murder of Pope John Paul I.* New York: Carroll and Graf, 2007.

The Vatican

Compton, Peirs. *The Broken Cross: The Hidden Hand in the Vatican.* London: Neville Spearman, 1983.

CHAPTER EIGHT: THE OCCULT AND MODERN POLITICS

Bilderberg Group

Eringer, Robert. *The Global Manipulators.* Bristol, England: Pentacle Books, 1980.

Heindel

McIntosh, Christopher. *The Rosicrucians: The History, Mythology, and Rituals of an Esoteric Order.* York Beach, Maine: Weiser, 1997.

International Order of Chivalry, Solar Tradition

Delaforge, Gaetan. *The Templar Tradition in the Age of Aquarius.* Putney, Vt.: Threshold Books, 1987.

Organizations for World Peace and World Government

Wilgus, Neal. *The Illuminoids.* Albuquerque: Sun, 1978.

Rudolf Steiner

Bancroft, Ann. *Modern Mystics and Sages.* Chicago: Academy Chicago, 1981.

Other Topics

Webster, Nesta. *Secret Societies and Subversive Movements.* Whitefish, Mont.: Kessinger, 2003.

CHAPTER NINE: THE NEW WORLD ORDER

Skull and Bones, Princess Diana, Princess Grace of Monaco

Levy, Joel. *The Little Book of Conspiracies: 50 Reasons to be Paranoid.* New York: Thunder's Mouth Press, 2005.

NATO and the New World Order, Operation Gladio, the Iraqi War, Princess Diana, Bohemian Grove, Skull and Bones

Burnett, Thom, ed. *Conspiracy Encyclopedia.* New York: Chamberlain Brothers, 2005.

Murder of Roberto Calvi, P2 Lodge

McConnachie, James, and Robin Tudge. *A Rough Guide to Conspiracy Theories.* London: Rough Guides, 2005.

Bohemian Grove

Ronson, Jon. *Them: Adventures with Extremists.* New York: Simon and Schuster, 2002.

Real Origins of the Priory of Sion

Picknett, Lynn, and Clive Prince. *The Sion Revelations.* New York: Touchstone, 2006.

American Religious Fundamentalism and the Christian Right

Hedges, Chris. *American Fascists: The Christian Right and the War on America.* New York: Free Press, 2007.

INDEX

Page numbers in *italics* indicate illustrations.

Abdullah, 33
Abraham, 32, 33
Adam, 9, 33
Adams family, 101–2
  Brooks, 104
  John, 101–3
  John Quincy, 103–4
Adonis, 16–18, 27
agape, 30
Agarthi, 158–59
Agrippa, Henry Cornelius, 49–50,
  55
Ahriman, 27
Ahura Mazda (Ormazd), 26
Aion, 27
Akhenaton, 175
Alamut, 34
Albigensi. *See* Cathars alchemy
Alexander I, Czar, 113–122, 131
Alexander II, Czar, 122–23
Alexander II, Pope, 35
Alexander III, Pope, 38–39, 172
Alexandra, Czarina, 139
Althotas, 74
Amenhotep II, 55
America. *See also* United States

Committee for a United Europe
  (ACUE), 186–87, 205
  freemasonry in, 91
American Philosophical Society, 97
Ancient Arabic Order of Nobles and
  Mystics, 108
Andrea, Johan Valentin, 62–63,
  64
Anjou, Duke of, 61
Anthroposophical Society, 209
anti-clericalism, 133
anti-monarchism, 100
anti-Semitism, 127, 133, 152, 197
d'Anton, duc, 66
Anubis, 44
Apollo, College of, 67
Apollonius of Tyana, 5
Aquarian/New Age, 100–101, 110, 127,
  210–13, 215–16
Arabia/Arabs, 10, 31, 33, 51, 56
Architects of Africa, Order of, 70
architecture, 4, 11, 12, 20–21, 22, 209
Armanenschafft, 128, 131
Arthur, King, 57, 101
Aryan race, 135–36, 131, 155, 157, 159,
  162

Ashmole, Elias, 63–65
Asiatic Brethren, 77
assassinations, 60–61, 68, 107, 126,
    133–36, 141, 176, 194, 220
Assassins, 33–35, 40, 42, 80–81, 179
Astarte (Aserah), 7, 9–12, 15, 17–19, 44
astrology, 90, 152, 168, 178, 208, 210,
    211, 213, 218
Attis, 16, 27
Augustus, Caesar, 21
Austria, 62, 71, 81, 136, 154, 191. *See also*
    Habsburgs

Baal, 9, 11, 19
Babel, Tower of, 5, 232, 233
Babylon, 8, 25, 230, 233
Bacchus. *See* Dionysius
Bacon, Sir Francis, 85–88
Bailey, Alice, 212
Bakunin, Mikhail, 133–34
Baldwin II, King, 35–36
Bamuel, Father, 81
Banco Ambrosiano, 191–94
Baphomet, 41–46
Barbarossa, Frederick, 178
Bast, 46
Batimis, 33
Bavarian Mystics, Order of, 154
Beatrix, Crown Princess, 205
Bennett, J. G., 32
Bernhard, Prince, 187, 204–5
Besant, Annie, 126–27, 170, 208–9
Bilderberg Group, 204–7
Black Hand, Order of the, 135–36
Blake, William, 92
Blavatsky, Helena, 124, 126, 127
Bogomils, 30
Bonaparte, Joseph, 81
Bonaparte, Lucien, 81
Bonaparte, Napoleon, 81–82, 117–18,
    170, 190
Book of Lies, 130
Book of Wisdom, 9
Booth, John Wilkes, 107
Boyle, Robert, 55

Britain, 90, 93–95, 119, 134, 137, 163–71,
    197–202
Broken Cross, The, 184
Brotherhood of Saturn (Fraternitus
    Saturni), 165
Bruno, Giordano, 55
Brzezinski, Zbigniew, 206
Bulgaria, 30, 35, 134
Bush, George H., 227, 228, 231–32
Bush, George W., 224–28, 231–35
Bush, Jeb, 231–32
Bush, Prescott, 228
Byblos, 15

Caaba
Cagliostro, Comte, 55, 74–77, 80
Calvi, Robert, 191–92, 193, 221
Canaan, 7–8, 9, 12, 15, 17, 19, 96
Carbonari, 120, 172, 182, 184
Carlos I, King, 134
Carter, Jimmy, 202, 206
Cassidens, 20
Cathars alchemy, 29–31
Catherine II, 114–15
Catholic Church, 172–95
    and freemasonry, 66
Cernunnos, 44
Chaldea, 25, 26, 28
Charlemagne, Emperor (Charles the
    Great), 55, 177
Charles II, King, 63, 86
Charles V, Emperor, 180
de Chartres, duc, 66
Chartres cathedral, 104
cherubim, 12–14
Childeric III, King, 177
Christianity, 24–47
    Celtic, 173–74
    Coptic, 174
    esoteric, 26, 37, 63, 127, 208, 216
    Syriac, 48, 68
Churchill, Winston, 166, 167, 171,
    186–87, 191
CIA, 186, 188–91, 194, 204, 205, 220,
    227

Civil War
  America, 105
  English, 56, 65, 81, 89, 94, 181
  Russian, 142
  Spanish, 188
de Clement, comte, 66
Clement of Alexandria, 174
Clement V, Pope, 40, 47, 56
Clement XII, Pope, 181
Clovis, King, 177
Clutterbuck, Dorothy, 170
Clymer, R. Swinburne, 106
codes/ciphers, 61, 85
Columbus, Christopher, 84–86
Comacine Masters, Order of, 21–22
Coming Race, The, 127
Communism, 110, 187–90, 197
Community of Truth Seekers, 158
Compton, Piers, 184–85
Constantine, Emperor, 175–76
Constantine, Grand Duke, 115–16, 129–30
Constitutions, 91
Corbett, Boston, 107
Corpus Hermeticum, 50, 59
Council on Foreign Relations (CFR), 186
Councils, 26, 28, 173
Cromwell, Oliver, 65, 94, 107
cross/crucifix, 29–31, 37–42
Crowley, Aleister, 147, 130, 163–68
crucifixion, 28–29
Crusades
  anti-Cathar, 30–31
  anti-masonic, 183
Cybele, 107

Damascus, Emir of, 39–40
Dante, 55, 85
Dashwood, Sir Francis, 91–94, 145
David, King, 6
Dead Sea Scrolls, 20, 46
Death, Order of, 226–28
Debussy, Claude, 56
Decembrist movement, 121–29
Dee, Arthur, 63
Dee, John, 45, 55, 59–62, 65

Denmark, 165
Derwentwater, Lord, 66
Devoted, Order of the, 33–34
Diamond Necklace Affair, 75
Diana, Princess, 223–25
Dilettanti, Society of, 91
Dionysian Artificers (Sons of Solomon), 19–21
Dionysius, 16–17
Disraeli, Benjamin, 126
dollar bill, 108–11, 110
Donovan, William "Wild Bill," 186
Douglas-Home, Sir Alec, 204
Dragon, Order of the, 95
druids, 92, 230
Druid Universal Bond, 92
Druses, 33
dualism, 29, 31, 43

Eckart, Deitrich, 153, 157
ecology, 103, 212
Edward II, King, 47
Edward III, King, 57, 58
Egypt, 14–16, 54–56
El, 9
Eleusian mysteries, 33, 70, 93
elixir of life, 56, 68, 106
Elizabeth, Empress, 133
Elizabeth I, Queen, 61, 85
Emerald Tablet, 5
Encausse, Gerard, 137–39
Engels, Friedrich, 129
England, 59–61
Enochian language, 45, 62
Ephesus, 20
Eringer, Robert, 204
Essenes, 20, 46, 68
Europe, 158–69, 177–82, 185–87
  Central, 123, 209
  Eastern, 217, 219, 234
  united, 205–6
  Western, 124, 158, 206
European Union, 216, 217, 235
excommunication, 180, 181
Ezekiel, 17

Fama Fraternitatis, 51, 62–63
Farley, James, 111
Fasciculus Chemicus, 63
Fascists, British Union of, 197
Fatimites, 33
feminine principle, 12, 25, 31, 63, 212
Ferdinand, King, 128
fertility cults/rites, 8, 12, 18, 19, 26
Flagellants, Society of (People of God), 118
flags, 95–96, 155
Fleming, Ian, 167–68
Flemming, Walter, 108
Flood, 4–5, 8, 17, 19, 33
Florence, William, 91–92, 108
de Fonseca, Manuel, 190
Fortune, Dion, 163, 170–71
France, 66, 74–83, 104, 106, 114–20, 127,
    129, 134, 137, 180, 182–83, 189–91,
    214–15, 221–23
    freemasonry in, 66
Francis II, Emperor, 181
Franklin, Benjamin, 55, 67, 90–91, 93,
    95, 97
Franz Ferdinand, Grand Duke, *148,*
    134–36
Frederick II, Emperor, 34, 39, 178
Frederick the Great, 70, 76, 108
Freemasonry, 2–7, 17–19, 66–71, 74,
    79–82, 181–93
    Scottish Rite, 66, 108
Friars of St Francis of Wycombe (Hell
    Fire Club), 91, 92
Frick, Wilhelm, 153
Friends of Truth, 67

Garden of Eden, 8, 233
Gardner, Gerald, 170
Garibaldi, 108
Garter, Order of the, 57–59, 63, 161
Geller, Uri, 111
Gelli, Licio, 188–89
geometry, 4, 6, 19, 20, 102
George I, King (of Greece), 134
George III, King, 91, 93
George V, King, 152

Germany
    freemasonry, 71, 74, 128
    Workers Party, 152–57
Germer, Karl (Frater Saturnus), 164–65
Gilani, Abdelkadir, 51
Global Manipulators, The, 204
Gnostics, 26–31, 49–50
goddess worship, 7–11, 14, 25, 40, 42
Godunov, Boris, 113
Goethe, 108
Goliniewski, Mikael, 190
Gonne, Maud, 129
Grabianka, Count Thadeus, 114
Grand Orient, 66–67, 74, 81, 82, 127,
    136, 152
Grant, Joan, 166
Great Seal, 95–100, *99,* 108–11
Great White Brotherhood, 109–10, 124
Greece, 25, 33, 35
Gregorius, Gregory, 165
Gregory, Pope, IX, 178
Gregory, Pope, VII, 178
de Guaita, Stanislas, 137
guilds, 3–4, 21–23
Gurdjieff, George Ivanovitch, 32, 157–59
Gurtner, Franz, 153
Gustav III, King, 69, 77
Gusyeva, 140
gypsies, 162

Habsburgs, 73, 112–14, 131–32, 136–37,
    153–55, 179, 181
    Franz Josef von, Emperor, 119, 123,
    185
    Otto von, Dr., 191
    Rudolf von, Prince, 132
Hall, Manly Palmer, 90
Hamilton, duke of, 167
Harrison, Michael, 246
Hartman, Franz, 128
Hasan-i-Sabbah (Sheikh el Jebal), 33
Hatshepsut, Queen, 54
Hausofer, Karl, 157–59
Hebrew Goddess, The, 246
Hebrews, 6–19. *See also* Jews

Hecate, 176
Heindel, Max, 213
Heliopolis, 11
Helmet, Order of the, 85
Henry, Prince, 101
Henry II, King, 39
Henry IV, Emperor, 178
Henry VIII, King, 63
Hermes Trismegistus, 5, 59
Hermetic Brotherhood of the Light, 105
Hermetic Order of the Golden Dawn, 106, 109, 125, 129–30, 137, 162–63
Hess, Rudolf, 131, 157–58, 163, 166–68, 171
Himmler, Heinrich, 160–61
Hinduism, 33, 124
Hiram Abiff, 6, 11, 14, 17–19, 28, 40, 68
Hitler, Adolf, 151–69
Hohenzollerns, 112, 113, 137
Holy Alliance, 119–20, 131
Holy Blood, Holy Grail, 221, 222
Holy Grail, 31, 36, 110, 160–61
Home, D. D., 131
Honorius, Pope, 37–38
Horns, 44, 108
House, Col. E. M., 200–201
House of Rothschild, 80, 196, 227
von Hund, Baron, 67–69
Hungary, 71, 139

ideologies, 112, 202, 203
Illuminati, 70–83
images, 22
Imperial Constantine Order, 155
India, 26, 34, 44, 90, 107, 124, 126, 134, 157, 158
initiation ceremonies, 25, 42, 71, 135
Inner Light, Fraternity of, 171
Innocent VIII, Pope, 49
Inquisition, 49, 55, 74, 80, 86, 92, 180, 193
Institute for International Affairs (IIA), 201, 205
intelligence services, 163–70
Invisible College, 65, 86, 97, 207

Ionians, 20
Ireland, 97, 174, 217
Ishmael, 33
Isis/Ishtar, 12, 17–18, 25, 44
Islam, 31–33, 219, 232–34
Ismailis, 33
Israel/Israelites, 7–15, 20, 96, 217
Italy, 39, 50, 91–92, 120, 126, 186–89
Ivan the Terrible, Czar, 63, 65

Jack-in-the-Green/Green Man, 16–17, 22
Jackson, Andrew, 103
Jacobins, Society of, 75
Jacobite, The, 133
Jacobites, 66, 68, 69, 76, 125, 130
James I, King, 87–88, 101, 104
Japan, 199, 200, 203, 206
Jefferson, Thomas, 55, 96
Jehovah, 4, 7, 19, 29. See also Yahweh/Yahwehism
Jennings, Hargreaves, 125
Jeroboam, 10
Jerusalem, 6, 9–11, 28, 35, 40
Jesuits, 60, 70, 80, 161, 184
Jesus, 24–32, 37, 42–43, 47, 55, 68, 69, 172–74
   secret teachings of, 5, 26, 30, 39
Jews, 24, 108, 153, 155–56, 162, 196
   World Congress, 155–56
Jezebel, 10–11
John Paul I, Pope, 192–93
John Paul II, Pope, 193–94
John XII, Pope, 177
John XXIII, Pope, 184, 194
Jones, John Paul, 67, 91
Joseph of Arimathea, 173
Joyce, William, 167
Judaism, 1, 8, 174
Julian, Emperor, 176
Juliana, Queen, 205

Kabbalah, 8, 33, 50, 86, 89, 124, 127, 208
Kant, 108
Karl von Hesse-Kassel, Prince, 77
Karmathites, 33

Kellner, Karl, 128–29
Kelly, Edward, 62
Kelly, Grace, 225
Kelpius, Johannes, 89
Khlysty (People of God), 138
Kilmarnock, Lord, 68
Kitchener, Lord, 131
Knight, Maxwell, 166–68
Knights of Christ, 84
Knights of Light, 70
Knights of Malta, 191
Knights of St. John, 38, 47
Knights of Templar. *See* Templars, Order
    of Knights
Knights of the Solar Cross, 214
Kohn, Frederick, 155
Koot Hoomi, 124
Koshelav, 118–19
Kramer, Heinrich, 49
von Kruderer, Madame, 117–18
Ktav, Raphael, 12–13

de Lafayette, marquis, 91
de Lage, Savalette, 67
Lamech, 4, 12
Larmenuis, 47
de La Rochefoucauld, duc, 67
Lascaux, 32
Last Days of Pompeii, The, 126
Leadbeater, C. W., Bishop, 125
League of Nations, 109, 200–203
League of the Three Emperors, 123
Legitimists, 125
Legitimists, Society of, 66
Lenin, 142
Leo III, Pope, 177
Leo X, Pope, 179
Leo XIII, Pope, 182
Levi, Eliphas (Alphonse Constant), 43,
    45
Lewis, H. Spencer, 106–7
von Liebenfels, Lana, 130–31
Lilith, 9
Lilly, William, 63, 65
Lincoln, Abraham, 105

Link, the, 167
von List, Guido, 128, 154–55
    de la Molte, comtesse, 75
Lobster, 189
*L'Ordre Internationale Chevalresque
    Tradition Solaire,* 215
Louis Philippe I, King, 82
Louis XVI, 75
Louis XVII, 82
Lucheni, 133
Lucifer, 17, 44
Luther, Martin, 179
Lytton, Lord Edward Bulwer, 124–27

Maat, Order of, 214
Mafia, 186, 188, 191–92, 219, 221
Magi, 55
magic, 9–10, 43–45, 49–51, 128–30,
    137–39, 162–66, 170–71, 208, 211,
    212, 214–15
Malleus Malefiracum, 49
Mani/Manicheans, 29, 98
Marcinkus, Archbishop, 191, 193
Margaret, Princess, 224
Marie Antoinette, 75, 77
Mark, 37, 174
Marquis de Luchet, 77
Marshall, Jonathan, 189
Martinists, 67, 115–17
Marx, Karl, 129, 134
Mary Tudor, 59
Masonic Rites of Memphis and Mizraism,
    136
masons, 2–7, 21–22, 55, 57, 59, 65–68, 77,
    79, 82, 93, 120, 127, 160, 170, 182
Massie, Jacques, 189
Masters of Wisdom, The, 32
Mathers, Samuel McGregor, 125, 130, 137
McKenzie, Kenneth, 125
de Medici, Cosmos, 50
de Medici, Lorenzo, 85
Mein Kampf, 155–56, 160
Melnik, Constantin, 189
*Memoires pour serir de l'histoire du
    Jacobinisme,* 81

Mendes, 16
Mesmer, Dr., 74, 77
Mexico, 87, 199, 204
de Mirabeau, comte, 73–74, 78, 80, 108
Mithras, 26–28, 31, 72, 78
de Molay, Jacques, 40–41, 46–47, 69,
   80–81
   The Tomb of Jacques de Molay, 80
Monad, The, 61
Montalban, Madeline, 45
de Monte Carmel, Charles, 68
Mont-Saint-Michel and Chartres, 104
Moors, 50
Morning Star, Order of the, 44, 45
Morris, William, 129
Morton, Thomas, 88–89, 101, 102
Moses, 12, 33, 96
Mosley, Sir Oswald, 197
Mountbatten, Lord, 191
Muhammed, 31–33, 108
murders, ritual, 133
Mystères de la Franc Macconerie, Les, 183
mysteries, pagan, 3, 14, 30, 59, 66, 107,
   173, 174, 176

Napoleon III, 82–83
nationalism
   German, 112, 127, 152, 157, 163, 198
   Irish, 125, 130
   Magyar, 131
   Polish, 115
   Serbian, 131, 136
National Socialism, 123, 131, 155, 157,
   160, 171, 196, 198
Neitzsche, 159
neo-paganism, 131, 160, 218
Neoplatonism, 174
Neuf Soeurs lodge, 67, 91
New Atlantis, The, 65, 86, 88, 97
Newton, Sir Isaac, 181
Nicaea, Council of, 25, 173
Nicholas I, Czar, 122
Nicholas II, Czar, 134, 152, 156, 158, 189
nihilists, 133–34
Nimrod, King, 5–6

Ninevah, 5
Noah, 4, 33
North, Lord, 93
Nostradamus, 157, 169
Nu-Isis Lodge, 214

oaths, 2, 36
De Occulta Philosophia, 49
Ordo Novi Templi (ONT), 130–31
Ordo Templi Orientis (OTO), 106,
   128–30, 162, 164–65, 185, 214–15
d'Orléans, duc, 80–82
Ormus, 37, 174
Orthodox Church, 120, 142, 190
Osiris, 14–19, 174

P2 lodge, 188, 191–93, 196, 198, 215,
   219–21
paganism, 25, 28, 43, 119, 174, 176
   neo-paganism, 131, 160, 218
de Pairaud, Hugh, 46
Paladin, Adrien, 137
Paladin, Josephin, 137
Pallas Athena, 85
pantheism, 33
Papacy, 80, 177, 185, 187, 192, 219. *See
   also individual headings*
Paracelsus, 55
de Pasqually, Martinez, 67
passwords, 3, 19, 22
Path of the Rose, 51
Paul, Czar, 116–17, 121
Paul VI, Pope, 185, 187, 192, 194, 205
de Payens, Hugh, 35–36, 38, *143*
Perfectibilists, Order of, 71
Persia, 26, 29, 33–34, 69, 134, 157, 159,
   176
Peter, St., 181
Peter the Great, 76
Peter the Hermit, 35
Petitpierre, Dom Robert, 163
Philadelphia Eucharistic Congress, 184
Philip of Nablus, 45
Phillip, Prince, 205, 229
Phillip IV, King, 40, 46–47, 68, 173

Philo, 13
Phrygian cap, 27, 67, 72, 78
Pietists, Order of, 89–90
Pius X, Pope, 182
Pius XI, Pope, 186
Pius XII, Pope, 218
Plato, 33
Pohner (police commissioner), 153
Poland, 77, 114, 120–21, 165, 194, 200, 205
political doctrines, 19, 112, 171
Portugal, 47, 84, 134
Princip, Gavrilo, 133–36
Priory of Sion, 36–37, 172, 174, 216, 221–23
Protestantism, 62
Protocols of the Elders of Zion, 155, 159
Prussia, 70, 76–77, 81, 112, 119, 123
psychic powers, 105, 168–69
Psychic Self Defense, 163
Psychological Warfare Department, 168–69
Puharich, Andrija, 111
Puritanism, 9, 102
Pushkin, Count, 121
pyramids, 97–100, 108, 109
Pythagoras, 70

Quakers, 105, 118

racism, 203
radicalism, 77, 79, 114, 115, 122, 182
Radio Free Europe, 189
Ramsay, Chevalier Andrew, 66, 67
Rand Corporation, 189
Randolph, Pascal Beverly, 105–6, 214
Rasputin, Gregori Efimovitch, *146,* 138–42
Raymond VI, Count of Toulouse, 55
Reformation, 62–63, 67, 117, 180–82, 194
reforms, 52, 62, 65, 77–79, 82, 86, 101, 117, 123, 126, 182, 185, 190
reincarnation, 25, 30, 101, 118, 124, 173, 197
Renaissance, 21, 50, 180

Restoration of the Decayed Temple of Pallas, 51
resurrection/rebirth, 3, 14, 16–18, 21, 24, 27, 98
Retinger, Joseph, 204–5
Reuss, Theodor, *150,* 128–30, 164
revolution
    American, 55, 70, 83, 87, 90–91, 95–96, 100–102, 112, 202
    Austrian, 120
    French, 73–81, 91, 98, 114–15, 125, 132, 197, 211
    German, 112–42
    Russian, 156, 198
Reynard, Lord, 92
Rhodes, Cecil, 200–201
Richard the Lion Heart, 34
rituals, 16, 21, 25, 34, 51, 120, 130–31, 133, 171, 176
Robespierre, 78
Roerich, Nicholas, 109–10
de Rohan, Cardinal, 75
Romains, Abbé Pierre, 81
Roman Empire, 20–25, 29, 100, 174–76
    College of Architects, 21–22
    Holy, 55, 155, 177–80, 185
Romanovs, 112–13, 123, 139–41, 190–91
Rompalla, Cardinal, 185
Roosevelt, Franklin Delano, 108–9, 111, 191
Rosenberg, Alfred, 159–60
Rosenkreuz, Christian, 51–53, 56
Rosy Cross/Rosicrucians
    Ancient and Mystical Order of Rosae Crucis (AMORC), 108
    Corona Fellowship of, 170
    Kabbalistic Order of, 137, 138, 214
    Lectorium Rosicrucianum, 213
    neo-, 65, 105–6, 124, 127–28, 165, 170
    Order/Fraternity of, 213–14
    Societas Rosicruciana Anglia (SRIA), 124
    Societas Rosicruciana Civitatibus Foederatis, 106
    Temple of, 127, 170

Rothovius, Andrew B., 101
Rothschild, Lord, 201
Round Table, 200–201
　Fellowship of, 57, 161
Royal Society, 63, 65, 86, 97, 181, 207
Rudolf, Count, 179
Rudolf, Crown Prince, 132
Rudolf II, Emperor, 59
Ruskin, John, 201
Russia, 112–23, 134–42
　freemasonry in, 114

sacrifices, 11, 18, 30, 34, 44, 105, 119, 223, 224, 227, 230–31. *See also* murders, ritual
de Saint-Germain, Comte, 76–77, *149*
Saint-Martin, Louis Claude, 67
St. Bernard of Clairvaux, 36, 37–38
Samborsky, André, 115
Saracens, 35, 38, 40, 42, 48, 226
Sarmoung Brotherhood, 158
Satan/Satanism, 17, 29, 31, 49, 183, 224
scapegoat, 28–29, 44
Schonfield, Hugh, 46
Schutzstaffel (SS), 160–62
Scotland, 38, 48, 66, 68–69, 120, 125
von Sebottendorf, Baron, 152–53, 155
Secret Committee, 117
Secret Doctrine, The, 158
Sekhmet, 46
Selivanov, Kandvah, 118
Serbia, 139, 142–45
Service d'Action Critique (SAC), 189
Set (Typhon), 14–15
sexuality, 10, 30, 98, 192, 193, 218
Shah, Idries, 45, 51
Shakespeare, William, 21
Shaw, Gilbert, 163
Sheba, Queen of, 10
Sheela-na-gig, 22
Shekinah (Bride of God), 8
Sibyline books, 100
Sidon, 10, 15, 42
du Simitière, Eugene, 96–97
Sinai, Mount, 12

Skoptsi sect, 107, 118
Smith, Morton, 174
Sol Invicta cult, 175
Solomon, King, 6–7, 9–11, 18, 20–21, 28, 35, 46, 178
　Key of, 9
Soviet Union, 111, 142, 186, 206, 217
Spain, 35, 38, 44, 50–51, 127
Spanheim, Abbot of, 61
Spinoza, 55, 108
Spiritualism, 19–26, 30–33, 49–51, 87–105
Sprengel, Anna, 125
Sprenger, James, 49
Stalin, Josef, 110, 157
Starck, Johann Augustus, 69
Steiner, Rudolf, 160, 162, 208–10, 212
Strict Observance Rite, 68
Stuart, Charles, Prince, 68, 69
Sublime Perfect Masters lodge, 82
Sufis, 31–35, 42, 45, 51, 109, 152
Sumeria, 8–9, 17
Summers, Montague, 45
sun worship, 10, 128
swastika, 124, 131, 155, 160, 161
Sweden, 69, 77, 119, 165
Swedenborg, Emmanuel, 117–18
Switzerland, 42, 62, 71, 133, 155–56, 163, 209, 214
Syllabus of Errors, 182
symbolism/symbols, 11, 25, 48, 57, 71, 74, 95, 98, 105, 111, 130, 161, 175, 181, 183, 196
Syria, 15–16, 34, 39, 45, 48, 54, 68

Tammuz. *See* Adonis
Tantrism, 76, 105–6, 124, 128
Tatarinova, Catherine, 118
Taxil, Leo, 182–83
Templars, Order of Knights, 5–6, 20, 31, 35, 48, 68, 80, 84, 109, 130, 161, 172, 222–25
　neo-Templars, 68–70, 80–81, 189, 215
Temple of Solomon, 6, 11–12, *13,* 68–69, 86, 88, 156, 179, 196, 226

terrorism, 34, 74, 211, 220, 232–36
Teutonic Knights, 38–39, 115, 161, 179
Theodosius, Emperor, 21, 176
Theosophical Society, 109, 124–28, 158, 160, 208–9, 213
Thomas, Diana, 183
Thomson, Charles, 97–98
Thoth, 5, 54–55
Thothmes III, Pharaoh, 11–12, 53–55, 124
Three Wise Men, 52
Thuggee, 34
Thule Society, 131, 152–56, 188
von Thum und Taxis, Prince, 154
Tomb of Jacques de Molay, The, 80
Treatise on Naval Defense, 60
Treaty of St. Petersburg, 77
Trilateral Commission, 186, 204, 206
Turin Shroud, 43
Turkey, 35, 134, 152, 184–85, 189
Tyre, 6–7, 11–15, 18, 20, 40, 42
    King of, 6, 7, 18

underworld, 17–18, 25, 44, 189, 223
unification, religious, 207
Union and Progress, Society of, 153
United Nations, 202–3, 234
United States, 55, 90, 102, 105, 106, 111, 164, 165, 187–90, 199–206, 213–14, 217, 219, 226, 232–35
United World Federalists, 203
Utopia/utopianism, 17, 19, 20, 22, 63, 71, 85–86, 96–97, 100, 101, 127, 129, 207, 211

Vatican, 172–95
    and freemasonry, 187, 192
Vaughan, Diana, 183
Venus, 17, 28, 32, 44, 92
da Vinci, Leonardo, 85
Virginia Company, 87–88
Virgin Mary, 25, 36, 39, 46, 57, 63
Viril Society, 127
Vitrivius, 21
Volkisher Beobachter, 157
Voltaire, 67, 132

Wallace, Henry, 109–11, 202
Walsingham, Sir Francis, 60–61
war
    American Independence, 83, 91, 95–96, 227
    Balkan, 153, 234
    Napoleonic, 81, 190
    Seven Years, 76
    Sino-Japanese, 200
    World War I, 109, 120–21, 123, 127, 131, 134, 137, 151–65, 196–99
    World War II, 182, 202, 218, 222
Washington, George, 94–96, 100, 102, 145, 224
Webster, Nesta, 196–97
Weishaupt, Adam, 70–74, 130, 184, 201
Wentworth Little, Robert, 124–25
Westcott, William Wynn, 125, 130, 183
Wheatley, Dennis, 165–66
Whitby, Council of, 173
White, William, 124–25
widow, sons of, 6, 18, 28, 49
Wilhelm, Kaiser, I, 123, 151, 153
Wilkes, John, 94, 107
Wilson, President Woodrow, 199–200, 204
witchcraft/witches, 45, 49, 60, 89, 113, 169–70, 218, 224
de Wohl, Louis, 168–69
world government, 199–201, 203, 206, 209, 212
Wotan, 128
Wren, Sir Christopher, 55

Yahweh/Yahwehism, 7–12, 16–17, 33
Yarker, John, 128
Yeats, W. B., 129
Younger, Bill, 121, 141, 166, 218
Yugoslavia, 30, 35, 217–18
Yusupov, Prince Felix, 141

Zanoni, 126
Zoroaster, 26, 29, 59
Zoroastrianism, 26–27